Best Practice in a Global Context

Best Practice
Upper Intermediate

Bill Mascull and Jeremy Comfort

Coursebook

United Kingdom • United States • Australia • Canada • Mexico • Singapore • Spain

Contents

Best Practice is a business English series designed for both pre-work and in-work students. Its topic-based modules train students in the skills needed to communicate in the professional and personal sides of modern business life.

MODULE 1 — PEOPLE
pages 4–33

	Business Inputs	Language Work	Communication	Business across Cultures
1 Leadership	**Listening**: An interview about leadership styles **Reading**: Top Seven Leadership Mistakes	**Grammar**: Modals	Profiling your own communication style	International leadership
2 Dream teams	**Listening**: A conversation about problems within a team **Reading**: An article about a teambuilding session	**Expressions**: Idioms	Active listening	Understanding the team
3 Independence	**Listening**: Attitudes towards independent working **Reading**: Would you make a successful freelancer?	**Grammar**: Conditionals	Influencing	Motivation at work
4 Are you being served?	**Listening**: An interview about private and public sector services **Reading**: A report on customer service in the UK	**Grammar**: Relative clauses	Getting your message across	Organisational cultures

Business Scenario 1 Mediaco

Review and Development 1–4

MODULE 2 — MARKETS
pages 34–63

	Business Inputs	Language Work	Communication	Business across Cultures
5 Entering new markets	**Listening**: Different ways of getting into new markets **Reading**: Joint ventures in India	**Grammar**: Determiners and quantifiers	**Presentations**: Engaging your audience 1	India
6 The right look	**Reading**: Zara: The future of fast fashion	**Grammar**: The passive	**Presentations**: Engaging your audience 2	Dress
7 Brand strategy	**Reading**: Extending a brand **Listening**: Consumers compare local and global brands	**Grammar**: Making comparisons	Interviewing	Branding nations
8 The hard sell	**Reading**: Product placement in films **Listening**: An interview about reaching the Hispanic market in the US	**Grammar**: Making predictions	Feedback	Global marketing

Business Scenario 2 Dua

Review and Development 5–8

MODULE 3 — MONEY
pages 64–93

		Business Inputs	Language Work	Communication	Business across Cultures
9	A thriving economy	**Reading**: An article about the private sector in China **Listening**: The growth of the Chinese economy	**Grammar**: Cause and effect	Leading meetings	China
10	Foreign investment	**Reading**: Foreign direct investment **Listening**: An interview with a country-risk analysis specialist	**Grammar**: Referring and sequencing	Participating in meetings	Russia
11	The bottom line	**Reading**: Tips on how to beat a recession **Listening**: Talking about budgets	**Grammar**: Prepositions	**Negotiations 1**: Bargaining	Brazil
12	Escaping poverty	**Reading**: Factors associated with poverty **Listening**: An interview about microfinance	**Grammar**: Reported speech	**Negotiations 2**: Handling conflict	Africa

Business Scenario 3 Katabaro Hotel

Review and Development 9–12

MODULE 4 — WRITING RESOURCE
pages 94–99

13	Developing people	Advertisements, Emails
14	Local partners	Business reports
15	Getting away from it!	Press releases

Student B material	*pages 100–111*
Audio script	*pages 112–125*
Answer key	*pages 126–147*
Communication	*pages 148–150*
Business across Cultures	*pages 151–153*
Grammar overview	*pages 154–165*
Glossary	*pages 166–170*

PEOPLE

1 Leadership

> If you have an army, it's no good just having a general – you need leadership all the way through the system.

Start-up

A With a partner, discuss these questions.

1 To what extent do you agree with the quotation opposite? Explain your reasoning.
2 What are the qualities of a good leader?
3 How much does the success of an organisation depend on its leader(s)? Is it the same for all types of organisation?

Vocabulary and listening

A Look at the adjectives below. Which are positive characteristics and which are negative? Which can be a mixture of both? Use a dictionary if necessary.

charismatic   inspiring   visionary   authoritarian   audacious   intimidating   subservient   motivated

B Use the adjectives above to complete the gaps in the sentences below. (Not all adjectives are used.)

1 That guy is always thinking 20 or 30 years into the future. His ideas are quite _____ .

2 Laura has such a _____ personality. She has this magic quality that makes everyone admire her and want to work with her.

3 He's a bit of a bully. I hate going into his office as he can be quite _____ .

4 Your new boss seems very _____ . Employees just do what she tells them.

5 What an _____ woman! She makes people want to work harder and exceed their expectations.

6 That new employee is more than obedient, he's _____ . All the managers treat him like a doormat!

🎧 1.1 **C** You are going to listen to an interview with James Bartley, a specialist on leadership styles. Listen to the first part of the interview and answer the questions.

1 Which of the characteristics in A does he mention?
2 According to James, is leadership something inborn, or can it be learnt?

🎧 1.2 **D** Listen to the second part of the interview and answer the questions.

1 What is the first leadership style called?
2 How does James Bartley describe it?
3 What is a disadvantage of this first leadership style?
4 What's the second type of leadership style and why is it better?
5 What's the difference between leadership and management?

E Think about the organisation in which you work or study. To what extent does its leader involve employees / students in its strategy? Do you feel there is a clear sense of leadership? Which of the characteristics listed in A would you apply to the leader of your organisation?

LEADERSHIP

Reading and speaking

A We have probably all experienced examples of poor leadership, or at least read about them. Think of some examples of ineffective leadership. What kind of mistakes did the leaders make?

B Read the article below about leadership mistakes. Match each paragraph (1–7) to its heading (a–g).

a Afraid to change
b Knowing everything
c Lack of focus
d Not being able to handle criticism
e Neglecting workers
f Procrastination
g Unable to delegate responsibilities

Top Seven Leadership Mistakes

Leadership and management skills are something that rarely come naturally to most people. But if you follow some basic rules and are willing to learn how to work with people, you will have things running much more smoothly in the workplace in no time.
Here's a list of some the things you should not be doing.

1 _e Neglecting workers_

Your workers are your business and they have to be treated that way. Failing to send this message to workers can be a financial and productivity drag for any business. Our workers are people with feelings and emotions and need to be told in many ways how important they are to the company.

2 _____

Just because you are in a leadership position does not mean that you suddenly become immune to making the wrong decisions. As a leader you must listen to constructive criticism and make the necessary changes. If a worker cares enough to share criticism, the least you can do is listen.

3 _____

We have to trust that our workers can do the things we have done for so long. A big part of leadership and management is about making sure that things run smoothly and efficiently, and that does not mean running from job to job doing everything yourself.

4 _____

Many of the world's greatest leaders are people of average intelligence who don't know all there is to know in their industry. They understand that they can't possibly know everything and they hire people who between them do know everything! The success of any business is in the hands of its workers and the leading managers and entrepreneurs of the world all try to hire the best in their field.

5 _____

Putting something off till tomorrow that should be done today. This is often a result of having no plan or list of priorities. Time management and goal setting are two ways to overcome this problem.

6 _____

Obviously there will be things that come up during the day which require immediate action that will distract us from our work, but we must have a clear set of priorities to follow. Doing a little bit of everything gets nothing finished, causing stress and feelings of being overwhelmed.

7 _____

Holding on to old ways of doing things just because they've always been done that way is a sure way to lose business. If any aspect of the business can be improved then there has to be change, even if this means getting rid of a poorly performing worker or a product range that is no longer profitable.

C True or false? Based on the advice in the article, leaders should …
1 be considerate towards workers' feelings.
2 keep criticism from workers to a minimum.
3 regularly 'get their hands dirty' by helping workers with their jobs.
4 understand they can't be experts about everything.
5 leave time management and prioritising tasks to their personal assistant.
6 be prepared to take hard and unpleasant decisions sometimes.

D Do you agree with the list of leadership mistakes in the article? Can you think of any others?

E Work in small groups. Decide on the three worst mistakes that leaders can make. Compare your selection with that of other groups and justify your choice.

MODULE 1

Grammar

Modals

A Modals are used to indicate functions such as necessity, obligation and possibility, for example, *As a leader you must listen to constructive criticism* (obligation). Read the article about seven leadership mistakes again. Underline all the modals you can find. What form of the main verb follows the modal?

> Modals are always followed by an infinitive. This is often a simple infinitive like *do*, *be*, *listen* or *find*.
> We **must have** a clear set of priorities to follow.
>
> The infinitive also has passive, continuous and past forms:
> Procrastination is when we put something off till tomorrow that **should be done** today.
> Here's a list of the things a leader **should not be doing**.
> You **could have given** me better advice on how to run this company!

B Fill in the gaps using an appropriate infinitive of the verb in brackets.

1 Every business should _____ (try) to be operationally effective, for example by performing better than its competitors.

2 A business leader needn't _____ (worry) about not knowing everything!

3 Employees must always _____ (give) help and encouragement by their leaders.

4 The management might not even _____ (know) at that time how the workforce felt.

C Look at some of the functions of modals in the box below. Match them with sentences 1–7.

| possibility | obligation | lack of obligation | permission | lack of ability | deduction | past habits |

1 Employees may seek the advice of their line manager at any time.
2 Graham has a personal charm which must have helped him develop good relations with his team.
3 When she was in charge here, she would continually stress the importance of ethical leadership.
4 If the supporting team is effective, the leader needn't always be checking up on them.
5 As a leader you must be self-aware, and understand your own strengths and weaknesses.
6 The company's poor performance might be a result of incompetent leadership.
7 Why couldn't she establish a good relationship with her employees, do you think?

> **Questions**
>
> You usually form questions by putting the modal before the subject, as in 7 above. *Have to*, however, is different. It is known as a phrasal modal, and questions are formed by using an auxiliary, as with any regular verb.
>
> Why **does** a leader **have to** learn about time management and goal setting?

D Work in pairs.

Student A: You are a manager at the start of your career. Ask your mentor, Student B, for advice about how to be an effective leader and how to avoid making mistakes in your future leadership roles.

Student B: You are Student A's mentor. Try to use as many modal verbs as possible in your discussion.

▶ Review and development page 31

▶ Grammar overview page 154

You should delegate as much as possible.

LEADERSHIP

Communication

Profiling your own communication style

In order to develop your communication skills, it is important to understand what your main style is first. Then, you can decide which areas you need to work on.

🎧 1.3

A Listen to seven extracts. Match the extract (1–7) with the style (a or b).

1 a direct b **indirect**

Indirect language *I wonder if we could think about this* v Direct language *We need to think about this*.

2 a personal   b impersonal
3 a formal   b informal
4 a simple   b complex
5 a asking questions b giving advice
6 a active listening b passive listening
7 a emotional   b neutral

B Look at the Key language below which shows some typical characteristics of different communication styles. Match each characteristic (1–7) with one of the seven styles above.

Key language

1 Long sentences with specific vocabulary	The system is supported with a continuous feed which is piped through the external network of conduits which are installed variably around the peripheral environment.
2 Questions which show interest or seek to clarify what the speaker is saying	So, if I understand you, you believe we should stop this project?
3 Showing how you feel about something or someone	It's really nice to see you again. I enjoyed working together last time.
4 Getting straight to the point	OK, we need to look at the reasons for this downturn.
5 Telling people what they should do	You need to slow down.
6 Keeping a distance from people	My name is Smolensky. Professor Smolensky.
7 Using 'official' language	According to the procedures, all lights must be switched off during the process.

C Work in groups of three. Two members of the group should role-play the situations below while the third observes. At the end of the role-play the 'observer' should give feedback on the communication style.

1 A colleague at work is going to leave because of personal reasons. She has been with the company for 20 years and you want to make short farewell speech.
2 Call a client to tell them that a delivery will be late because of production problems.
3 Explain to your colleague how to use a new piece of equipment (e.g. a specific service on your mobile).
4 Advise your colleague about how to develop his / her career.
5 Tell your colleague about a crisis at work you have recently faced.

D What is your dominant style? In which areas would you like to develop?

▶ Review and development page 33

▶ Communication page 148

International leadership

Leaders can't do everything. They have to make sure the followers (employees) are motivated and skilled enough to implement their strategy. In this section we look at three cases in order to explore how the leadership style influences the culture of an organisation.

Leadership styles

🎧 1.4 **A** Listen to Maria López, an independent financial consultant, talking about two companies she's worked for, Invesco Investment and Markhams Derivatives. As you listen match a word in the box to the company.

| male-oriented   competitive   personality-driven   impersonal   fair   results-oriented |
| hierarchical   managing results   process-driven   long hours |

B Listen again and make notes on each company. Use the words in the box to help you.

C In pairs, prepare a short profile of the culture of each company. Use the words in the box and add others. Include your opinion about the company culture when you present the profile.

D Describe the cultural profile of the company you currently work for, or would like to work for in the future. Present the profile to your partner.

Cultural fit

Many mergers and acquisitions fail because they fail to take account of the 'cultural fit' between the two companies.

E Work in pairs. Discuss what are some of the typical mistakes companies can make when trying to integrate an acquisition or a new merger partner.

F Mays International, a leader in recruitment and personnel services, has recently bought Penfold, Peters and Delaney (P, P & D), a headhunting company. Read about the two businesses and then look at the list of integration strategies which follow. What advice would you give the Mays management on how best to integrate P, P & D?

MAYS INTERNATIONAL

Mays International was established 35 years ago and since then has built itself up to be a leader in its field. It acts as recruitment consultants for large international and multinational clients. Its head office is in Boston but it has offices in many capital cities and its current headcount is 2,450 worldwide. It was founded by Arthur Mays although the family is no longer involved in the business. The company is highly structured with six layers, starting with office staff and rising up to board level. It has a rigorous reporting system and also very transparent HR processes. It is very results-focused and all managers and employees have performance-related pay.

PENFOLD, PETERS AND DELANEY

Penfold, Peters and Delaney has built itself up over the last few years to occupy the highly profitable niche of international executive head-hunting. It finds CEOs and senior executives to run global businesses. The offices are in London and there are 120 employees. The three partners have agreed to sell their business to Mays International but would like to see it continue to succeed. They have built up a very strong network based on relationships with board members of top international companies. They are a typically person-based company which operates flexibly with few systems. They have just three layers – partner, consultant and assistant. All three partners have a very informal leadership style.

LEADERSHIP

Mays management should:

- support and develop the culture of P, P & D
- focus on results
- increase the number of layers to make the organisation more structured
- appoint strong charismatic leaders
- maintain a distance from their staff
- put Mays managers in charge
- encourage independence in P, P & D employees and staff
- change the culture to adapt to the Mays culture
- focus on relationships
- reduce the number of layers to reduce costs
- appoint participative and cooperative leaders
- stay close to the staff
- promote P, P & D managers to run the business
- build a strong network between P, P & D and Mays managers

plus .... (your ideas)

Values and leadership

Culture is like an iceberg. Above the surface, we observe aspects of the culture such as the way people dress, what they eat and how they drive. Deep below the surface are the values, which are like an unwritten code which most people understand but don't talk about. Values are also the invisible part of a company culture.

G NorskOil is a major oil company. Read its values below.

Imaginative
Hands-on
Professional
Truthful
Caring

1 Match the words in the box to one of the five values above.

| creative | open | concrete | qualified | pragmatic | supportive |
| frank | innovative | practical | expert | honest | nurturing |

2 In pairs, expand on these values and explain what they mean.

3 How can leaders encourage and maintain these values?

4 Does your institution or organisation have a written set of values? If so, what are they? How are they communicated to employees? To what extent do employees put these values into practice?

▶ Business across cultures page 151

Checklist
- ✓ adjectives to describe leaders: *inspiring, intimidating, visionary*
- ✓ leadership styles and mistakes
- ✓ modals: *leaders needn't know everything, employees must be given guidance*
- ✓ profiling your communication style
- ✓ international leadership

PEOPLE

2 Dream teams

Start-up

A How would you define a *team*? Work in a small 'team' with two or three other people and agree on a one-sentence definition. Explain your definition to the other teams.

It's better to have a great team of minds, rather than a team of great minds.

Vocabulary and speaking

A Look at the different types of working styles below. Where would you place yourself on the scale?

1 I like working with other people. — I prefer working on my own.
2 I am 100 per cent involved throughout a project. — I often lose interest towards the end of a project.
3 I regularly speak to my colleagues about work matters. — I am always too preoccupied with my own work.
4 I often come up with new and innovative ideas. — I prefer to stick to ways of doing things that are tried and tested.
5 I organise and plan my work carefully. — I often have to rush at the last minute to get things done.
6 I always take other people's feelings into consideration. — The way I do things sometimes upsets the people I work with.
7 I'm a perfectionist in everything I do. — It's better to do each task in a 'good enough' way, depending on its importance.

B Discuss your answers with a partner. Which positions on the scales are particularly good or bad for effective teamwork? Why?

C Look at some of the key issues affecting team work in the box below. Match the issues to the relevant statement from the scales (1–7) above.

| communication | time management | conflict avoidance |
| creativity | performance | commitment | independence |

D Think about good and bad team members you have worked with. Use the key issues in C to talk about them.

Listening and speaking

A Bob Fisher, a team leader, talks to Helen Clarke, a management consultant, about some problems he is having with his team. Listen to the conversation and answer the questions.

 2.1

1 Which key issue from above is mentioned for each team member?
Nadine   Janet   Karen   Oliver   James
2 Which two members get the most positive feedback?

B Complete the statements about teams and team members below. Then listen again to check your answers.

1 If team members like each other, they _____ on well with each other.
2 Someone who prevents arguments between people is said be good at reducing _____ and conflict.
3 Someone who is a bit of a _____ prefers to work on their own.
4 Someone who leaves things to the last moment is prone to last-minute _____ .
5 Someone who contributes a lot is an _____ to the team.
6 When people are not working well together, someone might say that they need to _____ as a team.

10

Reading and vocabulary

A Have you attended a teambuilding course yourself? Did you find it useful? Look at some of the benefits of teambuilding courses below. Can you think of any others? Compare your list with a partner and rank the benefits in order of importance.

motivate people   have fun   boost morale

B You are going to read an article about a teambuilding session. Look at the headline of the article. What type of teambuilding session do you think it is?

Getting staff thumping to the same beat

THE roar goes around the conference hall like the sound of an army going into battle. Beat after beat reveals the drummers are *engrossed in* an activity they are deeply passionate about. They mean business.

'Whoops' and 'Ows' are heard from the chief drummer, *whipping the group into a frenzy* of exhilaration and excitement.

No, this is not a company of soldiers practising. Nor is it an African tribe performing a ceremonial dance. The group gathered in the conference hall at Ayr Racecourse are employees from the Scottish Executive's Accountant in Bankruptcy department.

Their office in Kilwinning opened in early March. All 80 employees have assembled inside the hall on a snowy March morning to beat 350 African drums. Why?

Enter Drumming Up Business, an enterprise set up by Suleman Chebe to boost motivation, morale and teambuilding in the workplace. The activity is by no means just another *gimmick* aimed at breathing life into a workforce. Far from it.

The sessions, he says, are ideal for *breaking the ice* between new members of staff, opening and closing conferences, corporate away days, or internal teambuilding.

These sessions help new employees build rapport. Most of the workers here today have only known each other for two weeks. However, looking at the group today, you'd think they had known each other for two years, not two weeks.

From executives to receptionists, the sessions are an effective way of *breaking down barriers*. Similar to singing from the same song sheet, all employees hit the same drumbeats.

'Unlike some teambuilding schemes where people have a different level of commitment, the drumming sessions are universal,' explains Chebe. 'We're not teaching people how to drum, we're teaching people how to have fun.'

'The drumming sessions are not what I expected and they certainly *get the pulse going*,' says Peter Hyslop, an employee of the company. 'I was a little *sceptical* before I got here, although I can now see the sessions are excellent at boosting morale and team work.'

'Che-che-ku-lae,' calls Chebe. This translates to 'Are you having fun?'

You can tell by the look on their faces the question doesn't need an answer.

C Look at the words and expressions in the article in *italics*. First, try to work out their meaning from the context. Then, match each of the words or expressions with one of the definitions or explanations below.

1 helping people from different backgrounds to get to know and understand each other better
2 doubtful, unbelieving
3 giving all your attention to something; totally absorbed
4 make you excited
5 something that is not serious used to attract people's interest
6 putting people into a state of uncontrolled and excited behaviour
7 making people who have not met before feel more relaxed with each other

D Work in small groups. Discuss the following questions:

1 Could you imagine participating in a 'drumming day' like this with your colleagues?
2 Do you think this kind of teambuilding session would work well in all cultures?
3 What other types of activities are used in teambuilding sessions? Which would work best for you?

MODULE 1

Vocabulary

A Business English is full of idioms. The article you read was about a company called Drumming up Business. What do you think to *drum up business* means?

B Complete the expressions below with a verb in the box.

| cut | pull | go | touch | think | take | face | be | pull | have |

1. _____ the plug on something
2. _____ rushed off your feet
3. _____ to the chase
4. _____ out of the box
5. _____ the music
6. _____ your weight
7. _____ base with someone
8. _____ something on board
9. _____ a lot on your plate
10. _____ through the roof

C Match the expression (1–10) above with its meaning (a–j) below.

a think about something in a new and creative way
b accept criticism or punishment for something you have done
c exchange news with someone about the latest situation
d have a lot to do
e talk about or deal with the main issue
f be very busy
g stop a project
h rise to a very high level
i understand or accept an idea or piece of information
j contribute your fair share as a team member

D Read the email below from Bob Fisher to Helen Clarke. Complete the sentences with the correct expression from B.

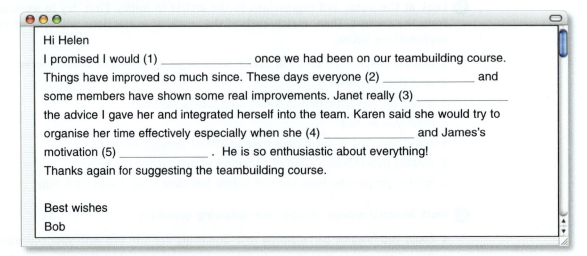

Hi Helen

I promised I would (1) _____ once we had been on our teambuilding course. Things have improved so much since. These days everyone (2) _____ and some members have shown some real improvements. Janet really (3) _____ the advice I gave her and integrated herself into the team. Karen said she would try to organise her time effectively especially when she (4) _____ and James's motivation (5) _____ . He is so enthusiastic about everything!

Thanks again for suggesting the teambuilding course.

Best wishes
Bob

E Work in pairs. Replace the idioms in the email with more everyday or common expressions.

▶ Review and development page 31

DREAM TEAMS

Communication

Active listening

Good listening can often be more effective than good speaking. Good listeners have the skill of getting people to trust and respect them. They are also usually better negotiators, as they check and clarify to make sure they fully understand the other party.

2.2

A Listen to a salesperson talking to a customer. Answer the questions.

1 What type of product is the customer interested in?
2 How does the salesman build a trusting relationship with the customer?

B Look at the Key language below. Listen again and, using the audio script on page 113, mark the moments when the salesman supports the customer's decisions.

Key language

Open questions	What sort of job do you have to do? What are you looking for?
Clarifying questions	So, you're looking for something …? So, if I understand you, you are looking for …? So, you mean that …?
Confirming comments	I'm sure. You're right. Of course. I see. OK.
Showing interest	Really? That sounds interesting.
Summarising	Let me just make sure I've got the picture. You … Can I summarise …?

C The skill in active listening is responding actively to what your partner is saying. Work in pairs. Student A looks at this page. Student B looks at page 100.

> **Student A**
> 1 Tell Student B about a challenge you face at work or at your institution (e.g. a difficult boss / colleague, a tough project / task)
> 2 Listen to Student B telling you about a recent success. Make sure you listen actively and can summarise at the end.

D Work in groups of three or four. Choose one of the topics below for discussion. One student should lead the discussion and show good active listening skills. The other participants should also show that they have understood each other. Make sure you focus both on listening and speaking.

- Teamwork is a nice idea but in the end it's about individuals doing the work.
- Team members should be chosen on the basis of their competence to do their job, not according to their personality or team skills.
- Teams should be rewarded rather than individuals. Bonuses for good performance should go to teams, not to individuals.

▶ Review and development page 33

▶ Communication page 148

Understanding the team

Building a strong international team depends on the individuals understanding each other – both the different personalities and backgrounds. In this section we focus on one team and the diversity in that team.

A When working in a team it is important to recognise the individual personalities. Look at the different personalities below. Match the personality type (1–5) to its preference (a–e).

1 Controller 2 Seller 3 Negotiator 4 Organiser 5 Creator

a Likes communicating, persuading and influencing
b Likes innovating, experimenting, finding new ways
c Likes structuring, planning and doing things
d Likes quality, making sure everything is correct
e Likes getting people together, building relationships and consensus

B Match the personality type in A (1–5) to its potential weakness below (a–e).

a Gets bored quickly, does not follow through to the end
b Can be obsessed with getting it right. Takes too long on projects
c Wants to plan everything. Does not allow enough flexibility
d Always wants agreement. Does not push strongly enough for results
e Talks too much. Doesn't always listen

C In pairs, match your personality to one of the personality types. You may find you are a mix of more than one. Build a short profile of yourself and your partner.

🎧 2.3 **D** Manthis Biotechnology has formed a project team to work on the international launch of a new anti-viral drug. The team is cross-functional and cross-border, bringing a wide variety of experience to the project. In their first meeting, they introduce themselves. Listen to the start of the meeting and complete the team wheel.

MANTHIS BIOTECHNOLOGY
Scientific research
Ludmilla — Controller
Meiling — Creator
Singapore
José
Brazil
Karl — Organiser
Lena
Austria
Public affairs

E The goal of this project is to develop a strategy for launching a new drug. The whole team wants to succeed in this goal. However, they all have very different backgrounds and will have different priorities. Match the team member to the priority.

1 Ludmilla   a decisions based on accurate research data
2 José   b clear scientific basis for product claims
3 Lena   c good media stories to support the launch
4 Karl   d an effective marketing campaign
5 Meiling   e a clear route to market and the end consumer

F Read the short profiles of the five countries from where the project team members come. Where do you see the biggest clashes happening?

DREAM TEAMS

Sweden
Sweden is one of the most egalitarian societies in the world. There are relatively small differences between people in terms of income and background. Their culture has always stressed the importance of compromise, gaining consensus between people and not imposing an individual's priorities on others. The state has traditionally played a large role in looking after the Swedish people.

Russia
Following the collapse of Communism, metropolitan Russia (Moscow, in particular) has become very commercially minded. There are not so many established rules which govern behaviour. Many people who were used to a more rule-governed society have found this difficult to adapt to.

Austria
Austria has had to adapt to no longer being the centre of a large and powerful empire. It is now a small player in the world but nevertheless has an important role in bridging cultures of Western Europe with those of Central and Eastern Europe. Some people say it still has a strong conservative streak, probably a result from times when it had a very considerable imperial bureaucracy.

Brazil
Brazil is a remarkably multicultural society with a mix of people with different ethnic origins. Brazilians pride themselves on their flexibility and entrepreneurial skills. They are used to making things work in a society where things still often go wrong.

Singapore
Singapore has moved a long way from its colonial past when it was part of the British Empire. It is a small country with a very competitive economy. The people have a very strong work ethic and also place enormous value on education and qualifications. It is a quite strongly rule-bound society, where the government keeps a strong hold on public behaviour.

G Work in groups. Discuss the questions.

1 Does this team need a team leader, especially if all the members are highly experienced?
2 If you had to choose a leader for this team, which of the five team members would you choose? Why?

H Work in groups of five. You work for a company which uses projects as the main way of getting things done. Your team has been asked to decide whether this is necessary and have organised a brainstorming session to decide what should be done.

Student A: Turn to page 100.
Student B: Turn to page 101.
Student C: Turn to page 102.
Student D: Turn to page 103.
Student E: Turn to page 106.

▶ Business across cultures page 151

Hold your meeting. Try and decide which member of the team plays which role.

Checklist
- ✓ key issues affecting teamwork: *performance, commitment*
- ✓ team building
- ✓ business idioms: *cut to the chase, face the music*
- ✓ active listening
- ✓ understanding the team

15

PEOPLE

3 Independence

Start-up

A What do you understand by the term 'self-employed'? What types of jobs do self-employed people usually do?

B Look at the figures opposite. Do they surprise you? Are there many self-employed people in your country?

C What types of activities do companies outsource? What are the benefits of using freelancers and contractors? Are there any downsides?

> 16 per cent of Europeans and 10 per cent of Americans are self-employed. And in a recent survey, 69 per cent of Americans and 51 per cent of Europeans said they would prefer to be self-employed.

Listening and speaking

A With a partner, discuss the advantages and disadvantages of being self-employed.

B Listen to four people talking about their attitudes to independent working. Complete the table.

🎧 3.1

	Freelance job	Training	Main advantage	Main disadvantage	Secret of success
1	Writer of children's books				Self-discipline
2			Independence		
3	IT Specialist	Degree			
4				Difficult customers	

C Work with a partner. Ask and answer questions about your job or studies using the prompts below. Then, tell the class about your partner's answers.

- qualifications / training? *What exam grades did you need in order to go to university?*
- special skills / talent?
- main advantages and disadvantages of your job / studies?
- the key to success?

D In pairs, discuss the following aspects of freelancing from your own point of view:

- working from home
- dealing with IT issues yourself
- dealing with a lot of paperwork
- job insecurity
- being self-disciplined
- networking and making lots of contacts
- not having any feedback on your work from your boss or colleagues

INDEPENDENCE

Reading and speaking

A Do you think you have what it takes to go freelance? Do the quiz below to find out whether you would make a successful freelancer.

Would you make a successful freelancer?

1 **If I had a customer who never paid his invoices,**
   a I would explain that I am approaching a cash flow crisis.
   b I would chase the debt at regular intervals. First I'd request payment by telephone and then by letter.

2 **If I wanted to expand my client base,**
   a I would let an agency deal with it.
   b I would look for my own work.

3 **Imagine the following situation:**
   You have a small consulting company and employ an experienced and reliable team of three people. However, you prefer to deal with the important task of customer contact and correspondence yourself.
   If this took up a lot of my time and I got behind schedule on several contracts,
   a I would train my staff to perform some tasks relating to client contact.
   b I would work at weekends to catch up.

4 **If I was working at a customer's site and I met an employee there who could do the task I was contracted to do,**
   a I would tell my customer he does not need me.
   b I would keep quiet. It is bad business to turn down work.

5 **If I was going to my first networking event and felt nervous,**
   a I would arrive early when there are very few people.
   b I would get there a bit later when it is quite busy.

6 **When it comes to getting ahead of my competitors, my philosophy is …**
   a 'Customers are attracted to low prices like bees to honey.'
   b 'Customers want a high quality product at a price that is fair.'

B Compare your answers with a partner, then find out whether going freelance is for you on page 128.

C A freelancer should be *independent* and *self-disciplined*. Think of other adjectives which could be used to describe a successful freelancer.

D With a partner, prepare a presentation on 'Going freelance' to be given at a seminar for 20 individuals who are considering setting up their own businesses. First, read an email from a participant on page 100.

MODULE 1

Grammar

Conditionals

A Look at sentences (1–4) below. Match them to a heading in the box.

a possible event in the future
an imagined or hypothetical situation
something that didn't actually happen
something that you usually do

1 If I had gone freelance sooner, I would have built up a bigger client base by now.
2 If I wanted to expand my client base, I would research the possibilities and make new contacts.
3 If a client doesn't pay on time, I email them and then phone a week later.
4 If a contractor charges a fair price the first time, the client will offer him more work.

B Match the sentences 1–4 in A with a conditional type: zero, first, second or third.

C Underline the correct answers.

1 If we *look / looked* at this chart, we see steady growth for the past two years.
2 If we don't get this product onto the market immediately, our competitors *will steal / would steal* our market share.
3 It *would be / had been* easier for consumers to navigate our website if we redesigned it.
4 If I'd been more adventurous, I *would have started / would start* my own retail business.
5 If I *am offered / will be offered* that job, I'll definitely take it.

"If I have to be at these boring meetings, I might as well get something out of it."

"Plus, if you do a good job we'll give you some furniture."

D Match a situation in the box below to a sentence in C.

strong recommendation   past regret   unreal future situation   fact   prediction

E Work in pairs. Ask each other questions based on the prompts below.

1 be self-employed   *What would you do if you were self-employed?*
2 find a job abroad
3 have more free time
4 study something different at university
5 can work wherever you like

▶ Review and development page 31
▶ Grammar overview page 155

INDEPENDENCE

Communication

Influencing

In business we need to influence colleagues, customers, bosses, suppliers and others. We may need to persuade them to work longer, accept a higher price, deliver more quickly or give you a promotion. There are two broad approaches to influencing, the *push approach* (presenting a strong argument in a forceful way) and the *pull approach* (asking the right questions to come to an agreement).

A Read the text below.

Katja Landmesser has been working for BLK Property for the last two years. She is responsible for writing reports on potential property acquisitions and developments. She understood when she joined BLK that she would be visiting properties and making assessments.

Phil Black is a Key Account Manager for Mackton Philips, a leading consultancy firm. His main customer is a supermarket chain, Costsavers. Mackton Philips has an annual contract with Costsavers to provide sales training.

 3.2

B Look at the Key language below. Listen to both Katja and Phil trying to influence and persuade someone. As you listen, answer these questions.

1 Who do you think they are trying to influence?
2 Do they use the push or pull approach?

C Listen again. What arguments do they use? Do you think they use the right approach?

Key language

The push approach	
Be well prepared	I'd like to talk about …
Make sure the objective is very clear	Could we review …?
Use a transparent process to move to your objective	There are two points I want to make.
Summarise and get a decision	So those are the main points. Can we decide?

The pull approach	
Be well prepared	Could we start with …?
Negotiate the objective	Shall we look at …?
Use questions to lead the process	How do you see the problem? What do you think are the priorities?
Ask for conclusions and action	What do you think is the next step?

D Work in pairs. Choose one of the situations below to practise the two approaches to influencing. Student A looks at this page. Student B looks at page 100.

1 You have been employed in the marketing team for seven years by your company and are responsible for organising exhibitions and trade fairs. You want to continue to do this work but on a freelance basis. Your partner is moving to another country and you would like to move with him / her. However, you are sure you can continue to organise events from abroad. You have the contacts and the experience. You can also travel for meetings where it is not possible to work by phone or videoconference. You think this is a win-win situation. The company will lose a salary and just pay for the results and you will have the freedom to live abroad.

2 You work closely with a team. One of your colleagues would like to reduce their working hours and so would you. You would like to do a job share with this colleague. You have analysed the workload and believe that you could do the two jobs in six days, with each of you working three days a week. The three days would have to be flexible to allow for personal commitments (e.g. children). You think this is a win-win situation for your boss because he / she gets more flexibility and lower salary costs.

▶ Review and development page 33
▶ Communication, page 148

BUSINESS ACROSS CULTURES

Motivation at work

Motivating people to work hard and effectively is a key factor for success in business. McClelland identified three motivational needs that work must satisfy (beyond the basic need to earn enough to live). These needs are acquired over time and are shaped by an individual's life experiences. They are found to varying degrees in everyone, and they influence our behaviour and the ways in which we are motivated.

A Apart from earning enough to survive, what motivates you at work?

B How important is each of the following to you?
- Power (a sense of having power over others)
- Achievement (a sense of reaching your goals)
- Affiliation (a sense of belonging to a group)

C People with a high need for affiliation like to feel accepted by other people, and they perform well in customer service and client interaction situations. Work in small groups. Brainstorm the characteristics and behaviour of:
- people with a need for power
- people with a need for achievement

Turn to page 129 to check your answers.

D According to McClelland's three motivational needs theory, how would you classify yourself?

Power

People with a high need for power have a strong need to lead and influence people. Power may be a common need across most cultures but the way we see power varies considerably.

🎧 3.3 **E** Listen to Georg and Suzanne talking about their jobs. As you listen, decide if these statements are true or false.

Georg
1. Georg worked for a state-owned company
2. The bosses were hands-on managers
3. The bosses kept close to their workforce
4. Georg could meet his targets
5. The new French managers are hands-on
6. The new management supports training

Suzanne
7. Suzanne was employed by a fashion house
8. Suzanne liked working with her colleagues
9. She now works for one of the top fashion houses
10. The fashion industry is not status conscious
11. The women treat men badly

F Look at the different styles of management below. Which have Georg and Suzanne experienced in their jobs?
- power distance (distance between bosses and workers)
- hierarchy (number of layers of management)
- management support (hands-on or hands-off)
- trust and respect (delegating and handing over responsibility)
- independence (working on your own, without a boss)
- servicing the customer / client (meeting business needs)

G What kind of organisation would you prefer to work for?

INDEPENDENCE

Personal and professional achievement

There is a lot of pressure on all of us to be results-oriented. However, not all of us are driven just by achieving financial results.

H Read about four entrepreneurs below and decide which factor drives them.

quality   security   community spirit   money   fame   size

1 Peter started his fitness business five years ago. His ambition is to establish his company as a local market leader in the fitness field. He feels passionate about fitness and wants to make a difference to the well-being of local people.

3 Hassan comes from a wealthy Lebanese family. He could have gone into the family business. Instead, he started his own online trading business. His aim is make his first million by the time he is 30.

2 Ira has set up her own design consultancy in Singapore. She wants to build a reputation for innovative design. In five years' time, she would like ARI Design to be synonymous with high-class design.

4 Imelda already runs Spain's largest financial consultancy – IME Asociados. Her aim is to expand internationally in order to build a really significant business. She already has partnerships in the UK and Germany. She is now looking at acquiring a consultancy business in Italy.

I Work in groups. Discuss what you are motivated to achieve. Use the factors above as a starting point.

Affiliation

Affiliation means feeling part of a group. Businesses often talk about 'stakeholders' as key members of the group – these include customers, employees, shareholders and the community. Building good relationships with key stakeholders is usually a major success factor.

3.4 **J** Listen to Matt talk about his key relationships at work. Which of these stakeholders does he mention?

customers   colleagues   community representatives   suppliers   investors   government authorities

K With a partner, discuss how involved you like to be or would like to be at work. Ask yourselves these questions.

1 Are colleagues important to me? Do I need to interact frequently with colleagues?
2 Do I need to belong to a team or do I prefer to work independently?
3 Do I like meetings or do I see meetings as necessary but painful?
4 Do I like to build social relationships with stakeholders or do I prefer to keep things on a professional level?

▶ Business across cultures page 151

Checklist
- ✓ advantages and disadvantages of being self-employed
- ✓ would you make a successful freelancer?
- ✓ conditionals: *If I'd gone freelance, I would have had more independence.*
- ✓ influencing
- ✓ motivation at work

PEOPLE

4 Are you being served?

Start-up

A In your country, which of these businesses are in the public sector (owned by the government), and which are in the private sector? Which might be in either sector?

car makers
postal services
train services
education
healthcare providers
telecoms providers
energy provider
bus services
electricians
banking and financial services

> Public sector or private sector? Competition, which flourishes in the private sector, guarantees lower prices and higher quality, while monopolies, common in the public sector, provide more expensive and less efficient services.

B Look at the statement above. What is a monopoly? Do you agree with the statement? Why / why not?

Listening and speaking

A Are you happier overall with the service you receive from the public sector or from the private sector? Explain why.

B In small groups, discuss the benefits and drawbacks of privatising public services.

🎧 4.1 **C** Listen to Laura Wright being interviewed about public and private sector services. Decide whether the following statements are true (T) or false (F).

1. The German company, DHL, is now running the UK's National Health Service (NHS).
2. Now, NHS clinical staff can spend more time in the stock room and less time on patient care.
3. Services or industries which provide social benefits usually have a monopoly.
4. As a result of privatisation of the UK railways, customers are now offered a broad range of services to the same destination.
5. In 1998, the Brazilian government sold off Telebras, the state-run phone company, as a pre-election bid for popularity.
6. Despite the privatisation of Telebras, telecommunications services in Brazil have not improved.

D In small groups, look at the boxes below. What is your experience of these public and private sector services in your own country and abroad? Have you ever had to complain about any of them?

Public
street cleaning
rubbish collection and recycling
public transport
a tax office
a hospital
a school
an embassy

Private
plumbing
a car repair centre
an airline
an electric goods company
a supermarket
a restaurant
a bank

E Imagine that your group is responsible for developing a strategy to increase customer satisfaction with one of the services above. Discuss what steps you will take and present your plan to the rest of the class.

ARE YOU BEING SERVED?

Grammar

Relative clauses

You use a relative clause after a noun to give more information about it. There are two main types: defining and non-defining.

The information in defining relative clauses is essential to the meaning of the sentence.
> Services or industries **which provide social benefits** usually have a monopoly.

In non-defining relative clauses the information is extra or non-essential, and is separated from the main clause by a comma.
> Then there's the privatisation of the water industry, **which has been a total failure for similar reasons.**

Relative clauses are usually introduced by the **relative pronouns** *who*, *whom*, *that*, and *which* (though *whom* is becoming rarer), as well as *whose* (+ noun) *when*, and *where*.
> *That* is not used to introduce non-defining relatives.

A Look at the sentences below from the interview. Identify the relative clauses and say whether they are defining or non-defining.

1 There is a great deal that public sector organisations can learn from private sector methods.
2 Supply chain management is the way that an organisation obtains and manages the supplies that it needs in order to run its operations. (Two relative clauses here).
3 Services which provide social benefits tend not to thrive under private ownership.
4 In 1998 the Brazilian government, which was trying to gain popularity before the elections, sold off Telebras.

B With a partner, discuss how you could complete the relative clauses in these sentences:

1 The public sector in a nation's economy consists of enterprises which _____

2 The people who _____ are not employed by the state.

3 Industries providing social benefits are often monopolies, which means _____

4 The postal service is an industry that _____

5 The telecoms industry, which _____, has been successfully privatised in Britain.

▶ Review and development page 32

▶ Grammar overview page 156

Reading and vocabulary

A In your culture, do people complain when they are not satisfied with a product or service?

B You are going to read a report about a survey on customer service in the public and private sectors in the UK. Several verb-noun collocations appear in the text. Match up the following verbs and nouns:

Verb	Noun
1 Deliver	a a high standard of customer service
2 Face	b tools
3 Meet / exceed	c customer service initiatives
4 Implement	d challenges
5 Deploy	e customer expectations

Now read the report on page 24 and check your answers.

C Read the report again and answer the questions that follow.

Awareness of rights causes expectations to rise

UK citizens are increasingly likely to complain when faced with poor service, according to a recent survey. This research comes as the public sector focuses increasingly on delivering a high standard of customer service.

The independent survey of customer service directors in public and private organisations across the UK commissioned by global customer service software company, Touchpaper, reveals that 85 per cent believe rising customer expectations about service levels are among the main challenges they face. 79 per cent point to greater awareness of consumer rights and 74 per cent highlight a cultural shift, with Britons losing their famous reserve, making them more confident about speaking up for themselves when they experience poor customer service.

'Meeting and exceeding the expectations of citizens is now central to public sector service delivery. Our research demonstrates that citizens have truly found their voices when it comes to complaining. More than ever citizens must be treated as valued customers,' commented Marina Stedman, Marketing Director of Touchpaper.

76 per cent agree that customer service could be improved through increased investment in technology. 80 per cent feel that they could benefit from more support from the IT department when implementing customer service initiatives.

'Technology has long had a role in customer service. Some of the exciting areas which are starting to make an impact include self-service systems which empower customers to resolve many simple enquiries themselves. Additionally, companies are now deploying intelligent self-learning tools that provide customer care staff with information that is most appropriate to specific customers,' explained Marina Stedman.

Worryingly, despite increasingly demanding customers, there is evidence of complacency. 51 per cent of those questioned complained of a lack of budgets for customer service, while 31 per cent admitted that boards and the organisation as a whole failed to understand the importance of customer service.

1 How has consumer behaviour changed in the UK?
2 Why are customer expectations rising?
3 How can technology have an impact on customer service?
4 What may prevent organisations from delivering a high standard of customer service?

D The report claims that UK consumers are becoming more aware of their rights. Do you know your rights as a consumer? With a partner, look at the situations below. What are your rights? If you are not sure, can you guess?

- A product becomes faulty within six months of purchase.
- A train is two hours late and you miss an important meeting with a client.
- You go on a terrible holiday that did not meet the description in the brochure.
- For the past four months, your bank has been charging you $12 a month for a special account which you don't have.

ARE YOU BEING SERVED?

Communication

Getting your message across

Successful communication depends on the sender and receiver of the message understanding each other. There are many things which can go wrong, for example, the sender might not encode the message clearly or the receiver might misinterpret the message. One way to be sure that your message gets across is to 'package' it so that the receiver is warned, before he or she receives it, what type of message it contains.

🎧 4.2 **A** Listen to Pablo Romero talking to his American manager, Carrie Styles. Pablo has a difficult message to communicate to Carrie.

1 What is the message?
2 Do you think Pablo communicated it well?

B Look at the Key language below. Listen again and, using the audio script on page 116, mark the moments when Pablo 'packages' his message.

Introducing the subject	I'd like to talk about … I wanted to mention … It concerns / It's about …
Structuring the subject	There are two points. The first …, the second … Before we come to that, can I … The other issue is …
Showing feelings	I'm worried / I'm disappointed / I'm very pleased.
Giving background	You may remember … As you know …
Bad news coming	Unfortunately, I'm afraid to say …
Good news coming	I'm pleased to say …
Making a suggestion	I'd like to suggest / propose …

C In pairs, practise getting these messages across. Student A looks at this page. Student B looks at page 101.

1 You want to tell your boss (Student B) about a problem you have with a colleague. Your colleague is making life very difficult for you and the rest of the team, because he / she is often late to work and does not work productively like the rest of the team. You think he / she is lazy and doesn't care about the job. You have mentioned that to your boss before but now it is becoming a risk to an important project. You think he / she should be moved out of the department or even the company.

2 You are the customer of Student B. You are waiting for a delivery of PX55s – an important order for you.

▶ Review and development page 33

▶ Communication page 148

BUSINESS ACROSS CULTURES

Organisational cultures

The culture of an organisation depends on many factors such as history, size and sector. In this section, we explore some of the differences between organisational cultures.

A Think of an organisation or institution where have you worked or studied. What did you like about it? What did you dislike?

4.3 B Marco Pestalozzi has applied for a job with BBN, an international food company, with its head office in Switzerland. He currently works in Italy for a Government Food Safety Committee. He is being interviewed by Regula Tschudin, an HR Manager. As you listen, make notes on the job description and organisational cultures of his current and possible new job.

FSC	BBN
Working on study of obesity in children	Advise Central Marketing Department on food safety issues

C Work in pairs. Compare your own work or study experiences. Cover the following areas:

- type of work / study
- processing speed of work
- targets and budgets
- team / individual work
- bureaucracy of organisation / institution

D Read the two job advertisements and answer the questions.

EXECUTIVE SALES CONSULTANT

Munro Systems is the world's leading international logistics company. Our global clients use our services to meet all their transport and supply needs.

We are looking for a dynamic individual with a strong background in sales. You will like working in a competitive environment with short deadlines and tough targets. We are looking for individuals who can make a difference to our business. Individuals must be self-motivated and be able to push their teams to really great performance.

PVA HEALTH INSURANCE

PVA are leading providers of health insurance to the private sector. Many major companies secure the health of their people by opting for one of PVA's packages. We are looking for Relationship Managers who can help to build our business. The role involves maintaining relationships with existing clients and building new relationships with prospects. PVA is an equal opportunities employer and we welcome applications from any candidate with experience of sales in the commercial sector. You will need to share our key values of integrity and caring and will join a team of professionals who are devoted to building a better and more secure future for our clients.

1 Could the same candidate apply for both jobs?
2 What sort of candidate would be attracted by the Munro Systems job?
3 What sort of candidate would be attracted by the PVA job?
4 Which job would you prefer and why?

ARE YOU BEING SERVED?

E Read the four descriptions of organisational cultures. Match the diagrams (1–4) to the culture.

1   2   3   4

A **power culture** concentrates power in a few pairs of hands. Control is from the centre. Power cultures have few rules and little bureaucracy; quick decisions can be made.

In a **role culture**, people have clearly delegated authority within a highly defined structure. Typically, these organisations form hierarchical bureaucracies, with many layers. Power comes from a person's position.

In a **task culture**, teams are formed to solve particular problems. Power comes from expertise and only lasts as long as a team requires expertise. These cultures often work on a matrix basis, with employees reporting to more than one person.

In a **person culture** the individual is the central point and its structure is as minimal as possible. Some professional partnerships can operate as person cultures, because each partner brings a special expertise and clients to the firm.

F Read about four companies. Match the organisational culture to one of these employers.

1 Mazine Electric Corporation has a flat but complex organisation. Most managers report to at least two bosses – their direct line manager and also a functional boss such as Operations Manager. A lot of the direction and progress in the company is provided by project teams.

_____ culture

2 The National Oil Company is a massive company, employing around 500,000 people. Nobody knows exactly how many people are employed and what they all do. Each department is like a separate empire, guarding its people and its survival.

_____ culture

3 Peters, Mallin and Buckshore is a second generation law firm. There are 18 partners, 40 associates and around 50 paralegals.

_____ culture

4 Enzoni is a family-owned business. Mario Enzoni, who is now in his seventies, still runs the company with an iron fist. The company occupies a profitable niche and has been able to survive the many fluctuations in the market.

_____ culture

▶ Business across cultures page 151

G Work in groups. Discuss the advantages and disadvantages of the organisational cultures above for both organisations and employees.

Checklist
- ✓ public and private sector
- ✓ relative clauses: *Services or industries which provide social benefits usually have a monopoly.*
- ✓ customer complaints
- ✓ getting your message across
- ✓ organisational cultures

BUSINESS SCENARIO 1

Mediaco

Background

Mediaco is a mid-size media company with 170 employees based in Bath, England. The company makes short films for local companies and advertisements shown on regional TV stations. The company has been in existence for five years. Recently morale among employees has been low. It is felt this is because within the various teams, people do not get on very well together and there are rumours that employees feel they are badly led.

Speaking

The CEO, Stella Wilmot, sent out an anonymous questionnaire to all employees. Read the responses to the questionnaire below. If you were the CEO, what you would do to improve the scores?

questionnaire

	Maximum 10
There is good communication within my team.	7.2
There is good communication between the various teams.	4.0
I feel that I am valued as an employee.	4.2
My manager is competent.	3.4
I get regular feedback from my manager.	4.1
I am given lots of responsibility.	4.5
I am motivated to reach my goals.	5.3
The organisation recognises employees' needs.	3.8

Stella has called a meeting with the HR Director and an outside consultant to discuss how morale can be improved and productivity increased. The ideas which will be considered are:

- Regular staff meetings
- Flexible working hours
- Team building events
- Six-monthly appraisals
- Management courses for new and old managers

MEDIACO

Language

Use the expressions below to talk about the different options.

- This would really help us to …
- I think this would be great for …
- This is just what we need to …
- I think that … would really improve with this.
- This would really help us to build our performance in the area of …
- If we do this, we …

- I don't think this would help because …
- I don't see how this can …
- What's the point of …ing?
- This might be counter-productive because …
- This could have negative effects because …
- If we do this it will only …

Role play

Work in groups of three. You are in a meeting to discuss all the options and decide which two options will be introduced.

Student A: You are Stella Wilmot, the CEO of Mediaco. You lead the discussion. Turn to page 101.

Student B: You are the HR Director, Brian Owen. Turn to page 103.

Student C: You are an outside consultant, Serena Tomkins. Turn to page 104.

Writing

Imagine you are the HR Director, Brian Owen. Write an email to all employees stating which two procedures have been implemented and why.

REVIEW AND DEVELOPMENT

1–4

Vocabulary Leadership characteristics

A Look again at the vocabulary on page 4. Then complete the crossword.

Across

6 If you aren't very friendly or approachable, you are _____ . (12)

8 If you like to control everyone and everything, you are _____ . (13)

Down

1 If you are a pushover you can be _____ to others. (11)

2 If you are enthusiastic about your job and keen to do it well, you're _____ . (9)

3 If you have a quality that attracts and inspires people, you're _____ . (11)

4 If you have strong and original ideas about the future, you're _____ . (9)

5 If you make people feel enthusiastic and interested, you're _____ . (9)

7 If you are courageous and not afraid to take risks, you're _____ . (9)

30

REVIEW AND DEVELOPMENT 1-4

Grammar

Modals

A Look again at the rules and examples on page 6. Underline the correct answer below.

1 The last boss was really approachable. He *would / will* talk to even the most junior trainees as equals.
2 It's hard to know how this new product will perform. It *must / could* turn out to be a real winner.
3 Your English is really good. You *must / might* have lived in the States in the past.
4 As a leader you *may not / shouldn't* be running around doing every single job.
5 You *must / can't* delegate tasks if you have too much work to do.

B Match each of the sentences in A to a function in the box below. (One of the functions is not used.)

| ability   prediction   deduction   obligation   past habits   advice |

▶ Grammar overview page 154

Vocabulary

Idioms

A Look again at the idioms on page 12 and correct one word in each of the sentences below to make it correct.

1 The programme did not have enough viewers, so the TV company withdrew the plug on it.
2 I wanted to finish the proposal by this evening, but I've been rushed off my legs all day.
3 OK, let's stop talking about secondary issues and go to the chase.
4 We've ignored the problems for a long time, but now we need to confront the music.
5 The department is overstaffed: half the people there are not pulling their share.
6 She was very quick to pull the new situation on board.
7 I've been meaning to call you, but I've eaten a lot on my plate recently.
8 I need to touch heads with the US office and let them know how things are going.

Grammar

Conditionals

A Look again at the rules and examples on page 18. Match the two parts of each sentence.

1 If I hadn't worked in publishing for 20 years,
2 If you qualify as a teacher,
3 He'll go freelance
4 I wouldn't have been able to look after my daughter during the holidays
5 If we had enough people to do the work,
6 In some countries you pay more in tax

a when he earns enough money in his salaried job.
b I wouldn't have had the knowledge to become a freelance editor.
c you can get a job where you mainly work independently.
d we would do it all in-house.
e if you become self-employed.
f if I had still been working in my office job.

B Match the sentences (1–6) with a conditional type.

C Say what you would do in each of these situations, using the first or second conditional appropriately, depending how likely or unlikely it is to happen to you.

1 You are made redundant. *If I'm made redundant, I'll easily find another job.*
2 You become self-employed.
3 You are appointed CEO of your company.
4 You take early retirement.
5 You are offered a job abroad.

D It's five years later. Imagine that the situations in C really occurred. Say what happened as a consequence.

Example
1 *If I hadn't been made redundant, I wouldn't have found this better job.*

▶ Grammar overview page 155

31

MODULE 1

Grammar

Relative clauses

A Look again at the rules and examples on page 23. Match the sentences below and then insert an appropriate relative pronoun from the box below.

| that   where   which   who   whose |

1 The drug _____
2 The City is the leading financial centre in London, _____
3 Paul Bishop was a company executive _____
4 The privatisation of the post office, _____
5 The candidate _____

a was invented last year will save thousands of lives.
b CV was outstanding was offered the job.
c has not been discussed much in the media, could be next.
d you'll find hundreds of international banks.
e was shot in mysterious circumstances last year.

▶ Grammar overview page 156

Vocabulary

Verb-noun combinations

A Look again at the examples on page 23. Match the verbs (1–5) to the correct nouns (a–e).

Verb	Nouns
1 deliver	a assets / resources / troops
2 face	b decisions / measures / reforms
3 exceed	c results / goods / services
4 implement	d limits / quotas / targets
5 deploy	e bankruptcy / criticism / difficulties

B Now put the verb in brackets in the correct form and choose the most suitable noun from above to complete each of these sentences. (One of them is in the passive.)

1 There was chaos when China was accused of _____ (exceed) _____ for imports of clothing into Europe, and millions of pounds of clothing was held up in warehouses.

2 All employers are expected to _____ (implement) safety _____ to minimise hazards in the workplace.

3 The Internet grocery _____ (deliver) fresh _____ to customers in specially designed vans, but it went bankrupt in 2001.

4 Considerable _____ _____ (deploy) to ensure the success of the product launch last year.

5 In the last few months, the ministry _____ (face) _____ over its failure to prevent the outbreak of the disease.

REVIEW AND DEVELOPMENT 1–4

Communication

Look again at the communication skills pages in Units 1–4. Then complete the exercises.

A Look at the sentences below. Change the style to its opposite in brackets. The first one has been done for you as an example.

1 The answer is no. (Indirect)   *I'm afraid I'm not sure about this.*
2 The system needs to be reviewed. (Personal)
3 You should resign before it is too late. (Asking questions)
4 The performance was good. (Emotional)
5 Good morning, Mr Spencer. How do you do? (Informal)

B Read the dialogue below and add appropriate questions and comments (1–5).

A: 1 _____ (open question)

B: I work for a food company. I am in charge of quality control. This means that I have to oversee all production and make sure it all conforms to the quality standards

A: 2 _____ (show interest)

B: It's becoming more and more demanding as there has been a lot of legislation in this area, especially in the area of food safety and hygiene.

A: 3 _____ (clarify the job scope to include food safety)

B: When I started, it was just me in charge of quality. Now I have a team working throughout the plant. I have to manage the team and that's not so easy.

A: 4 _____ (confirm understanding)

B: The problem is that they all have their specialities and it's difficult to get them working as a team. They tend to do their jobs but not really talk to each other.

A: 5 _____

(summarise two main issues: demanding legislation and team management)

C Read the text below about trying to persuade a freelancer to become a salaried employee. Does it use a 'push' or a 'pull' approach?

'This is a great opportunity for you. This company is really going places and you could be a key member of the team. As a freelancer, you aren't really involved in the decision-making process and you are allocated tasks we need you to do. As a salaried employee, you'd become much more involved. I want to really use your potential and I am sure you can contribute a lot to the future success of the team. We have an attractive benefits package on offer – your salary will be in line with your current freelance fees and on top of that, you'll be part of the company pension and bonus scheme. I think you've got a real future with this company.'

D In pairs, prepare some questions based on the text in order to use the opposite approach.

Example *Could we talk about the possibility of becoming a salaried employee?*

E Your company wants to improve the customer service it offers. It has decided to train all employees in this area. Your job is to present this initiative to the management committee. Use the notes opposite to help you get your message across.

> Introduction: new training course for all employees on customer service
> Structure: two key areas, communication and attitudes
> Showing feelings: this is key area for the future of the company
> Giving background: negative feedback from customers
> Bad news coming: poor attitudes of certain employees
> Good news coming: good results from this training in other parts of the company
> Making a suggestion: managers should attend first to show commitment

▶ Writing resource 13
page 94

MARKETS

5 Entering new markets

Start-up

A In pairs, think of some foreign companies or foreign brands that have entered the market in your country. How successful have they been? Did they do it alone or with local partners?

> $10 million of international trade is conducted every minute!

Vocabulary and listening

A Look at the different methods of market entry below. Match each method (1–6) to its definition (a–f).

1 Indirect export
2 Direct export
3 Licensing
4 Joint venture
5 Direct investment
6 Franchising

a The company buys or merges with a company in the country or sets up its own subsidiary there.
b Companies sell the rights for a local company to operate a business using the original brand name and range of products or services.
c Companies deal with their own exports, for example by setting up sales offices in the country.
d Companies sell the rights to use a trademark or patent.
e Two companies, for example an overseas firm and a local one, work together to develop a particular market.
f Exporters sell goods through intermediaries such as export agents.

B Work in pairs. Try to list at least two examples for each method where a foreign company or brand has entered your home market.

5.1

C Listen to an export manager talking about three different ways of getting into new markets. Match each extract to one of the methods of market entry in A.

D Listen again and complete the table.

	Method	Advantage	Disadvantage
1			
2			
3			

E What phrases did the speaker use to refer to advantages and disadvantages? Write down as many as you can remember, then check the audio script on page 117.

Example
It has its downsides.

F Can you think of any other expressions for advantages and disadvantages?

34

ENTERING NEW MARKETS

Reading and speaking

A What are the advantages and disadvantages of joint ventures? Discuss with a partner.

B Read the article about joint ventures.

Partnerships feel the Indian heat

'I love India – the opportunities are fantastic,' says Sir Anthony Bamford, chairman and owner of JCB, the UK excavator maker. Well he should, as JCB is a leader in India in mid-sized construction machines. But at least part of JCB's success in India comes from its general policy on joint ventures – it tries to avoid them. JCB likes to be in charge and, in the past seven years, it has ended its partnership with Indian engineering group, Escorts. Now the UK company is expanding operations in India, where it has two plants and recently announced a $50m (£27m) manufacturing expansion.

Until the late 1990s, when the rules were relaxed, the Indian government usually insisted that foreign investors must team up with a local company, mainly to ensure that India-owned businesses would gain access to technical know-how. In the past ten years, the Indian government has made it easier for foreign companies to have full control over their operations there. Before this, investors were required to set up joint ventures with local Indian companies.

Even so, joint ventures remain mandatory in several sectors, such as telecommunications, agriculture, retailing and insurance. Moreover, they hold several attractions for inward investors: they can share the investment risks and gain access to the local company's customer base. But often, says Shirish Sankhe, a manufacturing expert in the Mumbai office of McKinsey, the strategy consultancy, the arrangements have worked out poorly. A wholly owned operation means the multinational can keep better control of technology and 'push on with developments at a speed that suits what it wants to do,' he says.

India's fast growing motorbikes market illustrates some of the potential problems of joint ventures. TVS Motor, the third biggest motorbike maker in India, started a joint venture in 1984 with Suzuki, the Japanese motorbike and car maker. For TVS, the collaboration gained it expertise, particularly of Suzuki's engine technology. For the Japanese company, the alliance was the only way into the market because of government restrictions. But the co-operation worked out happily for neither side and five years ago TVS bought out Suzuki's share in the venture.

'We gained some engineering expertise from Suzuki, so in this sense we got something from the partnership,' says Venu Srinivasan, TVS chairman. 'But in terms of the most interesting new technical developments, Suzuki wanted to keep its technology for itself. It was frustrating as we were keen to develop our own capabilities.' TVS then expanded its technology, particularly in engines, and has made good progress while Suzuki started a wholly owned company to make motorcycles in India, which began production last year.

C Look at the statements below. Number the order in which they appear in the article. Then answer the questions at the end of each statement.

a India's regulation of foreign investment is becoming less severe. In what ways?
b TVS did not gain as much from its joint venture with Suzuki as it had hoped. Why not?
c India still regulates foreign investment in some industries. Which ones?
d JCB was involved in a joint venture with an Indian company. Who was it with and what happened to it?
e In TVS's collaboration with Suzuki, there were gains in both directions. What were they?

D Work in pairs or small groups.

Student / Group A: You represent TVS.

Student / Group B: You represent Suzuki.

TVS has had a joint venture with Suzuki for about 15 years, but now wishes to end the arrangement for some of the reasons mentioned in the article. Hold a meeting between the two companies, in which TVS presents its arguments for ending the joint venture. Suzuki can either argue for or against ending the joint venture. Make sure both sides give their reasons.

35

Grammar

Determiners and quantifiers

Determiners and quantifiers are words that are used before a noun to show which person or thing you mean, or to show the quantity of something. The commonest determiners are the **definite article** *the* and the **indefinite article** *a(n)*.

A Fill in the gaps with *the* or *a*.

1 JCB is _____ leader in India in construction machines. Now _____ UK company is expanding operations there.

2 TVS Motor and Suzuki set up _____ joint venture in 1984. _____ partnership ended with dissatisfaction on both sides.

3 In _____ past ten years, _____ Indian government has relaxed _____ investment rules. Before that, _____ foreign investor had to team up with _____ local company.

B Complete the text about joint ventures using the determiners in the box.

| a | enough | any | neither | several | this | another | little | both | other |

(1) _____ joint venture is a partnership between two companies and has (2) _____ advantages for (3) _____ parties, such as the spreading of investment risks. But are there (4) _____ major problems? One is that the foreign company may have (5) _____ knowledge of the local company's background, and (6) _____ knowledge may be difficult to acquire. (7) _____ drawback is that management styles and (8) _____ cultural factors may result in poor integration, so there may not be (9) _____ day-to-day interaction between the companies. In some cases, (10) _____ company ends up gaining from the partnership.

C Look at the determiners in B again. Are they followed by a singular count noun, a plural count noun, or an uncount noun? Complete the table.

Singular count	Plural count	Uncount

Quantifiers are often the same words as determiners, but they are followed by *of*, e.g *both of us work*. The words in **C** are also **quantifiers**, except for *every*.

The partnership illustrates **many of the problems** of joint ventures.
Suzuki shared **little of its technology** with us.
In the end, **neither of us** was satisfied with the arrangement.

D Work in pairs. Look at the sentences below and discuss which quantifiers are grammatically correct.

1 Asia contains (both of / neither of / all of / several of) the world's most highly populated and fastest growing major economies.

2 (Many of / Much of / Little of / A few of) the most successful European businesses operating in India and China produce and sell locally.

3 (Each of / All of / Neither of / Any of) the case studies showed that local consumers are the biggest beneficiaries of market-seeking investment.

▶ Review and development page 60

▶ Grammar overview page 157

ENTERING NEW MARKETS

Communication

Presentations: Engaging your audience 1

Presenters need to make sure there are no barriers between them and their audience. In this section, we are going to practise engaging your audience.

A Have you ever done a presentation? What did you do to engage the audience?

B Study the communication techniques below.

Technique	Example	
Make contact with your audience at the start	Tell them something personal about yourself, to show them you are human.	My daughter asked me where I was going today and I told her …
	Tell them something about your personal situation.	You see me standing here in the only clothes I have – the airline have the rest!
	Ask them a question.	I come from York. Have any of you visited this city?
Keep an eye on the physical distance from the audience	Make sure you do not stand far from the audience.	
	Make sure you do not stand behind a desk. Come to the front.	
	Make sure you do not 'hide behind' your slides.	
Slides	Give detailed information in handouts, rather than in slides.	
	Use slides occasionally; do not use them all the time; switch off the beamer if you are not showing a slide.	
Audience interaction	Get feedback from the audience. Don't wait until the end.	I'd like some feedback. What do you think about this?
		Before I go on, are there any questions?
		Is everything clear so far?

 5.2

C Listen to two extracts from two presentations. Which presentation engages the audience better? Why?

D Listen to the second presentation again. What techniques above does the presenter use to engage the audience?

E Prepare a presentation on one of the following topics:
- What you learnt from a recent business trip
- Main differences between doing business in your home market and your main export/foreign market
- Outsourcing trends in business
- Breaking into a new market

▶ Review and development page 63

▶ Communication page 148

F Give your presentation. Make sure you engage with your audience.

BUSINESS ACROSS CULTURES

India

India is set to become one of the world's super powers of the 21st century. In this section, we take a look at India and the challenges of doing business there.

A What do you know about India? In pairs, answer the questions. Compare your answers with the rest of the class. Then turn to page 133 to check your answers.

Quiz

1 The official religion in India is
 a Hinduism.
 b Islam.
 c There is no official religion.

2 Match the main Indian religious groups to the percentages.
 a Sikh   1 2.3 per cent
 b Buddhist, Jain, Parsi   2 13.4 per cent
 c Hindu   3 1.9 per cent
 d Muslim   4 80.5 per cent
 e Christian   5 1.8 per cent

3 When an Indian shakes his head once from side to side he means
 a no, I don't agree.
 b yes, I am listening.
 c I don't know.

4 Cows wander unattended along streets in the cities because
 a they belong to no one.
 b they are sacred.
 c they are sent by their owners to eat whatever they find.

5 The red dot, called a bindi, that Indian women often wear on their forehead
 a indicates they are married.
 b indicates they are devout Hindus.
 c is usually a fashion accessory.

ENTERING NEW MARKETS

B Read the article and answer the questions.

'Made in China' may be getting a new rival.

As global manufacturers seek new places to plant their flags, India – where factories have long been noticeable because of their absence – is seeing early signs of an industrial boom. The effects could be profound for India's vast number of poor people, and for the international sourcing of goods. For decades, manufacturing in India was restricted by old-fashioned labour laws, creaking infrastructure and paperwork. The new economy of call centres and software campuses has benefited the relatively privileged, but for many of the 75 per cent of Indians with less than middle-school education, few factories meant few jobs.

Special economic zones – the same type of areas of relative economic freedom that spearheaded China's export led industrialisation – are now spreading here, providing tax holidays, more control over infrastructure like water and power, and less regulation. At least 75 zones are in the pipeline, with more than a dozen already operating.

Hyundai Motor, which produces a new car in Tamil Nadu every minute, has made India its global hub for the Santro hatchback; it plans to ship 100,000 India-made cars to 60 nations this year, and 300,000 within two years.

'Geographically, it's close to the market, and the second thing is the very highly educated people in India,' said Heung Soo Lheem, chief of India operations for Hyundai, explaining why his company had invested in the country. Thirdly, he said, 'the suppliers here are – I do not say better than China, but maybe the same. And the labour costs are less than China.'

1. What is your image of Indian culture? Does the article reinforce this image?
2. What is India doing to attract the right types of industry? Do you think the developed world can continue to compete in traditional industrial areas?
3. What advantages does India have over China according to Heung Soo Lheem?
4. Do you think India will be able to build on these advantages?

C Doing business in India is not always straightforward for foreigners. Work in groups of 3 or 4. Make a list of some of the cross-cultural challenges you think people will face when working in India.

D You are going to listen to Arvind Patel talking about doing business in India. Look at the subjects in the box below. Are any of them the same as your list in C?

| Time | Money | Dress | Agreement | Initiative | Seniority |
| Hierarchy | Family | Relationships | Gifts | Bureaucracy |

5.3 **E** Listen to the interview. Which of the subjects in D does he mention?

F Listen again. Make notes under each headings.

G Work in pairs. Choose a culture you know well, and design a set of questions for each of the headings in D. Then role-play the new interview.

H Read the text below about time. In pairs, brainstorm all the ways that different attitudes to time can influence the way of doing business with another culture. Use the list below as a starting point.

The working day/week   Work breaks   Punctuality

Some cultures are very time dominated and measure much of their lives against the clock. Other cultures (such as India) are not as time conscious, don't consider it as such an important value and will be less led by the clock.

▶ Business across cultures
page 152

I Brief the rest of the class on attitudes towards time when doing business in your culture.

Checklist

- ✓ methods of market entry
- ✓ joint ventures
- ✓ determiners and quantifiers: *a, the, both, neither*
- ✓ engaging your audience
- ✓ India

MARKETS

6 The right look

Start-up

A Look at the quotation opposite. In pairs, list all the things a company can do to ensure that it achieves this goal.

> The secret of marketing is to have the right product in the right place at the right time.

Reading and speaking

A In small groups, list all the things you know about the clothes shop chain, Zara.

B Read the article and answer the questions.

THE FUTURE OF fast fashion

WHEN MADONNA recently gave a series of concerts in Spain, teenage girls were able to wear at her last performance the same outfit that she had worn for her first concert. Welcome to the world of instant fashion, in which a Spanish company is defying conventional wisdom and building a global brand: Zara.

Instead of trying to create demand for new trends in the summer and winter seasons using fashion shows, Zara studies the demands of the customers in its stores and then tries to deliver an appropriate design at lightning speed. In the process, Zara has become the most profitable arm of Inditex, a holding company of eight retail brands, and one of the biggest success stories in Spanish business.

How can Inditex thrive when Europe's entire textile industry is supposed to be under threat from cheap imports from China? At Inditex's heart there is a vertical integration of design, just-in-time production, delivery and sales. Some 300 designers work at the firm's head office in La Coruña in Galicia. They are in daily contact with store managers to discover bestselling items.

Fabric is cut in-house and then sent to a cluster of several hundred local, independently owned firms for sewing. When the finished product is returned, it is ironed, carefully checked and wrapped in plastic for transport on conveyor belts to a group of giant warehouses. Twice a week lorries deliver the garments to other European countries and by aircraft to the rest of the world.

Production is deliberately carried out in small batches to avoid oversupply. While there is some replenishment of stock, most lines are replaced quickly with yet more new designs rather than with more of the same. This helps to create a scarcity value. Shoppers cannot be sure that something that has caught their eye will appear in the store again – or can be found at another Zara store, even in the same city. On the other hand, they also know that everyone they meet will not be wearing it.

1 What does Zara do to create clothes that consumers want?
2 How does Zara's strategy differ from those of other designer clothes companies?
3 How quickly does Zara deliver new designs to the market?
4 Who owns Zara?
5 How does Zara know what is selling in its stores?
6 Where does Zara make most of its clothes?
7 Why is it sometimes not possible to find the same item in more than one store?

C Work in small groups. Decide what you think is Zara's USP (unique selling proposition) and invent a slogan or phrase that could be used in Zara's advertising.

Vocabulary

A Match the expressions from the article (1–10) to its meaning (a–j).

1 conveyor belt
2 cluster
3 vertical integration
4 just-in-time production
5 replenishment of stock
6 warehouse
7 in batches
8 garments
9 fabric
10 bestselling items

a when goods are produced as and when they are needed
b when new items are ordered to replace those already sold
c a group of companies in the same area with the same activities
d a building where large quantities of goods are stored
e a machine for moving materials, goods, etc. from one part of a company site to another
f when a company directly controls all the stages of its business, from design and production to distribution and sales
g material such as cotton, wool or linen from which clothes are made
h clothes designs which are the most popular
i in separate groups
j another word for clothes

B Complete the sentences below using the appropriate forms of expressions in A.

There is some (1) _____, but most new stock has a different design.

(2) _____ is cut in-house and then sent out to (3) _____ of local firms for sewing.

Store managers send back information about the (4) _____ items to the designers.

(5) _____ are delivered by lorry to stores all over Europe and by plane to the rest of the world.

The final product is prepared for transport and sent on (6) _____ to very large (7) _____.

Production is carried out (8) _____.

Speaking

A Rearrange the boxes above in the right order to create a flow chart of Zara's design, production and delivery process. Present the flow chart to your partner. Use words such as *first, next, then, after that, finally* to indicate the sequence of steps in the process.

B Draw a flow chart to show how the products or services of your organisation are produced and distributed, and explain it to your partner.

MODULE 2

Grammar

The passive

You form the **passive** using the auxiliary verb *be* in the appropriate tense + the past participle of the main verb. You can use a modal like *can* or *should* before *be*.

Latest sales trends **are communicated** *to Zara HQ by store managers.*
A new version of an existing model **can be found** *in the shops within two weeks.*

A Work in pairs. Look at the text again on page 40 and do the following:
1. Find uses of the passive where the verb *be* is omitted. Why is this?
2. Find passive structures that contain **adverbs**. What is the position of the adverb?
3. Find a passive structure that contains a **modal verb**.
4. Change the passive structures in the text into active ones. Is there any reason for using the passive?

B Complete the sentences below using the passive form of the verb in brackets.
1. The production process _____ rapidly _____ (set) in motion, controlled by Zara's head office in Spain.
2. A design team _____ (send) to copy and distribute the design at lightning speed.
3. After as little as five weeks, the outfit _____ (can buy) at Zara outlets all over the world.
4. A stunning dress _____ (wear) at a special event by a celebrity – a pop star or an actor.

C Put the sentences in B in the right order to show the correct sequence of steps. Link them using *first, what happens next is*, etc.

▶ Review and development page 61
▶ Grammar overview page 158

Information exchange

A One of Zara's biggest competitors is the Swedish firm H&M. Work in groups of three to exchange information about the two companies' business strategies.

Student A: Look at this page. Obtain information from Students B and C to complete the table.
Student B: Look at page 101.
Student C: Look at page 105.

Design and production	Zara	H&M
Designers	Recruits young unknown designers directly from top design schools.	Uses star designers like Stella McCartney.
Number of new items launched every year		
Time to produce a new garment from design to delivery		

Advertising and discounts		
Advertising spending		
Discounts		

Plans for growth		
Number of shops in US		
Number of new shops over next four years worldwide		

B Give a short presentation summarising the information.

THE RIGHT LOOK

Communication

Presentations: Engaging your audience 2

Presenters are most successful when they show that they have not only looked at a topic from their point of view, but also viewed it through the audience's eyes. In this section, we practise this two-sided approach.

6.1 **A** Geoff Peacock is the Marketing and Sales Director for an international food company. He is talking to a group of sales and marketing people working for one of the local subsidiaries. He wants to get them to accept a new structure for their function. As you listen, make notes on the old and new structure.

	Old Structure	New Structure
Reporting line	to the local market head	
Marketing plans		
Performance pay		

B Look at the Key language box below. Listen again to the presentation and write down the expressions he uses which are equivalent to the ones below. If necessary, use the audio script on page 118.

Key language

Opening with the situation	I know you are short of time so … I reckon / I guess you know why I am here.
Keeping people informed	I wanted to update you. Let me give you some background.
Recognising success	You have done a very good job. We are delighted with your results.
Acknowledging anxieties	Don't worry, we … I can see you are asking how …
Involving them in the challenge	We are sure you can make a contribution. This is a real opportunity to … We want to use your expertise to …

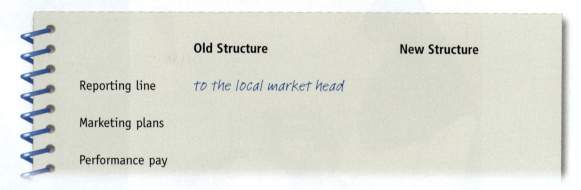

C Study the following situation from the employer and employees' points of view. Prepare a presentation to convince the employees about this change.

Maverick Clothing has always worked two shifts – 06.00 to 14.00 and 14.00 to 22.00. Now, Maverick Management wants to introduce a third shift, from 22.00 to 06.00. This is the result of increased sales but also a need to respond more quickly to the market. It will mean all employees will have to work a night shift. You are proposing four-day cycles followed by two days off. Currently they work five-day cycles with the weekend off. The new shift pattern will mean the factory can be run 24 hours, seven days a week. In this way, the company will be more competitive and responsive to the market.

▶ Review and development page 63

▶ Communication page 149

BUSINESS ACROSS CULTURES

Dress

The way we dress and the clothes we wear may seem like an unimportant part of our everyday lives. Yet in every culture, dress is one of the most powerful forms of communication. By using visual clues provided by dress, people quickly 'place' each other by making guesses about things such as the age, social status, occupation, religion, and ethnic or national identity of those they meet.

A Look at the photos below. With a partner, 'place' each person. Think about the following to help you build a profile: age, occupation, nationality, hobbies and interests.

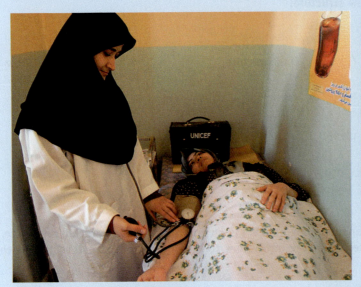

B Work in pairs. Read the sentences below and decide if the advice is true for your culture. Feed back to the rest of the class. Make any changes or additions that you think are important.

1. Dress smartly at work.
2. Choose conservative and sombre colours.
3. Never start a 'best-dressed competition' with colleagues.
4. Use your clothes to make a strong impression when first meeting people (e.g. at interviews or first meetings with clients).
5. Women shouldn't dress provocatively.
6. Always wear smart and clean shoes.

THE RIGHT LOOK

C Read the introduction to dressing across cultures. What's your view about people who pay a lot of attention to their appearance?

A brilliant IT strategist landed his dream job in Milan. While his plans and proposals were flawless and the company was destined for increased productivity, his ideas were greeted with only a small amount of enthusiasm. A native colleague politely informed him that his too-casual jeans, rumpled shirts, and unkempt hair were holding him back. Shocked that he should be judged on what he perceived as superficial, he looked around at his well-dressed counterparts. It was time for a change of attitude, and trousers.

Abroad we judge the dress; at home we judge the man. (Chinese proverb)

6.2 **D** Listen to Kate talking about attitudes towards dress in the UK. What advice does she give Dolores? Make notes under the headings below.

the seasons   colours in the office   dress-down culture   customer contact

E In pairs, prepare a briefing about dress that you could give to someone who has recently come to work or study in your country.

F Read the text below about a dispute between an employee and her employer. In groups, discuss the questions.

A devout Christian said today she planned to take legal action against her employer after they ruled that displaying her crucifix was against uniform rules. Gill Riley was sent home after refusing to remove the crucifix. The company upheld the decision and said Ms Riley had failed to comply with 'uniform regulations'. Ms Riley, who has worked with the company for five years, is suing her employer for religious discrimination after being suspended from work without pay for three weeks. The company's policy on uniform states that staff must not wear visible jewellery while at work.

1 Do employers have the right to dictate dress code at work?
2 Is it better to keep religion out of work?

G Read the scenario below. Work in small groups to decide what the company should do.

A young Muslim woman, who is a potential high-flyer in your company, based in Europe, has started to wear a headscarf (hijab), which she says is an important part of her Muslim identity. Her work is excellent, but her manager is worried how clients will perceive her. The company has no policy on this.

▶ Business across cultures page 152

H Work in pairs. Role play the interview with the young Muslim woman to communicate your decision.

Checklist

✓ the future of fast fashion: Zara
✓ words to do with fashion production: *vertical integration, warehouse*
✓ passive: *trends are communicated to the store's HQ*
✓ engaging your audience
✓ dress

MARKETS

7 Brand strategy

Start-up

A In your opinion, which brand names best sum up the idea of 'excellence' in these products and services? Explain why.

cars   men's suits   hotel chains   computers   airlines
furniture   cosmetics   banks

> 'Your brand is what people say about you when you're not in the room.'
> **Jeff Bezos, CEO, Amazon**

B How important are brand names to you? Are you willing to pay more for brand names? Do you think a higher price means better quality? Discuss your ideas with a partner.

Reading and speaking

A What are the benefits of extending a brand? What are the risks?

B Read the article and match the words in italics with the definitions (1–7) below.

When Bruce Stevens became president and chief executive of Steinway & Sons in 1985, he took charge of an *iconic* American brand that had been in existence for 132 years. From Manhattan to Moscow, the name Steinway *triggered thoughts of* 'top quality piano' and 'concert hall quality'. And there was a good reason. Virtually every top pianist in the world performed on a Steinway piano.

In the decade before Stevens took over, there had been a series of owners, and in 1984 Steinway was up for sale again. The fact that Steinway was on the market put the company *in limbo* for a full year. Not knowing who was going to acquire the company or when, Steinway dealers put orders on hold and inventories mounted. But instead of focusing on short-term solutions, Stevens began to lead the company on a slow, methodical climb back to stability. He carefully examined the sales structure and eventually *trimmed* the number of dealers by two-thirds. *Re-orchestrating* Steinway's marketing took five years.

Another major challenge, however, began to emerge. Steinway lacked entry-level and mid-level pianos, so its dealers would stock less expensive pianos from other manufacturers to satisfy lower price points. It would have been suicide to put the Steinway name on an entry-level piano, the company concluded. 'There is no such thing as a cheaper Steinway,' Stevens says.

To fill this need, the company agonised about how to create new lower-priced brands that would *leverage* the image of the Steinway brand, but not *tarnish* it. The result was 'Boston, designed by Steinway.' 'The worry that we went through when we came out with the Boston brand in 1991!' Stevens recalls. 'We came so close to not doing it for fear of hurting the golden success of the Steinway brand.'

But it worked so well for the mid-level Boston brand that the company also created an entry-level 'Essex, designed by Steinway' brand in 2000, with an even lower price point. Both the Boston and Essex pianos are manufactured in Japan for customers who can't afford $40,000 to $100,000 for one of the 4,500 'real' Steinway pianos produced each year.

And the future? Steinway & Sons opened a Shanghai operation two years ago, and Stevens sees markets in Asia as the major area of future growth, especially China. With the present sales breakdown of 65 per cent in the US and 35 per cent in the rest of the world, he sees this situation reversing in the next 10 years, driven by Chinese demand. He will develop the new Chinese business the same way he presently runs Steinway & Sons – slowly and carefully.

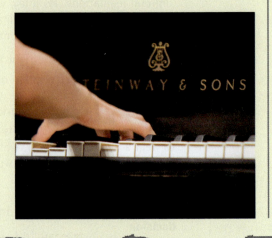

1 a state of uncertainty
2 to damage
3 famous and represents a way of life
4 to reduce
5 to make people think of something automatically
6 to improve or enhance
7 to rework

BRAND STRATEGY

C Read the article again and say who or what the following things are.

1 Steinway   2 Bruce Stevens   3 Boston   4 Essex   5 China

D Here are some examples of brand extension. What do you think of them from a marketing point of view?

- A maker of large saloon cars starts making small, compact cars under the same name.
- A travel agent specialising in cheap holidays in the sun in short-haul destinations starts to market upmarket holidays to long-haul destinations.
- The owner of a rock music record label uses the same name for a transatlantic airline.

E In pairs, discuss how the following brands could be extended.

Shell   Rolex   Nokia   Adidas   Wrigley

Listening

 7.1

A You are going to listen to four extracts of consumers comparing local and global brands. Listen to the extracts and decide which point in the box below is being discussed.

Quality and standards
Market relevance
Price
Value for money
Community
Consistency
Social responsibility
Credibility

B Listen again and decide if the following sentences are true or false.

1 The Chinese manufacturer TCL made fun of Motorola's handsets.
2 Chinese customers have exactly the same taste as Western customers.
3 She goes to her local farmers' market only because she believes importing food is bad for the environment.
4 Going to the supermarket is not as enjoyable as going to the farmers' market.
5 The first speaker isn't aware of a local PC maker who can provide after-sales support as efficiently as a large company.
6 The second speaker couldn't fix his PC himself because he hasn't got the technical skills.
7 When local companies exploit their employees, people pay no attention.
8 Global brand companies should follow the example of local brands by acting with integrity.

C Do you agree with the consumers' views and observations? Discuss with a partner.

Information exchange

A Work in pairs. You are going to find out about a company called Spruce Shirts. First, read the information below.

> Building brands is all about enhancing relationships with the customer and developing loyalty based on reputation and trust. Corporate social responsibility (CSR) is becoming increasingly important to brand image.

Student A looks at page 102.
Student B looks at page 106.
Exchange information to build a complete picture of the company's situation.
Student A should start.

B In small groups, study the information about Spruce Shirts. As the management of the company, hold a meeting to work out how you are going to improve your brand's image.

MODULE 2

Grammar

Making comparisons

When you make comparisons, you can use words like *slightly* and *infinitely* with a comparative adjective or adverb to emphasise the size of the difference between two things.

*Global brands are **infinitely better**.*

You use *as* to say that two things are the same or similar, and words like *just* or *nearly* to make the comparison more precise. For negatives you use *not as* or phrases like *nothing like as*.

*Treating your employees well is **just as important**.*
*Supermarket shopping is **nothing like as enjoyable**.*

To make an **explicit** comparison within a sentence, you use *than* or *as ... as*.

*TCL's handsets were **a lot flashier than** the ones made by their competitors.*
*Their after-sales support is **just as efficient as** anything a big company can offer.*

A Complete the table with words from the box below that have similar meanings.

| nowhere near | just | a little | much | far | a great deal | nearly | slightly |

a lot / a good deal / infinitely / considerably		more interesting	
1 _____ 2 _____ 3 _____		greater	(than ...)
a bit / marginally		less exciting	
4 _____ 5 _____		more efficient	
every bit / 6 _____	as	efficient	(as ...)
almost / 7 _____		important	
not / nothing like / 8 _____		sensible / cheaply	

B Look at the first two listening extracts on page 118. What are *local brands, TCL* and *supermarket shopping* being compared with? Write sentences using *as ... as* or *than*.

To make comparisons you can also use:

sentence linkers: *but, however, in comparison, in contrast, in the same way,* etc.
In comparison, Arab souks are a lot of fun.

both ... and and *neither ... nor* to say that two things are the same, either in a positive or a negative way.
Neither local **nor** international companies can afford to exploit their workers.

C Work in pairs. Compare the following things using appropriate comparison words.

Buying locally produced food   Buying imported food
Buying a PC locally   Buying a big brand PC
Treating your employees well   Exploiting your employees

D In pairs, compare different brands of each of the following products, using as many comparison words and phrases as possible.

mobile phones   newspapers   chocolate   soft drinks   sports shoes

▶ Review and development page 62

▶ Grammar overview page 159

BRAND STRATEGY

Communication

Interviewing

The skill of interviewing and being interviewed is a key to business success. The underlying skill is based on how you ask and answer questions. In this section, you can practise both interviewing and being interviewed.

A Work in pairs. Discuss your experience of interviews. Tell your partner about your last interview. What happened and what types of questions were you asked?

7.2 B Listen to an interview and answer the questions.

1 What sort of job has the candidate applied for?
2 What experience does he have?
3 What skills does he have?
4 How do you think the interview went? Do you think he will get the job?

C Look at the Key language box below, which shows the different types of interviewing questions. Then listen again and identify the types of questions the interviewer asks.

Key language

Opening	Would you like a coffee?
	Did you find us OK?
Background	Could you tell me about your career so far?
	Could you tell me something about yourself?
Professional experience	What made you become a …?
	Why did you choose the … business?
	What did you learn when you were at …?
	Which of your jobs has given you most satisfaction?
Competencies	What can you contribute to this company?
	How would you add value?
	What would you bring to the job?
Critical incidents	Tell me about a difficult situation you have faced.
	Could you describe a success / failure you have had?
Motives	Why do you want to leave your current job?
	Why do you want to join us?

D The interviewee also asks a question. What does he ask about? If you were being interviewed, what else might you ask about?

E Work in pairs. Student A looks at this page. Student B looks at page 106.

Student A

1 Interview Student B for a management post in your company. You are looking for someone to join the financial controlling part of the company. Student B has been recommended to you by a colleague. You haven't seen his / her CV, but you have heard that he / she has considerable experience and is looking for a new job.

2 Attend an interview with Student B for a work placement (internship) in his / her company. You know the company takes on one or two interns every year for six months. The company is a well-established medium-sized engineering firm, which manufactures electrical goods mainly for export. You are hoping that you can use your language skills and also get experience of working on the customer contact side.

▶ Review and development page 63

▶ Communication page 149

Business Across Cultures

✱ Branding nations

Nation branding aims to measure, build and manage the reputation of countries. It is based on the observation that the 'brand images' of countries are just as important to their success in the global marketplace as those of products and services. In this section, we explore what is involved in branding nations.

🎧 7.3

A Simon Anholt is one of the world's leading advisors to governments who wish to build global brands. Listen to his comments about nation branding and answer the questions.

1 Why do some people object to nation branding?
2 Which countries does he mention and what does he associate with them?

B What do people associate with your country?

C Read a success story about rebranding a nation. If you were asked to rebrand your country, what symbol would you use?

Nation-branding campaigns to date have been relatively limited in scope. During the 1990s, Spain, in what is often cited as the most successful nation-branding effort so far, took advantage of its exposure during the 1992 Barcelona Olympics to launch a national marketing campaign. This campaign promoted everything from newly privatised utilities to the films of Pedro Almodóvar to Ibiza, a Mediterranean party island. The effort, organised from Madrid, was a success. Twenty years ago Spain was thought of as a European backwater; today it's seen as a hip, high-design playground.

D Countries don't always have positive images associated with them. Read about how one company in China is trying to change its brand image and answer the questions.

It's never too late to right a wrong. Chinese goods have had to fight a worldwide perception of low quality. In a clear demonstration of the Chinese government's commitment to building up its country brand, no less than six government departments are currently working on several national branding initiatives and activities. The Chinese brand Haier, originally state-owned and producing  low-quality electrical goods for the domestic market, is a great example of reversing the poor image of Chinese goods. Haier's business philosophy and policy rested on three planks: Brand First, Innovation and World Class Quality. It now commands an impressive market share in the US with the manufacture of high quality goods. As a Chinese brand, Haier helps elevate the perception of Chinese goods.

1 How is Haier changing the image of China?
2 Which companies do you most associate with the following countries: US, Germany, France, Brazil and Russia?
3 Profile a company in your country. Present it to the rest of the class.

E Work in groups. Discuss what are some typical stereotypes of developing countries.

BRAND STRATEGY

🔊 7.4 **F** Listen to an interview about branding in the developing world and answer the questions.

1 In what way does brand image get in the way of economic development? *A bad image keeps companies from investing there*
2 What is brand strategy about? *Informing people about good things in the country to broaden understanding*
3 Is the brand image of developing countries changing? *Yes – Improvements in skills, infrastructure, Govt, biz envir.*

G Malaysia is a country which has worked hard on its image. Read the text below.

Malaysia is involved in a Vision 2020 effort, which hopes to put Malaysia into the ranks of developed nations. To achieve the brand vision, the 'Made in Malaysia' label should carry connotations of quality, excellence and innovation, while at the same time capture the Malaysian spirit.

Malaysian manufacturers such as Proton, Perodua and Naza have shown a remarkable commitment to quality, design and innovation. Malaysian services companies, especially insurance companies such as MAA, have been very innovative with their insurance products.

Malaysian Airlines, which together with the Malaysian Tourist Promotion Board has been the main standard bearers for brand Malaysia, has received multiple awards for its in-flight service.

Malaysia has also given the world celebrated brands including shoemaker Jimmy Choo, actress Michelle Yeoh, the Shangri-La Hotel chain, YTL Corp, and Sapura Corporation – clear proof that Malaysians and their corporations can compete on a global stage.

Malaysia's tag is currently 'Malaysia, Truly Asia'. The tagline was chosen to offer the tourist a multi-cultural experience.

H Work in groups. Decide on an image for your country or region. Develop the following elements.

- a brand vision (including label connotations and tag)
- brand ambassadors (companies)
- brand ambassadors (individuals)

▶ Business across cultures page 152

Checklist	✓ brand extension	✓ local and global brands	✓ making comparisons: global brands are nowhere near as good as local brands	✓ interviewing ✓ branding nations

51

MARKETS

8 The hard sell

Start-up

A Read the poem opposite. What is the message? What effect does advertising have on your life?

'I think that I shall never see
A billboard lovely as a tree.
Indeed, unless the billboards fall
I'll never see a tree at all.'

B Look at the different forms of advertising in the box below. How often are you exposed to each one? Have any of them persuaded you to buy a product or use a service? Discuss your answers with a partner.

| billboards   website   community events   press releases   word-of-mouth |
| sponsorship   telemarketing   public relations (PR)   TV and radio commercials |
| ads in magazines and newspapers   product placement (in films and on TV shows) |
| spam (unsolicited email advertising) |

C In your opinion, which ...

- is the most effective in reaching a niche market / the mass market?
- is the most cost-effective for the advertiser?
- is the biggest nuisance to the public?

Reading and speaking

A 'Product placement' is a marketing tactic in which real commercial products are used in films, soap operas and music videos. Match the film (1–4) to the product (a–d).

Films
1 *Mission Impossible 2* (2000)
2 *Superman 2* (1980)
3 *Harry Potter and the Goblet of Fire* (2005)
4 *James Bond – Casino Royale* (2006)

Products
a Marlboro cigarettes
b none
c Apple computers
d Heineken Beer

B You are going to read an article which was published on the release of the James Bond film *Die Another Day* in 2002. Before you read, discuss the following questions:

1 What are the effects of extensive product placement in such a film?
2 Why do you think advertisers are keen to place their products in films appearing at the cinema?
3 What types of audiences do Bond films appeal to?
4 What is the future of product placement?

C Read the article and check your answers.

THE HARD SELL

Bond film is 'a giant advert'

The release of the latest James Bond film *Die Another Day* is good business for firms outside the film industry. After 40 years of Bond films, winning a place for products within a scene has become big business. So much so that *Die Another Day* is, in some respects, one long advert – for vodka, watches and cars.

People looking for the usual Bond features will not be disappointed. *Die Another Day* has flash cars, gadgets, and, of course, plenty of action. But critics say some of the authentic Bond characteristics have been sacrificed on the altar of advertising. There is so much product placement in the film that people in the marketing industry are calling it *Buy Another Day*.

At a time when the advertising industry is in a downturn, it seems surprising that companies are falling over themselves to pay such huge sums. But brand consultant Steve King said that such a strategy made sense.

'Years ago you could expect to reach 80 per cent of TV viewers but with the proliferation of cable and satellite channels that figure has fallen. One of the unique things about cinema is its global appeal which means advertisers get the reach they cannot obtain elsewhere.'

Bond movies are especially popular with advertisers because of their appeal to the young and old. The 60:40 male–female ratio among Bond audiences is also appealing to many advertisers.

But where is product placement going? Experts say it may not be too long before interactive television and mobile technology link up. You will be able to buy the watch straight from Pierce Brosnan's wrist.

Listening

A Read the quotation below about mass marketing. Do you agree with it?

> The US advertising executive, Fairfax Cone, once said, 'There is no such thing as a Mass Mind. The Mass Audience is made up of individuals, and good advertising is written always from one person to another. When it is aimed at millions, it rarely moves anyone.'

B You are going to listen to the advertiser Antonio González being interviewed about reaching the Hispanic market in the United States. How do you think companies gain customer loyalty in this niche market? Discuss your ideas with a partner.

8.1 **C** Listen to the first part of the radio interview and answer the questions.

1 How much is the Hispanic market worth?
2 Antonio mentions one slogan and one motto. What are they?
3 What other tactics do companies use to tap into the Hispanic market?

8.2 **D** Listen to the second part of the interview and answer the questions.

1 Why are advertisers changing their approach in marketing to Hispanics?
2 How are they changing their approach?
3 Why isn't mainstream advertising effective in reaching Hispanics?
4 What is a fusion market? Which fusion market ad does Antonio describe?

E What are the main niche markets in your country? How are they likely to change in the future?

Speaking

A Work in small groups. You are responsible for advertising one of the following products or services to a specific niche market. Discuss how your campaign will show that your service meets their unique needs, and how you will speak their 'language', get their attention and, hopefully, loyalty.

1 A community subscription website → over 50s (mainly retirees)
   The site will feature interactive games to increase mental agility, news on entertainment and hobbies, a weekly IT literacy guide, and a discussion forum.
2 A political party (of your choice) → 18–25-year-old age group
3 International telecommunications services → newly arrived immigrants

MODULE 2

Grammar

Making predictions

To make predictions, you typically use *will ('ll)* or *will not (won't)* + infinitive. There are different ways of saying how sure you are that your prediction will come true.

A Look at these sentences and say whether you think they express certainty, probability, possibility or doubt.

1 I've no doubt we'll see more examples of this type of advertising in the future.
2 I very much doubt that there's a future in radio advertising.
3 The Hispanic market is worth about $700 billion, and is expected to grow to $1 trillion by 2010.
4 Interactive television may have a big role to play in advertising in the future.
5 I bet we'll see more fusion advertising in the future.
6 Your experience in the Hispanic market is sure to give you a head start.

> Here are some ways of predicting something you are **certain** about.
> *I'm (absolutely) certain / sure / positive / convinced that ...*
> *Definitely, certainly, inevitably ...*
> *I have no doubt that; there's no doubt that ...*
> *be sure to / bound to / certain to* + infinitive

B Complete the sentences using an appropriate phrase from the box above.

1 Markets will _____ become more global and multicultural.
2 _____ doubt that advances in communication technologies will open up new opportunities for advertisers.
3 I'm _____ that the use of scents in outdoor advertising will take off in the near future.
4 Niche marketing techniques are _____ become more sophisticated.

> Here are some ways of saying what you think will **probably** or **possibly** happen.
> *may, might, could* + infinitive
> *It's likely, probable, possible that ...*
> *Probably, possibly, perhaps ...*
> *be (widely) expected / predicted to ...*
> *There's a (good) chance / a (strong) possibility that ...*
> *I bet (that) ...*
>
> To express **doubt**, you say that something is *unlikely*, that it *probably won't* happen, or that you (*very much*) *doubt that* it *will*.

C Work in pairs. Use the words and structures above to give your own opinions about the statements.

1 Internet advertising will become more and more popular in the future.
2 Music and entertainment will play an increasing role in gaining customer loyalty.
3 The media will determine the future of advertising if current trends continue.
4 Advertisers will increasingly use interactive television to sell their products.

D Prepare a short presentation about one or more of the following points in relation to the future of your company or country. Use as many of the words and structures above as possible.

Example

*The population **is bound to** go on increasing and there **may not be** enough resources.*
*The company **is widely expected to** computerise the production process soon.*

advertising   popular culture   political changes   demographic changes   competitors
the environment   economic factors   technological developments

▶ Review and development page 62

▶ Grammar overview page 160

THE HARD SELL

Communication

Feedback

Here are two types of useful feedback.
- Affirmative – when you recognise something that is being done well, you point out that success and reinforce it.
- Development – when you recognise that something could be done better, you point out that gap and see how you can fill it.

In this section, we explore ways of giving feedback.

A Discuss how much feedback you get at work or studying. What type of feedback do you receive?

8.3 **B** Kate Milligan is Bill Carter's boss. Twice a year she holds performance review sessions for all her team. Today she is talking to Bill about his performance at work and any actions he needs to take. As you listen, complete the table.

	Targets	Progress	Further action?
1			
2			

C How did Kate manage this session? Did she give the feedback or did she get it from Bill himself? What type of feedback came out – affirmative or development?

D Look at the Key language below. Then listen again and tick the phrases that you hear.

Key language

Focus on progress	What were your targets? How's it going? How do you think things have gone, so far, this year?
Recognition of success	I've been making quite an effort. I feel I've made more of a contribution. I think I'm on the right track. From what I hear, it's going well.
Reinforcing success	I'm pleased about that. I can see you've made an effort.
Recognition of a gap / lack of progress	To be honest, not very well. I'm finding it difficult. I feel I've got nowhere. In fact I've gone backwards.
Showing understanding	I understand. I think we all do. It's not easy.
Obstacles	What's stopping you from …? What's getting in your way?
Next steps	How are you going to move forward? So what are you going to do? I wondered whether I could …?

E Work in pairs. Student A looks at this page. Student B looks at page 103.

Student A

1 Give Student B feedback on one of the following topics:
   - progress in learning (language, business, management skill)
   - progress in career (new jobs, opportunities)
   - challenge they face at work (deadlines, personalities, conflicts, etc.)
   Follow the process and use the language above.

2 Reverse roles and get feedback from Student B on one of the topics.

▶ Review and development page 63

▶ Communication page 149

BUSINESS ACROSS CULTURES

Global marketing

Companies sometimes assume that what works in their home country will work in another country. They take the same product and same advertising campaign and expect it to succeed. The result in many cases is failure. In this section, we explore how culture affects marketing.

A Work in groups. Discuss what you have to take into account when you want to reach local markets.

B Look at the photographs below. Discuss how you would market these products in your home market. Would it be the same in a foreign market?

C Work in pairs. Student A reads extract one. Student B reads extract two. Read the extract and summarise the main points to your partner.

Extract one

Global versus local advertising is a strategy marketers working in the international field have been wrestling with over the last few years. Finance executives find the costs that they can save by marketing products on a global scale very appealing. However, not all brands can be marketed internationally and many marketers are implementing local campaigns or adapting global ones in order to effectively sell their products abroad.

Product type is a key factor when deciding whether to implement a global campaign. Technology and clothing brands cross borders effectively while food, drink and packaged goods often encounter difficulties such as cultural differences, the overall brand experience, product development and the state of the local economy.

Extract two

When marketing products abroad, some companies like to have a common look and feel around the world. Keyvan Cohanim, the Vice President of marketing and communications for IBM Canada, says, 'We're really trying to portray ourselves as a single global company. The IT industry we participate in, the services area of consulting with customers, and the solutions we talk about are all applicable globally.' However, some global companies prefer to implement a local advertising strategy. An example of this is Unilever, one of the world's largest marketers. Stephen Kouri, the Vice President of brand development says that with a big company like Unilever it's very important to find the right balance of global and local advertising. Brand propositions travel well, but TV executions may not, he says.

D Work in small groups. Use the information from C and your own ideas to prepare a presentation about global versus local advertising.

THE HARD SELL

🔊 8.4 **E** Listen to extracts from three different markets. Use the table below to make notes.

Market	How they resist globalisation	Impact
Iran		

F Work in pairs. Discuss whether you think markets can resist globalisation. Do you think the government should protect their local market and culture? How?

G Work in pairs. First read the text below.
Student A looks at this page.
Student B looks at page 103.

Your task is to launch a new telecom service for both home and office use in Malaysia. Your target consumer is both the large expatriate community and local Malaysians. It is called HomeOffice and allows customers to work from home and the office. You want to use TV advertising and outdoor posters to launch this new product.

Student A

1 Read the information below. Group each point under one of the following headings:
work   status and titles   ceremonies   dining   gender   time   personalities

- Malaysians are very warm, friendly and hospitable, but may appear shy and reserved initially.
- Most Malaysians view the organisation as an extended family. Expats may find themselves being called 'Uncle/Auntie' by the children of their local colleagues.
- Malaysians consider ceremonies as part of their way of showing hospitality and building relationships.
- Don't mix business with food and refreshments. Business always comes second and should not take precedence over eating.
- Malaysians tend not to hurry and are quite easy-going.
- Malaysians respect titles and status. People with local status are often important for the long-term success of the business.
- When interacting with Malaysians, be aware of gender and sex role differences. Malaysia is still largely a male-dominated society and women must be prepared to be treated as number two.

2 Exchange the information with Student B to build a picture of Malaysia.
3 Use this information to brainstorm an advertisement for your product.

▶ Business across cultures page 152

Checklist
✓ product placement
✓ marketing to the niche markets
✓ making predictions: *I bet we'll see more Internet advertising in the future.*
✓ feedback
✓ global marketing

BUSINESS SCENARIO 2

Dua

Background

The UK bicycle producer Dua, founded in 1993 by Aarit Motala, is considering launching its high-end bicycles and accessories in India. The Indian company Sharp Edge Cycles would act as the exclusive distributor and, with its network of bike stations, it could create a country-wide presence of Dua.

Speaking

In order to assess the market potential, Aarit Motala has asked the marketing team at Sharp Edge Cycles to provide him with information about the cycling culture in India and India's 18–35 high-end market.

Work in groups of four. Divide yourselves into two teams.

Team A: You will give a joint presentation on the cycling culture in India. Look at page 104.

Team B: You will give a joint presentation on India's young high-end market. Look at page 107.

Useful language

Feel free to ask any questions as we go along.
Let me give you some background ...
As you can see on this first slide, ...
Let's move on to ...
Now I'd like to tell you a little about ...
Before I go on, are there any questions?

Discussion

Based on the presentations, discuss which of the following products would suit the young high-end market in India.

Mountain bike – Lightweight frame, and state-of-the-art multi-speed gears and disc brakes. Outstanding performance and great looks!

Tour bike – Lightweight and designed for long-distance bike tours. A Tour de France favourite!

BMX bike – Strong, low-maintenance race circuit bike.

Folding street bike – A trendy commuting tool that can be kept under the desk until the ride home. Available in a wide range of stylish colours.

Electric street bike – Designed for ease, speed and agility in the city. Commute without effort!

Dua sportswear – An enormous hit with alternative sports fans in Japan, Europe and the US.

Dua's own range of superlight camping gear – High quality tents and equipment. Ideal for bike tours and much cheaper than a hotel!

Meeting

Aarit Motala has arranged a meeting with the Sharp Edge Cycles marketing team to devise an advertising campaign. During the meeting, he is going to talk about the products he has chosen for the Indian market. There will then be a discussion about ways of creating a powerful marketing campaign. He has asked the team to prepare for the meeting by coming up with a variety of original marketing ideas beforehand.

Work in groups of four.

Student A: You are Aarit Motala. You chair the meeting. Look at page 105.
Student B: You are Amit Koduri. Look at page 107.
Student C: You are Shalina Dama. Look at page 109.
Student D: You are Ira Sumon. Look at page 111.

Writing

Write some brief notes of the decisions made during the meeting. Say what was decided and why.

REVIEW AND DEVELOPMENT

5–8

Vocabulary

Market entry

A Look at the words and expressions below associated with entering new markets. In each sentence, one of the words or phrases is not possible. Which one is it?

1 One way to get into a new market is to *enter into / construct / form* a joint venture with a local partner.
2 If you're not happy with your joint venture, it might be difficult to *end / withdraw / exit* from it.
3 When a company sets up its own operation without foreign partners, that operation is *absolutely / fully / wholly* owned by it.
4 With globalisation, the tendency is for governments to *lift / raise / abolish* restrictions on joint ventures with firms from abroad.
5 *Inner / inward / foreign* investors from abroad that plan to invest in a country should do as much research as possible before going ahead.
6 When one company works with another, it can gain knowledge and *experience / expertise / experiments* about a particular technology.
7 Some joint ventures do not *end / result / work out* happily.

Grammar

Determiners and quantifiers

A Look again at the rules and examples on page 36. Use the words in the box to complete the sentences below.

| few of   few   many of   either   neither   less   little |

1 Two surveys have been carried out, one in Africa and one in Latin America. _____ suggests that citizens are in favour of foreign investment.
2 British firms see _____ benefit from expansion of the European Union. In fact, almost a fifth believe enlargement will reduce foreign investment.
3 Indians have _____ time off work than Westerners.
4 When two companies negotiate the terms for a joint venture, _____ side can withdraw from discussions at any stage.
5 _____ the world's biggest global corporations have already taken advantage of India's new thriving economy.
6 A _____ the problems encountered in international joint ventures stem from cultural differences.
7 _____ industries are more global than the oil industry.

▶ Grammar overview page 157

Vocabulary

Production, distribution and delivery

A Look again at the vocabulary on page 41. Then match the words in each column to create a complete phrase.

Store	stock	to the customer.
Carry out	large quantity of goods	quickly.
Place	a prototype	in a warehouse.
Ship	an order	in small batches.
Replenish	production	according to specifications.
Develop	the finished products	for 1,000 components.

60

REVIEW AND DEVELOPMENT 5–8

Grammar

The passive

A Look again at the rules and examples on page 42. Then look at the sentences below. Use the passive and the sequence words in the box below to describe the process.

| first   next   then   after that   finally |

'Proto-X' is an industrial tool manufacturing service. Its in-house team develops prototypes and produces tools according to customer requirements.

1 Customer places an order for a customised tool
   First, an order for a customised tool is placed.

2 Do 'quality and production planning'
   _____

3 Develop the prototype based on the customer's specifications
   _____

4 Carry out a trial on the prototype to ensure that there are no flaws or weaknesses
   _____

5 Do a production trial run to confirm that the correct processes and machinery are in place
   _____

6 Carry out mass production
   _____

7 Inspect the tools for any irregularities
   _____

8 Pack the tools and ship them to the customer
   _____

▶ Grammar overview page 158

Vocabulary

A Study the vocabulary in Units 7 and 8 again. Then complete sentences 1–8 below with the words in the box.

| sponsorship   niche   extended   placement   telemarketing   billboard   fusion   iconic |

1 Levi Strauss is an _____ brand that strongly reflects classic American attributes such as authenticity, durability and toughness.

2 Many soap and shampoo brands have _____ their brand name by broadening their range of merchandise to include household cleaning products.

3 A _____ is a form of outdoor advertising which targets passing pedestrians and drivers.

4 A good example of _____ marketing is the way in which Rolls Royce and Bentley have specialised in the slender and limited luxury market.

5 _____ is a promotional activity by which a company provides an organisation with funds or services in exchange for publicity and visibility.

6 _____ is a form of direct marketing which many people consider to be an invasion of privacy.

7 Product _____ is a popular source of revenue for commercial broadcasters despite criticism that it detracts from the quality of entertainment.

8 Consumer expenditure from the Latino bilingual and bicultural market, also referred to as the _____ market, will double over the next ten years.

REVIEW AND DEVELOPMENT 5–8

Grammar

Making comparisons

A Look again at the rules and examples on page 48. Then study the bar graph below. Using the words in the box, compare the two brands of motor vehicle.

Example
Brand B is much more reliable than Brand A.

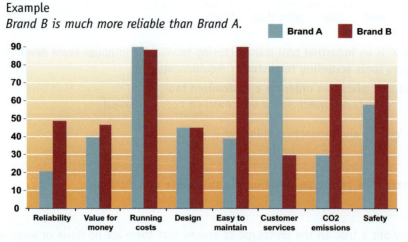

infinitely
considerably
far
much
slightly
a little
marginally
not as
nowhere near as
just as

B Choose one of the examples below. Using the words in the box, write six sentences comparing:

- The business culture / environment in India or China and that of your own country.
- The Spanish clothing brand Zara and a national clothing brand in your country.
- Two job interviews you have attended.

▶ Grammar overview page 159

Grammar

Making predictions

A Look again at the rules and examples on page 54. Then insert the following words and phrases in the table below.

I doubt …	…is / are likely …	… is / are unlikely …
should …	There's a good chance that …	I'm certain that …
I've no doubt that …	…is / are bound to …	may / might / could …

B Complete the following sentences using phrases from the table.

Certainty	Probability	Possibility	Doubt

1 If you shop at a certain supermarket, you ____*are likely*____ to use it for the rest of your life. (probable)

2 _____ most companies will eventually move to some variation of just-in-time production. (certain)

3 Africa has embraced foreign investment and privatisation, so it _____ prosper. (probable)

4 Although shopping malls with major outlets are becoming increasingly common in India, _____ they will be as vast as their Western counterparts. (doubtful)

5 Recently, there have been several takeovers of major UK companies, and there _____ to be more in 2008. (certain)

6 This niche market _____ be reached through online marketing. (possible)

7 Due to new anti-spam technologies, _____ spam will become a thing of the past. (probable)

▶ Grammar overview page 160

REVIEW AND DEVELOPMENT 5–8

Communication

Look again at the communication skills pages in Units 5–8. Then complete these exercises.

A Match the phrase (1–6) with its purpose (a–f).

Phrase
1 I'm really pleased with the progress you have made.
2 Let's just stop a moment. Have you got any comments?
3 This is a project which can make a real difference and your role is critical.
4 I can see you are worried about the next steps.
5 I woke up this morning with that funny feeling in my stomach.
6 Let's make sure we are all up to speed on this.

Purpose
a Make contact with the audience
b Get audience interaction
c Keep them informed
d Recognise success
e Acknowledge anxiety
f Involve them in the challenge

B Complete the interview questions below with the words in the box.

| career | join | background | contribute | add | faced | finding |

1 Can you tell me about some of the challenges you have _____?
2 What do you think you can _____ to our team?
3 What's your _____ in this sector?
4 Can you tell me why you've changed jobs a lot during your _____?
5 Did you have any trouble _____ us?
6 Why do you want to _____ this company?
7 Do you think you could really _____ value?

C Put the words in the right order. Punctuate correctly.

1 me   your   tell   targets   you   could   about
2 a   effort   you   big   I   see   can   made   have
3 I   backwards   am   going   feel   I
4 way   is   getting   what   in   your
5 it   is   going   how
6 I   right   on   think   I   track   am   the
7 difficult   finding   I   it   very   am

▶ Writing resource 14
page 96

63

MONEY

9 A thriving economy

Start-up

A Work in pairs. Discuss the following questions.

1 How widespread do you think the private sector is in China?
2 Which parts of China do you think have the highest concentration of private companies?
3 What do you think the Chinese government's attitude to the private sector is?

China is set to become the world's largest economy by 2026.

Reading and vocabulary

A Read the article. Find answers to the questions in the Start-up discussion.

Thriving but faced with uncertainties

When Hank Paulson made his first trip to China as US Treasury Secretary, his initial *port of call* was not the *corridors of power* in Beijing or the financial skyscrapers in Shanghai, but the provincial city of Hangzhou.

Best-known for its lake and its tea, Hangzhou has been celebrated by artists and poets through the centuries for its sense of refinement. But Mr Paulson went there for a different reason. The city is now one of the centres for China's *thriving* private sector economy.

The rise in the private sector has been one of the most important and least remarked upon aspects of the country's *spectacular* growth over the past two decades. The numbers are hard to *pin down*, but recent reports indicate that the private sector now accounts for 70 per cent of China's GDP and employs 75 per cent of the workforce.

Private companies have *flourished* in two regions in particular – around Shenzhen in the south and in Zhejiang province, south-west of Shanghai, of which Hangzhou is the capital.

The rise of Shenzhen and the other industrial cities in Guangdong province owe their dynamism in part to the proximity of Hong Kong and the heavy investment by Hong Kong and Taiwanese entrepreneurs in the region.

Zhejiang is more of a home-grown success story. Local businessmen say one of the main reasons that Zhejiang has flourished is because it was neglected. There were no large state-owned companies to absorb energies and draw attention from Beijing.

Private sector companies were only permitted in China in 1988 and for a number of years afterwards they still existed under considerable legal uncertainties. But recent changes in the law have altered the situation so much that private entrepreneurs now face few restrictions if they start a new company, unless it is in one of the heavily regulated sectors such as telecoms, finance or media.

Yet, there are still two big issues *hanging over* the private sector that might affect its ability to prosper. The first is the political climate. In the 1990s, under President Jiang Zemin, the official rhetoric gave huge encouragement to private entrepreneurs who were admitted to the Chinese Communist Party for the first time.

Under President Hu Jintao, however, the emphasis has been on reducing social inequality and some observers believe this has meant fresh political pressure on the private sector.

The other uncertainty concerns access to finance. In an area such as Zhejiang, most private companies *were founded* using funds from friends and family or underground banks, rather than the official banks, which have tended to concentrate on state-owned companies.

There are signs this is changing. Industrial and Commercial Bank of China says that it is focusing an increasing amount of its lending on small and medium-sized enterprises, which are mostly privately owned. Similarly, China Development Bank is setting up a new facility for SMEs.

B Answer the questions.

1 Where is Hangzhou and what is the city famous for?
2 Where is Shenzhen and why has it been successful in private business?
3 Why has Zhejiang been successful in private business?
4 When did the Chinese government first allow private companies to operate?
5 What restrictions do private entrepreneurs face?
6 What are the two potential difficulties that the private sector is faced with in China?
7 Where has the finance usually come from for private companies in China?

A THRIVING ECONOMY

C Match the words and phrases in *italics* in the article with their definitions below.

1 to discover exact details about something
2 developed very successfully
3 very successful
4 started (a company)
5 offering a potential threat
6 a place where you stop for a short time, especially on a journey
7 the higher levels of government where the most important decisions are made
8 amazing, unusually good

D Use the words and phrases from C to complete the sentences.

1 In China, many private companies are _____ with personal funds or loans from family members, rather than by bank loans.
2 When the president went on his Far East trip, his first _____ was Tokyo.
3 Private companies in China have really _____ in the area close to Hong Kong.
4 Both China and India have seen _____ growth over the past ten years.
5 The _____ the UK are in Whitehall, where the Prime Minister's office and residence are located.
6 Because of the lack of data, it is hard to _____ the exact number of private companies in China.
7 Because the Communist Party rules in China, there is still a degree of uncertainty _____ the private sector and its future.
8 Because of China's _____ economy, the number of affluent and middle-class Chinese has increased rapidly in the last decade.

E Work in pairs. Discuss how the development of the private sector in China compares with your country or another country you know well. Present your conclusions to the class.

Listening and speaking

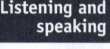

9.1

A Listen to an economist talking about the growth of the Chinese economy. Decide whether the following statements are true (T), false (F) or not given (NG). Give your reasons.

1 China currently imports more than $1,000 billion a year of raw materials.
2 China is the world's third largest economy.
3 Problems in the future will be caused more by politics than economics.
4 Most private companies have to work closely with state-owned enterprises.
5 The Chinese government prefers foreign multinational companies to domestic private ones.
6 Lenovo is China's biggest private company.
7 High growth will continue with or without an enlarged private sector.
8 The Chinese will soon be in control of many large multinationals.

B Work in small groups. Use the information from the interview and your own general knowledge about China to discuss the following questions:

- How will the Chinese economy develop over the next five years?
- Will it continue to expand as fast as it has been doing or will the bubble burst?
- What potential problems do you see – access to resources, environmental concerns, the political situation, etc.?

65

MODULE 3

Grammar

Cause and effect

To talk about the cause of something, you can use a conjunction like *because* or a multi-word preposition like *due to*. (Multi-word prepositions are practised in Unit 11.)

*In fact, **because** it sees foreign companies as less of a threat, China has gone out of its way to attract multinationals.*

To talk about the effect of something, you can use a sentence linker like *therefore*, or a verb like *lead to*:

*This should eventually **lead to** the rise of large Chinese companies which are genuinely global.*

A Insert the following words in the table below:

as a result	cause	as a result of	on account of	so
as	because of	owing to	result in	consequently
since	because	therefore	due to	lead to

Cause	Effect

B Complete the sentences using the words and phrases in the table. (There is more than one possibility.)

1 _____ the continued liberalisation of the Chinese economy, there is more room for private enterprises to develop.

2 Foreign companies are seen as less of a threat; _____ China has gone out of its way to attract multinationals.

3 _____ interest rates are currently low, there is an increased flow of money into the Chinese stock market.

4 The introduction of a capital gains tax for equity investments could _____ a collapse of prices.

You can also express causes and effects by using nouns like *cause* and *reason*, *effect* and *result*.

The reason that China has gone out of its way to attract multinationals is that it sees them as less of a threat.

C *Reason for* or *result of*? Complete the sentences.

1 China's recent stock market fall was partly the _____ speculative pressures.

2 One _____ Zhejiang's prosperity is that it was neglected by Beijing.

3 The _____ the changes in the law is that private entrepreneurs face fewer restrictions.

▶ Review and development page 90

▶ Grammar overview page 161

Speaking

A Work in pairs.

Student A: You are a wealthy private investor from the West who is interested in investing in China. Turn to page 105.

Student B: You are an investment specialist on the Chinese economy and stock market. Turn to page 108.

A THRIVING ECONOMY

Communication

Leading meetings

Meetings still occupy a lot of business people's time. Therefore, it is important to make them successful. To do this, you need to *prepare,* make sure people know the *purpose,* follow an effective *process* and make sure the *people* are involved. This is known as the four Ps.

9.2 A Listen to an extract from a business meeting. As you listen, make notes under the four Ps below.

Preparation – What has been done before the meeting?

Purpose – What are the objectives of the meeting and does everyone understand them?

Process – What is the process by which they are going to achieve their objectives?

People – What are the roles in the meeting? What is the participation like in the meeting?

B Look at the Key language box below. Listen again and identify the language used to manage the meeting successfully.

Key language

Preparation	Did you receive a copy of the document? Have you all seen the agenda? I think you've all seen the memo which I sent round yesterday.
Purpose	We are here today to decide … The purpose of this meeting is to … Our objective today is … I've called this meeting …
Process *Opening*	There are three items on the agenda. Let's take things in this order. Are there any other points you want to add? We'll start by … Then I'd like to consider … Finally we should …
During	I think we all understand … Let's now talk about …
Ending	I think that is clear. Let's move on to … Can we summarise? Let me sum up. So, what are the actions? Let's try to bring this together then. Let's stop there. We'll meet again next week.
People (roles)	… is going to … … will take the minutes. … will report back at the next meeting.

C Work in small groups. You are a committee which represents the employees of your company. There are two issues you need to discuss and report back to the board of the company.

1 Working from home – the company's policy is not clear. Some office workers work from home, some of the time. In other cases, their bosses do not allow it. You want to find out what the committee thinks about this and to make specific recommendations to the board.

2 Dress – again, the company's policy is not clear. Some employees are very formally dressed, some very informally. You would like to discuss what the committee feels would be the best policy.

A different person should lead each item. Follow the four Ps.

▶ Review and development page 93

▶ Communication page 149

BUSINESS ACROSS CULTURES

China

In this section we examine how smaller foreign companies are doing business in China. We also look at some key underlying concepts in Chinese culture.

9.3 **A** **Listen to a small businessman talking about his experience of doing business in China. Answer the questions.**

1 Which of the factors below does he mention?

| language   politics   relationships   loyalty   understanding |

2 Why does he think the Chinese like to say 'yes'? What is your own attitude towards confrontation?

B **What you would say in these situations? Discuss with a partner.**

- A friend (not close) invites you out to see a film. You think the film is terrible.
- A colleague asks you to cover for him because he wants to go to a football match. He wants you to tell your boss he is ill.
- You take a client out to a restaurant. The food is disappointing and you are overcharged on the bill.
- An important customer wants you to be present at a big meeting over the weekend. Your family expects you to be at home for a big anniversary.

C **Work in pairs. Read about some key concepts of Chinese culture on the opposite page. Then, match the situations (1–6) with the concepts (a–f). Compare your results with other pairs. Explain your choices.**

1 Ben had been working in China for a few months and had been out with his colleagues most evenings. Although back in the UK he prefers to keep his work and personal life separate, he found it very difficult to say no, as he was expected to go out.
2 Sarah was sent to China by her firm to research into possible new markets. She noticed that she never got to speak to the right person. She was always talking to agents and brokers, rather than the CEOs of companies.
3 What Stefan found really frustrating was that he couldn't tell what people really thought. He couldn't see whether they really agreed and liked his ideas. They were always polite but he thought they weren't always honest.
4 Victoria found the Chinese rude and a bit abrupt. If they didn't know you, they seemed to just ignore you.
5 Maria was really proud of what she and her team had achieved and she thought they should celebrate. However, she noticed that her Chinese colleagues were not so keen to do this.
6 Philip was sure he had the right product at the right price. He booked a short trip and attended the trade fair for two days. He left very disappointed that he hadn't signed any contracts.

A THRIVING ECONOMY

Key concepts

a Guanxi

The concept of Guanxi lies at the core of Chinese society. Guanxi can be seen as 'who you know and what they perceive to be their obligation to you'. In China, an established network of good contacts can help accomplish almost anything, so having good guanxi is a very powerful asset. People will ask for favours from those with whom they have guanxi. It is often explained as 'You scratch my back, I'll scratch yours.'

b Mianzi

Mianzi is the concept of 'face'. In Chinese culture, losing face, saving face and giving face is very important and should never be forgotten. A person can lose face as a result of losing his or her temper, confronting an individual, acting in an arrogant manner or failing to show appropriate respect. If you want to do business with someone you haven't met, you will often have to go through a host or intermediary.

c Lijie and surface harmony

Lijie is the art of maintaining surface harmony by remaining polite and courteous at all times. An argument in a public place or a manager publicly criticising a subordinate would cause a loss of face, so intermediaries are often used to deliver bad or unpleasant news.

d Keqi

The Chinese do not consider it polite to be arrogant and boast about your achievement and connections. Keqi is the concept of humility and modesty that is illustrated through being considerate, polite and well-mannered. 'Ke' means guest and 'qi' means behaviour. It not only means considerate, polite and well-mannered, but also represents modesty.

e Inner and outer circles

In general, rules of behaviour such as offering an apology after bumping into a person do not apply to those outside of your inner circle of friends. As a result, concepts very familiar in the West such as being kind to strangers and being charitable are not widely shared in this culture.

f Collective vs. individual interest

Another social belief is that the collective or group interest is more important than that of the individual. As a result, individuals should sacrifice their own interests in order to serve the needs or wants of the majority.

D In pairs, discuss how you would feel in each of the situations in C.

▶ Business across cultures page 152

E Work in pairs. Profile your own business culture in terms of the six concepts above. Where do think you would find the biggest challenges in doing business in China?

Checklist
- ✓ a thriving but uncertain economy
- ✓ words to do with growth: *spectacular, flourish* ...
- ✓ cause and effect: *this should lead to better interest rates*
- ✓ leading meetings
- ✓ China

MONEY

10 Foreign investment

Start-up

A Work in pairs. Discuss the questions.

- How do you interpret the quotation opposite?
- What are the different ways that foreign investment into a country can be made?

> Investing in Russia is like entering a rich gold field studded with land mines: laced with rich veins of rich treasure, and riddled with pockets of pure poison.
> Mark Mobius, *Passport to Profits*

Reading and speaking

A Read the article about foreign direct investment.

WHO GETS WHAT IN THE FOREIGN DIRECT INVESTMENT LEAGUE?

FOREIGN DIRECT INVESTMENT (FDI) is of major importance in helping a country's economy to grow, or to maintain its growth rate. Some FDI is a result of new investment to expand a company's activities in that country, which is particularly the case for China and India. But in Western countries, a lot of FDI is often a purely financial transaction, the result of mergers and acquisitions by foreign companies.

According to the UN Conference on Trade and Development (UNCTAD), cross-border investment rose by 34 per cent in 2006, reaching a level of $1.23 trillion, and the US regained its position as the biggest recipient of FDI in the world ($177.3m), a position it had lost to the UK in 2005.

One of the countries with the most foreign direct investment for new and expanding business activities is China, which received $70m in 2006. Less often mentioned is Russia, which along with Brazil, India and China forms the BRIC group of countries. In 2006 Russia was the recipient of $28.4m, just below Italy and Singapore.

FDI league table TOP TEN FOREIGN DIRECT INVESTMENT

	FDI $bn	% change
US	177.3	78.2
UK	169.8	3.2
France	88.4	39.0
China	70.0	–3.3
Hong Kong	41.4	15.4
Singapore	31.9	58.9
Italy	30.0	50.2
Russia	28.4	94.6
Mexico	18.9	0.0
Turkey	17.1	76.3
WORLD	**1,230**	**34.3**

B Answer the questions.

1. What does the figure $1.23 trillion represent?
2. What kind of FDI do India and China receive?
3. Which country received the most FDI in 2006?
4. What is one explanation for the high levels of FDI in some mature Western economies?
5. How much FDI did China receive in 2006?
6. What is the BRIC group of countries?

C Say the following figures aloud – 34 per cent, $1.23 trillion, $177.3m, $70m, $28.4m

D Work in pairs. List some of the changes that occur because of a foreign takeover.

E Work in groups. You are going to debate the advantages and disadvantages of giving foreign companies a free hand to take over domestic companies. First, read the text below.

The UK is one of the most open countries in the world to foreign direct investment from other countries, especially acquisitions of leading British companies by foreign buyers. Recent takeovers have included ones in such strategic sectors as banking, telecommunications and airports. But not all countries are so open. The US will not let foreigners buy airlines, television networks or, increasingly, any business remotely connected with security. France protects eleven sectors from foreign takeovers, including casinos and defence contractors.

Group A: Brainstorm the arguments in favour of giving foreign companies a free hand to take over domestic companies.

Group B: Brainstorm all the arguments against.

Hold your debate.

FOREIGN INVESTMENT

Vocabulary and listening

A Work in pairs. Brainstorm all the factors which need to be taken into account when investing in a foreign country and make a list of them.

B You are going to listen to an interview with Richard Parker, a specialist in country risk analysis. Before you listen, match the phrases *in italics* (1–10) with their definitions (a–j).

1 if something *works out*
2 when something is *on offer*
3 if something *comes into the equation*
4 if something is *fully fledged*, it is
5 to *descend into chaos* means
6 to *live with* something means
7 to *remit* (money) means
8 if something is *closer to home*, it is
9 to *have your fingers burnt* means
10 if you *weigh something up*

a to accept a difficult situation
b to send it to someone (usually electronically)
c completely developed
d it is available
e it happens in a satisfactory way
f to become unstable and lawless
g you balance one thing against another before taking a decision
h nearer to where you are
i you suffer unpleasant results of an action, especially loss of money
j it enters the calculation

10.1

C Listen to the interview. What factors does Richard say you should take into account when investing abroad? Compare them with your list in A.

D Listen again. Which country is mentioned as being high-risk? Does Richard recommend investing there? Why?

E Match two words to form noun groups from the interview.

1 oil and gas
2 skill
3 exploration
4 inflation
5 government
6 labour
7 exchange
8 risk
9 money
10 oil
11 labour

a force
b giants
c incentives
d projects
e factors
f laundering
g industry
h costs
i levels
j rates
k control

F Say the words aloud, making sure you put the main stress on the correct word or syllable in each case. Listen to the interview again to check the pronunciation.

MODULE 3

Grammar

Referring and sequencing

You often use *this*, *that* and *these*, with or without a noun, to refer back to what you have just said or written. For example, in the interview, Richard Parker says.

The first thing to consider is political stability. This doesn't mean that the country has to be a fully fledged democracy, only that it's relatively stable.

A Look at sentences 1–3 below from the interview. Match a sentence with an item in the box.

> This factor ...   This problem ...   These ...

1 Then there's the government attitude to foreign investment.
2 The risks of investment in certain parts of Africa are well known.
3 There's still a lot of corruption and money laundering going on.

You can sequence a text using words like *first(ly)*, *second(ly)*, *then*, *also* and *finally*.

You can use *what about ...?* and *related to that ...* to introduce a new aspect of a topic.

▶ Review and development page 91

▶ Grammar overview page 162

B Read the audio script on page 122. Answer the questions.

1 What are the 'two angles' Richard Parker mentions at the beginning, and which words or phrases are used to introduce them?
2 Within each 'angle', which words are used for sequencing?

Information exchange

You are members of the management board of an international supermarket group from the US. You have already opened stores in a number of developing countries, and now you are considering expanding to other countries. The two countries being considered are Brazil and India.

A Work in pairs. Student A looks at this page. Student B looks at page 109.

Student A

	Brazil	India
Political climate	Stable after four years of economic crisis	
GDP growth rate		8.5%
GDP per capita		$3700
Unemployment	9.6%	
Inflation rate	4.2%	
Population below poverty line		30%
Mobile phones users	86.21m	
Internet users	25.9m	
Retail sector	Highly fragmented	
Legal issues		Direct foreign ownership of retailers not allowed
Infrastructure	Good roads between cities in the south	
Consumers		Increasing urbanisation and rise of middle class with aspirations

B Work in groups. Hold a meeting to decide which country to invest in.

FOREIGN INVESTMENT

Communication

Participating in meetings

Asking questions in meetings is an effective way to participate and to influence decisions. In this section, we introduce and practise a range of questions you can use in meetings.

A Look at the Key language box below. Then, match the question (1–6) to a question type (a–f).

1 So, in other words, you think we should …?
2 Would you mind telling us more about …?
3 Can't we just decide to …?
4 What should I do next?
5 Do you follow me?
6 Can we have a show of hands?

Key language

a	Clarifying	Do you see what I am saying? What do you mean by? Could you go over that again?
b	Reformulating	So you're worried about …? If I understand you, you're saying …? So you feel we should …?
c	Showing interest	Could you tell me about …? I'd be interested to know … Could you say a little more about …?
d	Leading	Shouldn't we move …? Don't you think we should …?
e	Seeking agreement	Can we agree to …? Does everyone agree that we …? We all seem to agree …?
f	Suggesting action	So, what actions do we need to take? What are the next steps?

🎧 10.2 **B** Listen to six extracts from a meeting and identify the question type (a–f) you hear. Compare your answers with a partner.

C Work in pairs. Student A looks at this page. Student B looks at page 109.

Student A

You have arranged a meeting with Student B. He / she wants to persuade you to invest in his country. Make sure you ask all six question types during the meeting. Student B will want to also find out more from you. First, decide on an investment project below.

- kitchen design and building
- Internet distribution for books
- a chain of night clubs
- a middle-market hotel chain
- warehouses for distribution
- other: _____

▶ Review and development page 93

▶ Communication page 149

Business Across Cultures

Russia

Russia is a country with enormous business potential. In this section, we explore the country and its culture. We also take a look at investment opportunities in this part of the world.

A Read the article. Draw up an investor's checklist for Russia.

Advantages
rich natural resources

Disadvantages
high unemployment

A nation with rich oil fields, coal mines, mineral reserves, natural gas and timber, Russia has long been an economic power house. Russia ended 2005 with its seventh straight year of growth, averaging 6.4 per cent annually since the financial crisis of 1998. High oil prices and the cheap rouble helped this economic gain. Nevertheless, serious economic problems persist; inflation and unemployment are high and industries badly need modern equipment. Also, Russia's international image as an investment location has suffered from accusations of politicians interfering in business.

Despite the problems facing the nation, Russia is still an attractive business destination. Its large natural resources, which are yet to be fully exploited due to geographic constraints, are a major attraction. With modern equipment and technical manpower, they could be harnessed to generate great profit. With almost 100 per cent literacy, the country has potential to be an outsourcing hub. Compared to India and China, it has better infrastructure and its geographic proximity to Europe is an advantage. The large Soviet-era nuclear power stations which are now mostly abandoned due to lack of proper management and upkeep could be used to generate energy for potential markets in Eastern Europe.

FOREIGN INVESTMENT

B Work in pairs. You want to invest in Russia but you need to decide whether there is the necessary 'cultural fit'. Student A reads extract 1. Student B reads extract 2. Exchange information to decide if you could work effectively with people from this culture.

Extract 1
Climate
Living for centuries in a very harsh climate explains the Russians' strength, their ability to endure extreme hardship, and their bleak outlook on life. It also explains their patience and submission. Climate has also contributed to a cautiousness they exhibit.

Geography
Russia has only limited access to the sea, deterring development of a trading mentality. Russia's size has made it often inward-looking and its people not always aware of what is going on in the rest of the world.

Community
Communal spirit and togetherness distinguishes Russians from Westerners. The affinity for the group can still be seen today in everyday life and physical contact with strangers. In restaurants, Russians will not hesitate to join a table with strangers rather than dine alone. Men kiss men and show affection, women hold hands while strolling. Recreation is often arranged in groups, often with colleagues they work with. They prefer organised sports with set teams. In general, in a collective society, everybody's business is also everyone else's.

Extract 2
The law
The law in Russia has served to protect the state and the community rather than the individual. The leaders had the tradition of being above the law. Many Russians do not take the law very seriously. With the fall of Communism, there are often conflicting laws and police choose when to enforce them.

Behaviour and attitudes
In public and at work, Russians can be brusque and they watch what they say. At home, within the intimate circle of family and friends, they feel secure and relaxed, warm and hospitable, sharing and caring, and they speak their minds. Some Russians expect things to go poorly and have learnt to live with misfortune. However, they have an admirable durability and resilience, a proven strength and endurance.

Negotiating
Russians regard compromise as a sign of weakness, a retreat from a correct and morally justified position. They often seem inflexible and unwilling to compromise. Only at the end, will they agree to concessions.

C Work in pairs. Draw up an investor's checklist for your country. Use the ideas below to help you.

- Climate
- Geography
- Economy (inflation, unemployment, etc.)
- Natural Resources
- Literacy / Education
- The Law
- Government
- Values (competition, co-operation, individual versus group)
- Attitudes (optimism, conservatism)

▶ Business across cultures page 153

Checklist
- ✓ FDI league table
- ✓ words to do with FDI: *works out, on offer* ...
- ✓ referring and sequencing: *this, that, firstly, secondly* ...
- ✓ participating in meetings
- ✓ Russia

MONEY
11 The bottom line

Start-up

A What do you understand by the title of this unit? How does it relate to budgets, expenditure and revenue?

A budget tells us what we can't afford, but it doesn't keep us from buying it.

B Have you ever had to budget for something special, such as a wedding, a party, or a holiday? Or have you ever been responsible for a budget at work? Tell a partner how you planned your budget.

Reading

A What are the causes of economic downturns or recessions? What are the effects on small businesses? Discuss with a partner.

B Read the article below about how small businesses can boost their bottom line and survive a recession.

C Match a heading from the box below to a tip in the text (1–9).

| Skills | Inventory | Staffing levels | Overheads | Cash flow |
| Premises | Investment | Staff input | Promotional expenditure |

D Work in small groups. Think of other recommendations that could be added to the list above.

Beating a recession

Here are a few tips for small business managers to follow during economic downturns.

1 _____ Monitor your company's financial health, and make monthly forecasts to ensure that expenses and planned expenditures are in line with accounts receivable. Be able to project where you will stand three months in advance.

2 _____ Examine your capital spending. Consider delaying the purchase of high cost items, upgrading equipment, and expansion plans that will take a long time to pay off.

3 _____ Consider reducing stock of slow-moving products. Observe the results, and look out for products that should be eliminated from your stock. This way if sales plummet, less of your cash is secured in unproductive assets.

4 _____ Many businesses reduce advertising during hard times. However, increasing ad outlays during slowdowns helps a business to get ahead of rivals who cut back.

5 _____ You could generate extra income by subletting excess office space.

6 _____ A business can save huge amounts of money by buying recycled printer cartridges and used computer equipment, copiers, and office furniture.

7 _____ Organisations often cut back on training during recessions. However, slow periods are the optimal time to conduct training, especially low-cost, on-the-job instruction.

8 _____ Do not compromise service by being understaffed. If full-time employees are stretching your budget, take on freelancers. During a slowdown, taking on part-time staff is easy due to layoffs in other organisations.

9 _____ Meet with staff regularly to exchange ideas on boosting productivity and other issues. Create an incentive scheme for good suggestions, and encourage team spirit for survival.

THE BOTTOM LINE

Listening and speaking

A You are going to listen to Tom Finchley talking about the budget for a conference in Chicago. Before you listen, insert the following expressions under the correct heading below:

To be $ maximum   To add up to $ To be just over $ To set us back $
To be approximately $ To be almost $ To exceed $ To work out at $ To come to $
To cost $ To be just under $ To be just short of $ To be in the region of $
To be $ at most   To total $ To amount to $ To be around $

Equal to $	Approximately $	More than $	Less than $
To work out at			

11.1

B Listen to the presentation. Fill in the missing information in columns 1–4. Compare your answers with a partner.

C Listen again and make notes relating to each budget item in the Notes column. The first one has been done for you as an example. Compare your answers with a partner.

Two-day professional motivation conference					
1	**2**	**3**	**4**	**Notes**
Budget item	Unit cost	No. units	Estimated cost	Charlotte Hotel. Downtown Chicago. Right atmosphere.
1 _____	$9,000	1	**$9,000**	
2 **Promotion / Invitations**				~
_____	$100	8	$800	
_____	$_____	50	$_____	
Invitations/Postage	$_____	3,000	$_____	
Subtotal	~	~	$_____	~
3 _____				~
Fees	$3,000	_____	$_____	
Subtotal	~	~	$_____	~
4 **Handouts**	$_____	2,000	$_____	
5 _____	_____	1	$_____	~
		Total	$_____	~

D Work in pairs. Use the language in A to talk about the costs of one of the ideas below.

- The process of hiring someone
- A three-day off-site staff development course
- An advertising campaign for a product or service

MODULE 3

Grammar

Prepositions

Look at these examples from the listening.
Together with envelopes and postage, ...
With regard to nice, glossy posters, ...

They are multi-word prepositions. They consist of two and three words functioning together. (For multi-word prepositions expressing cause and effect, see Unit 9.)

A Read the audio script on page 123. Underline all the other prepositional phrases that begin with multi-word prepositions.

B Match a preposition (1–5) to a preposition with a similar meaning (a–e).

1 except for   a near to
2 with regard to   b in addition to
3 close to   c as for
4 in accordance with   d apart from
5 as well as   e in line with

C Complete the sentences using the prepositions in the box. (Sometimes there is more than one possibility.)

| with regard to | in addition to | thanks to | apart from | in terms of | in spite of |
| as for | according to | except for | as well as | in view of | depending on |

1 _____ costs, we have to pay $9,000 for the venue alone.

2 The venue charges different rates _____ the day of the week.

3 $12,000 will cover the cost of the speakers, _____ their travel expenses, which will be budgeted separately.

4 _____ how far some of the speakers have to travel, we should provide travel expenses.

5 _____ a good offer from our local printer, we'll be able to get some glossy posters at low rates.

6 The costs of the conference may well increase _____ our attempts to limit them.

7 We plan to promote the conference through a series of advertisements in local journals, _____ posters and leaflets of course.

Look at these examples from the listening. These are prepositional phrases (preposition + noun group) that are fixed **idioms**, working as a unit.
by no means, *at the most*, and *beside the point*.

D With a partner, find these three phrases in the audio script and discuss other ways of saying the same thing.

E Work in pairs or small groups. Create a budget for one of the following:

a team-building event   an office party   a business trip   a project of your choice

F Present your budget to the rest of the class, using as many prepositions as possible.

▶ Review and development page 92

▶ Grammar overview page 163

THE BOTTOM LINE

Negotiations 1: Bargaining

Whatever the culture and style of business partners, the heart of a negotiation is the bargaining. The bargain is the deal which satisfies both parties. At this stage in a negotiation, an offer is usually linked to a condition.

11.2 **A** Listen to four extracts of negotiations. Match the offers to the conditions using one of the connectors in the box below.

| if | provided that | so long as | on condition that |

Offers	**Conditions**
a discount	guarantee regular orders
better payment terms	promote the products nationally
an exclusive deal	order a minimum quantity
a smaller order	place your first order today

11.3 **B** Look at four ways of responding to offers in the Key language box below. Listen again to the four extracts and the responses that are given. Match the extract (1–4) to the response (a–d).

Key language

a	Acceptance	That is acceptable. We can agree to that. That sounds OK. All right.
b	Refusal + a new offer	We can't agree to that, but we could … That would be difficult. However, would you consider …? I'm afraid that's not going to work. Perhaps we could …
c	Acceptance + a condition	That's fine if … Provided you can …, then we can agree to … OK, as long as …
d	Rejection	I'm afraid we can't agree to that. Despite your generous offer, we could not accept … I don't think we can go any further.

C Work in pairs. Read the situation below and then prepare for the negotiation. Remember that it is in both your interests to reach a deal.

Movula is a small company which provides a specialist translation service for medical people – translating medical letters and documents. At the moment, it is providing this service for local doctors and hospitals. However, Movula would like to offer its services more widely and has started negotiations with Medcare, a large medical services company, which serves the whole country. Movula and Medcare are in talks about integrating their services.

Student A: You represent Movula. Turn to page 110.
Student B: You represent Medcare. Turn to page 111.

▶ Review and development page 93

▶ Communication page 149

BUSINESS ACROSS CULTURES

Brazil

Brazil is the fifth largest country in the world, taking up over half the land mass of South America. It has 19 cities and a population of over 170 million. After severe economic problems, Brazil is making a comeback.

A Work in pairs. Discuss what role rules and regulations (e.g. laws, tax regulations) have on doing business in your country.

B Read three extracts about Brazilian culture. What do they tell you about:

1 government bureaucracy?
2 economic growth?
3 business transactions?
4 attitudes towards tax?

> *Brasil cresce de noite.* Brazil grows at night. This is a well-known truth. No matter what the government does to hold people back, Brazil will get by and grow, even if at night. The idea here is that during the day, the government machinery stifles economic growth, but when the bureaucrats sleep, real progress occurs. This is also the idea behind the concept of '*jeitinho*', in which you can also find 'a little way' around rules and regulations.

> *Despachante* is the term used in Brazil to refer to the 'middleman' or facilitator of business transactions. This contact has the ability to introduce you to the right people, set up meetings and deal with paperwork. The terms of the facilitator are simple. He wants your friendship and he wants it now. Another important aspect to this friendship is the giving and taking. Whether it is of money, favours or gifts, it is a way of life.

> Many businesses have a *Caixa 2*. Translated, this means 'Cash Account Number 2'. It is all the money or assets that are kept off the books and official records. This, of course, keeps it away from the eyes of the tax authorities.

C Work in pairs or small groups. Compare the 'Brazilian way' with your own culture. Report back to the class.

THE BOTTOM LINE

11.4 **D** **Listen to an interview with Maria Fernandes about work and social life in Brazil. Which of the topics in the box below does she mention?**

time   negotiation   breaks   climate   titles   corruption

E **Listen again. What advice does Maria give about:**
1 being direct?
2 using first names?
3 punctuality?

F **Read the advice below about negotiating in Brazil. Match the extract (1–5) with a piece of advice (a–e).**

1 Brazil is a person-oriented culture where the organisation exists to help people achieve their purpose. Forming relationships is key to business success. This can be contrasted with a task-oriented culture which is more focused on specific jobs that need to be done and less with the people.
2 Brazil is a high-context culture where the environment (your dress, the way you sit, the use of humour) are just as important as what you say. Low-context cultures rely more on what people say and less on the context around them.
3 Brazilians are often suspicious of authorities and prefer to work with people they know. Some cultures have a more universalist approach where rules need to be obeyed and the law is seen as a support to society, rather than an obstacle.
4 Brazil is an emotional culture, where it is important to show how you feel. In more neutral cultures, people hide what they are feeling and they may be embarrassed by shows of emotion.
5 Brazil is a polychronic culture where people tolerate many things happening at the same time. In monochronic cultures, people expect punctuality and for time to be structured and measured.

a be patient
b think about your body language
c treat each member of the team as an individual
d use a local accountant and lawyer
e don't be afraid to make physical contact

▶ Business across cultures page 153

G **Work in small groups. Prepare some advice about negotiating in your culture. Present your advice to the rest of the group.**

Checklist ✓ beating a recession   ✓ words to do with budgets: *to be just over, to amount to ...*   ✓ prepositions: *except for, as well as ...*   ✓ bargaining   ✓ Brazil

MONEY

12 Escaping poverty

Start-up

A Read the statement opposite. What does it mean? What do you think of this philosophy?

> Give poor communities the opportunity, and then get out of the way!

Reading and speaking

A Read the text.

Factors associated with poverty

1. **Geography** Mountains, deserts, rivers and coastlines can help or hinder communication. This has slowed the spread of new technology to areas such as Central America and Sub-Saharan Africa.

2. **Natural disasters** Developing countries suffer much more as a result of hurricanes, earthquakes and tsunamis because of inadequate resources and antiquated emergency mechanisms.

3. **The 'resource curse'** Countries with an abundance of natural resources tend to have poor economic growth due to the volatility of revenues from the natural resource sector, and a decline in competitiveness within other sectors.

4. **Disease** Families are often forced to sell what few assets they have to secure even partial treatment. Caring for sick relatives means that many children cannot attend school, reducing their chances of a sound education and stable future.

5. **The 'brain drain'** Knowledge and expertise are 'drained' from the nation when thousands of trained individuals and graduates emigrate for higher wages and better opportunities.

6. **Corruption** This occurs when the authorities are not accountable to those they serve. Economic progress is impeded when leaders help themselves to funds that are intended for development projects.

7. **Lack of free trade** Goods and services cannot flow between countries obstructed by government-imposed tariff and non-tariff barriers.

8. **Infrastructure** Lack of roads, airports, utilities, and means of communication, including information technology, and development tools, hinders development.

9. **Financial services** In the West, easy access to loans with extortionate interest rates means many lives become debt-ridden, while in developing countries, lack of collateral prevents people from acquiring bank loans to help them set up a business.

B Find words in the text with the following definitions:

1 A government tax on imports or exports
2 Assets promised as security for a debt
3 Instability and unpredictability
4 To obstruct (× 2)
5 A more than adequate supply of something
6 To leave your home country
7 Obliged to answer for your actions
8 Highly excessive, especially in price
9 Extremely old

C Which of the above factors are 'causes' of poverty? Which are 'effects'? Discuss your views with a partner.

D How can these problems be dealt with? What can be done to pull people out of poverty? Discuss in small groups.

ESCAPING POVERTY

Listening

A If you were starting a small business, where would you go for finance? Discuss in pairs.

🎧 12.1 **B** Listen to the first part of an interview with Sanjay Chakraborty, a specialist in poverty reduction. Answer the questions.

1 What does he say about the results of international aid?
2 According to Milton Friedman, why do 'the poor stay poor'?
3 What is the term for lending small amounts to poor people?
4 When was the Grameen Bank opened? In which country did this happen?
5 Why are most of Grameen Bank's customers women?

🎧 12.2 **C** Listen to the second part of the interview and answer the questions.

1 How does microfinance differ from conventional financing?
2 How do microfinance loan repayment rates compare with those related to big business?
3 Why are large banks and investors becoming interested in microfinance?
4 Where in the world can you find microfinance lending institutions?

D Listen to the whole interview and write down the following figures:

> Proportion of world's population that live on less than $2 a day _____
> Amount of international aid given to developing countries in the last 50 years _____
> In relation to Grameen Bank:
> Number of borrowers ___
> Percentage of women borrowers ___ Rate of repayment of loans ___
> Number of customers using this form of finance worldwide ___
> Rate at which Grameen Bank's clients are escaping poverty _____

Speaking

The biggest challenge in extending financial services to the poor lies in persuading the financial sector that microfinance represents an opportunity. Many commercial banks perceive the poor as unbankable.

Work in pairs. Prepare a presentation to a privately owned commercial bank to persuade them to set up microfinance operations.

MODULE 3

Grammar

Reported speech

To report what someone has said, you can use a reporting verb like *say* or *explain,* followed by a *that* clause, although the word *that* is sometimes omitted.

When the reporting verb is in a past tense, you often take the tense of the reported verb 'back'.

'The Grameen Bank **was set up** in the mid-1970s.'

He **said** (that) the Grameen Bank **had been set up** in the mid-1970s.

When the reporting verb is in a **present tense**, you don't usually change it.

He **says** (that) the Grameen Bank **was set up** in the mid-1970s.

You often need to change pronouns, for example *I* to *she*.

'I'm hoping to get a bigger loan.'

She explained (that) she was hoping to get a bigger loan.

A Write the statements in reported speech. Use the verb in brackets.

1 'Traditional banks have not been willing to lend to poor people.' (stress)

2 'Microfinance emerged as a new approach to lending money.' (agree)

3 'Women are more likely to reinvest their earnings in the business.' (say)

12.3 **B** Listen to ten statements. Match each statement to an appropriate reporting verb in the box below. You can only use each verb once. Compare your answers with a partner.

| denies | warned | complains | predicted | confessed |
| replied | emphasised | explained | promises | added |

C Listen again. Report the statement back using the correct reporting verb.

To report questions, you often use *ask* and a clause introduced by *if, whether, how, when* etc.

'So, has the approach taken off in other parts of the world?'

Reported question: The interviewer **asked whether / if** the approach had taken off in other parts of the world.

How does the word order differ in the two sentences above?

D Look at the questions below from the interview with Sanjay Chakraborty. Rewrite the questions in reported speech.

1 How and when did this start?
2 So, how does microfinance work?
3 So, is microfinance the solution to beating global poverty?

E Work in groups of four. Two students should role play the situations below. The other two students observe and make notes. Then exchange roles. Report back to the class what your group said.

- You are managers meeting to discuss the fact that levels of job satisfaction among your employees seem to be falling.
- You are employees having an informal discussion about a plan to move some of your production of top-of-the-range rainwear to China.
- Student A is an entrepreneur who wants to open a new restaurant. You are making a pitch for financial backing to Student B, who is a private investor.

▶ Review and development page 92

▶ Grammar overview page 164

ESCAPING POVERTY

Communication

Negotiations 2: Handling conflict

In this second section on negotiations, we look at handling conflict. Conflict is a possible development in any negotiation and there are effective ways to resolve it.

A Have you ever experienced conflict at work or during your studies? How did you handle it?

 12.4

B Sean O'Donnell is an agent for an American company called Finsoft which produces customised accounting software solutions. Listen to a telephone conversation between Sean and Helen, an account manager for Finsoft, and answer the questions.

1 What is the conflict between Sean and Helen about?
2 What is Helen's position?
3 What is Sean's position?
4 What is Helen's solution?
5 What is Sean's solution?

C Look at the Key language box below. Then, listen again and identify:

1 How Helen tries to analyse the obstacle.
2 How Sean identifies the obstacle.
3 How Sean finds common ground.
4 How Sean introduces an option.

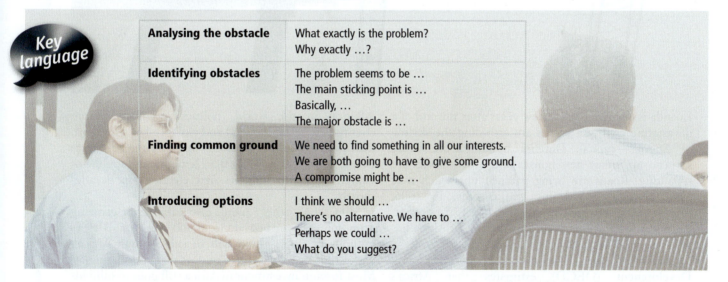

Key language

Analysing the obstacle	What exactly is the problem? Why exactly …?
Identifying obstacles	The problem seems to be … The main sticking point is … Basically, … The major obstacle is …
Finding common ground	We need to find something in all our interests. We are both going to have to give some ground. A compromise might be …
Introducing options	I think we should … There's no alternative. We have to … Perhaps we could … What do you suggest?

D Work in pairs. Student A looks at this page. Student B looks at page 111. You should try and find some common ground in this negotiation.

Student A

You are responsible for sales in your company. You have had the opportunity to bid for a contract with a large defence contractor. You know how business works in this sector and you want to make sure the purchasing people are well inclined towards your bid. You would like to have a significant budget (€2,500) to 'wine and dine' the customer. Your colleague in finance is very unwilling to let you have this money.

▶ Review and development page 93

▶ Communication page 149

Africa

Africa is often seen as a problem continent. In this section we discover some grounds to be more optimistic about the future, but also explore the problem of corruption which often halts economic development and hope for the future.

A Work in pairs. What image do you have of Africa?

B Read the article and then discuss with a partner.
- the reasons to be feel optimistic about Africa' future
- the reasons to feel pessimistic about Africa's future
- your own conclusions

Luanda is changing fast. A few years after the end of a devastating civil war, cranes are crowding the skyline of Angola's capital. Derelict buildings are being spruced up, smart new houses and office blocks are sprouting. Roads are being patched up, which may ease the city's maddening traffic jams. In 2006, Angola's economy grew by an estimated 15.5 per cent, the fastest on the continent. But the rest of Africa has also been doing well; a recent report by the Organisation for Economic Co-operation and Development (OECD) estimates that Africa's economy grew by almost 5 per cent in 2006, and is expected to do even better in the future.

The perky figures are partly due to a global hunger for oil, minerals and other commodities, whetted by demand from China and India. Africa produces much of what China wants, boosting trade and fuelling interest in the continent. But Africa itself deserves credit for the upswing. Inflation, now averaging 8 per cent a year, is at its lowest level in many countries since independence 40-plus years ago. With the striking exception of places as Côte d'Ivoire, Somalia, and Zimbabwe which has the highest inflation in the world, politics in most African countries is better handled and violence less prevalent. Peace seems to be breaking out in Angola, Sierra Leone and Liberia, while the Democratic Republic of Congo hopes to hold its first elections in decades shortly.

On the other hand, Africa's faster-growing economies have not done much yet for Africa's millions of poor; about half of sub-Saharan Africa's 750m-plus people still live on less than a dollar a day. Most foreign investment in Africa still goes to oilfields or mines, rather than factories, services or farming. Mineral riches provide governments with cash but do not create many jobs. Most people in Africa still work in the informal sector and unemployment is rife. The other huge check on growth is corruption. Some governments say they are trying to tackle it. Nigeria, whose economy has been devastated by the dishonesty of its politicians, has embarked on a high-profile anti-graft campaign. So has Zambia. But in the rankings index of Transparency International, a Berlin-based lobby, African countries are generally perceived as being the most corrupt.

ESCAPING POVERTY

 12.5 **C** Corruption affects a country's growth. Listen to a representative of a Swedish aid agency talking about the problems of corruption. What does she say about how corruption affects:

1 the law
2 politics
3 business

D Work in pairs. What are the attitudes towards these three areas in your country?

E Read about two types of culture and decide which you belong to.

People in **universalist** cultures believe that rules, procedures and standards are important and should be applied by everyone. The law is considered helpful to society and people, and makes the world a better place to live.

In a **particularist** culture, there may be lots of rules and laws, but people pay more attention to the particular situation and the relationships involved. They will follow the law if they have to but if there is a choice about what is right for their friends and relations as opposed to what is right according to the law, they will choose family.

F Read the following business situations and answer the questions. Discuss your ideas with a partner.

> You work in the Finance Division of your company. When you were leaving the office yesterday you saw a colleague from Purchasing carrying a half case of whisky (6 bottles). He made a joke about having a big party this evening. You know that one of your suppliers will have presented him with this gift.

What do you think the company's policy should be about gifts?

> Your company has never had anyone responsible for Public Relations. You were surprised to read that Sophie Menton has been appointed PR Manager. You later discovered that she is the niece of the Sales Director, fresh out of business school with little experience of business.

What do you think about this?

> You are a travel agent. One of your best customers has asked you to provide a receipt for a plane ticket to New York. He has asked you to make the receipt out for €2,150, the business class fare. In fact, he paid for an economy ticket costing €650. Your policy is not to provide these 'fake' receipts. However, you may well lose this client's business if you don't.

What do you do?

G Work in small groups. Discuss one of the topics below and report back to the class with your conclusions.

- Corruption is not just a problem in Africa. It is everywhere.
- All companies should be forced to offer fair trade arrangements with producers in the developing world.
- Business isn't fair. It's competitive.

▶ Business across cultures page 153

Checklist

✓ factors associated with poverty
✓ microfinance
✓ reported speech: *he confessed he was in a lot of debt ...*
✓ handling conflict
✓ Africa

BUSINESS SCENARIO 3
Katabaro Hotel

Background Read this newspaper report about the Katabaro Hotel in Dar es Salaam, Tanzania.

The five-star Katabaro Hotel in Dar es Salaam, Tanzania was once regarded as one of the most classically luxurious hotels in the world. It was an imposing building with 220 rooms and suites, many of which boasted panoramic views of the harbour or over the hotel's exotic gardens. Today, however, it is in an appalling state of disrepair – a shadow of its former self. When the country suffered great economic difficulties in the late 1980s, the hotel could not generate the cash flow to carry out renovations and found it increasingly difficult to compete with new hotels. Last week, its owner Akili Macha announced that he was seeking investment from the Middle East so that he can return the hotel to its former glory. Mr Macha said, 'We've gone through hard times, but I'm optimistic.'

KATABARO HOTEL

Negotiation

The wealthy Saudi investor Ibrahim Madani of the Madani Group has been in contact with Mr Macha and has expressed interest in investing in the famous hotel. Today they are meeting to find out what each side has to offer and to try to negotiate a deal.

Work in pairs.

Student A: You are Mr Macha, owner of the Katabaro Hotel. Look at page 108.
Student B: You are Saudi investor, Ibrahim Madani. Look at page 110.

> **Useful language**
> I can agree to that.
> That sounds OK.
> That would be difficult. However, would you consider ...?
> Provided you can ..., then we can agree to ...
> I'm afraid I can't agree to that.
> A compromise might be ...

Breakdown of costs

Item	Cost
Renovation of main hotel building	$1,800,000
Renovate the famous ballroom (for dances and functions)	$300,000
Renovate the existing small conference centre	$250,000
Transform the ballroom into a large state-of-the-art conference centre	$325,000
Create eight new meeting rooms (in addition to the existing ten)	$225,000
Create a travel agent and safari service	$325,000
Improve Internet access and business centre	$300,000
Landscape gardens	$325,000
Renovate and extend the health and beauty spa	$300,000
Build tennis courts	$100,000
Build new outdoor swimming pool	$250,000
Build a fitness centre	$350,000
Total	**$4,850,000**

Discussing a budget

Mr Madani has agreed to invest in the hotel, but less than $4,850,000. Renovation of the main hotel building is essential, but some other costs in the table above will need to be cut.

Work in groups of four. Hold a meeting to discuss which expenditures are priorities and which can be eliminated.

Student A: You are Mr Macha. You will chair the meeting. Look at page 102.
Student B: You are the hotel manager. Look at page 109.
Student C: You are Mr Madani. Look at page 110.
Student D: You are Mr Madani's business manager. Look at page 111.

Writing

You are Mr Macha. Write an email to your business partner, Haji Okeyo. Give him a brief summary of the outcome of the second meeting and explain why certain decisions were made.

REVIEW AND DEVELOPMENT

9–12

Vocabulary

A thriving economy

A Look again at the vocabulary on page 65. Then, read the definitions below (1–8) and find the correct word in the wordsearch.

M	P	F	L	O	U	R	I	S	H	E	L	A	M
Y	I	O	P	E	C	N	Z	P	W	J	N	C	U
I	T	H	R	I	V	I	N	G	D	E	E	S	L
S	P	E	C	T	A	C	U	L	A	R	R	B	T
P	E	S	T	O	A	U	V	F	L	P	U	M	H
I	S	N	J	T	R	O	K	O	D	U	D	C	A
N	R	I	Y	H	F	R	K	U	Z	U	Y	E	N
D	P	Q	O	X	B	U	I	N	V	Y	N	T	G
O	X	A	C	U	A	Y	Q	D	P	D	A	A	O
W	U	L	P	L	H	A	N	G	O	V	E	R	V
N	S	F	C	C	P	L	Q	U	I	R	I	X	E
R	E	S	T	R	I	C	T	I	O	N	S	G	R
P	I	N	E	Q	U	A	L	I	T	Y	M	E	L

1 A '_____ of call' is a place where you stop for a short time, especially on a journey
2 Very successful
3 To discover exactly what, where or when something is
4 Amazing, unusually good
5 To start (a company)
6 The '_____ of power' are the higher levels of government
7 To develop very successfully
8 To threaten something

Grammar

Cause and effect

A Look again at the rules and examples on page 66. Then, match the two halves of each sentence, linking them with an appropriate word in the box below. (Sometimes there is more than one possibility.)

consequently	because	due to	because of	owing to
as a result of	so	therefore	as a result	results in	as

Example.
Prices have fallen <u>due to</u> increased competition.

Effect	Cause
1 Prices have fallen	a there were so many government restrictions.
2 Young people in China have prospered	b increased competition.
3 Many governments pay close attention to foreign direct investment	c the country's booming economy.
4 Ten years ago, we couldn't invest in China	d the flow of money into and out of the country has an economic impact.

Cause	Effect
5 Inflation was very high	e China has made every effort to attract multinationals.
6 Foreign companies do not present a threat to the Chinese government,	f this industry will be internationalised and upgraded.
7 A flourishing business	g foreign investment decreased.
8 China has approved several joint ventures involving film and television production companies,	h the need for an expansion.

▶ Grammar overview page 161

REVIEW AND DEVELOPMENT 9–12

Vocabulary

Foreign investment

A Look again at the vocabulary on page 71. Then, replace the words in italics with a word or expression in the box below.

money laundering   weigh up   inflation   come into the equation

1 Russia's international image has been tarnished by stories of corruption and *illegally obtained funds being transformed into legal ones*.
2 Political stability should *be considered* when planning foreign investment.
3 A company has *to balance* the risks *against other factors* when planning to set up operations in war-torn countries.
4 Lower prices for basic goods have prevented *the economic situation where there are higher prices and a decrease in purchasing power*.

Grammar

Referring and sequencing

A Look again at the rules and examples on page 72. Use the words in the box to complete the sentence.

finally   first   these include   this is   then

1 The key factors driving foreign investment seem promising. _____ intensified competition and improved conditions for doing business in a rapidly increasing number of countries.

2 Africa's own investors tend to invest elsewhere. _____ one of the main reasons the continent has difficulty progressing.

3 The economic development of Russia since 1989 has gone through many stages. _____, the old Soviet economic system was dismantled. _____, short-term decisions were made concerning urgent economic policies. _____, long-term reforms were established to encourage greater economic stability.

▶ Grammar overview page 162

Vocabulary

Boosting the bottom line

A Look again at the vocabulary on page 76. Then complete the text below using the words in the box.

stretch   economic downturn   plummet   overheads   revenue   expenditure   lay off

There are signs of (1) _____: the long and stable growth of national output has finally slowed and higher interest rates have dampened down spending by households and businesses alike. The resulting fall in (2) _____ is forcing small business managers to consider strategies that will help them navigate their way through tough economic times. When sales begin to (3) _____, there is a tendency to (4) _____ skilled employees in order to bring down (5) _____. This may sound logical but it often proves risky as it can demoralise the staff who remain. Product development may also (6) _____ the budget but cutting back on it can result in a business falling behind innovative competitors and losing market share. In short, indiscriminate cost cutting can damage a business hugely. So how can costs be minimised? The most effective strategy is to cut (7) _____ such as rent of premises, gas, electricity, and stationery. These should not be reduced to the point where the business cannot operate any longer but they need to be assessed regularly to determine how every penny adds to or detracts from the bottom line.

B Now read the text again and identify five verbs that have the same meaning as *to reduce*.

MODULE 3

Grammar

Prepositions

A Look again at the rules and examples on page 78. Choose the correct option in italics to complete the sentences.

1 The company's performance is *in lines with / in line with / in line of* our expectations.
2 *In terms of / In any terms / In no terms* the proposal, it is just a draft.
3 We are not suffering from the recession *in the view of / in view of / in the views of* the fact we were well prepared.
4 *With regard to / With regards to / In regard* to a strategy, he seems very unclear.
5 If we're cutting our advertising budget, any discussion about our promotional campaign is *besides the point / beside of the point / beside the point*!

▶ Grammar overview page 163

Vocabulary

Escaping poverty

A Look again at the vocabulary on page 82. Then, match words from each column to create a complete sentence.

1 Strict tariffs	emigrate	third world countries to maintain impossible interest payments.
2 The educated	brings about	development and progress.
3 Extortionate world interest rates	force	the free flow of goods between countries.
4 Poor infrastructure	prevent	the spread of new technology.
5 Due to antiquated emergency mechanisms, the third world	encourages	more when natural disasters occur.
6 Awkward geographic features	slow	market volatility.
7 An abundance of natural resources	require	collateral to get a business loan.
8 Entrepreneurs	hinders	for better opportunities abroad.
9 Lack of accountability	suffers	corruption.

Grammar

Reported speech

A Look again at the rules and examples on page 84. Use the following reporting verbs to report the speech in sentences 1–7 below. The first one has been done for you as an example.

promise   admit   predict   argue   inform   complain   ask

1 'There's no evidence that microfinance actually lifts people out of poverty.'
   He argued that there was no evidence that microfinance ...
2 'This week, I will arrive on time for the meeting. I give you my word!'
3 'I haven't received the report yet. This really isn't good enough.'
4 'Like other entrepreneurs, I'm capable of making mistakes. Unfortunately, I invested in the wrong equipment.'
5 'Does poverty strengthen corruption?'
6 'Your company is too small for us to invest in.'
7 'By 2050, China, India, Brazil and Russia will probably be larger than the six biggest economies today, the US, Japan, Germany, the UK, France and Italy.'

▶ Grammar overview page 164

Communication

Look again at the communication skills pages in Units 9–12. Then complete these exercises.

A Complete the following questions and expressions by matching the start and finish.

1 Have you all
2 I've called this meeting
3 There are four
4 Are there any points
5 Let's now turn to
6 Can we summarise by
7 Peter has agreed to
8 Susan will report

a items on the agenda today.
b take the minutes.
c the second item on the agenda.
d identifying the main action points?
e seen a copy of the memo?
f to make a decision about the budget.
g back on progress at the next meeting.
h you would like to add to the agenda?

B Change the statements into questions.

1 I'd like you to go over that again. → Could _____?
2 I think you are worried about the budget. → So, _____?
3 Tell me more about the project. → Could _____?
4 I think we should limit travel this year. → Don't _____?
5 We all agree that the budget should be cut. → Does _____?
6 There are three vital steps to take. → What _____?

C Put the dialogue into the right order.

Matt: That could be interesting for us. Can you put this in writing?

Anna: That will be difficult as you do not buy some of the products in the right quantity.

Matt: That sounds interesting. What sort of discount?

Anna: So we have proposed our new prices. What do you think?

Matt: Perhaps. Provided the discount is across the full range of products.

Anna: I'm sorry to hear that. Would you consider them if we offered a quantity discount?

Matt: I'm afraid we can't agree to them.

Anna: We can't really agree to that but we could offer you a significant discount on your five main product categories.

Matt: Well, that may be so. But we can't go any further without an across the board discount.

Anna: Well, as long as you can guarantee minimum orders, we could offer a 15 per cent discount linked to early payment.

D Match a word in the box to one with a similar meaning (1–8).

| offer | sticking point | shared interest | middle way | propose | option | difficulty | answer |

1 obstacle
2 problem
3 suggest
4 common ground
5 compromise
6 alternative
7 solution
8 bid

▶ Writing resource 15
page 98

WRITING RESOURCE 13
Developing people

Email exchange

A Read the advertisement.

DREAM TEAM COACHES

Are you looking after the key personnel in your organisation properly? If not, you might be damaging the future of your organisation's success! The decisions they make today will affect your organisation for years to come. Your leaders are under enormous pressure, and are more likely to suffer from stress and an unbalanced work-home life as a result. Can you afford to leave their success to chance?

Dream Team Coaches offers the following services:

Performance Coaching	We promise to increase your managers' effectiveness and productivity.
Skills Coaching	We can tailor-make our coaching sessions to develop your managers' core business skills.
Executive Coaching	We guarantee to improve your financial results, by enhancing the performance of your key leaders.
Team Facilitation	We will ensure smooth running of your most strategic moments by facilitating budget and strategy meetings or coaching your team before a big team presentation.

Our coaches have internationally recognised business management qualifications and years of experience in coaching and mentoring. They possess a powerful combination of knowledge and professional experience, which makes them excellent leadership models for the top decision-makers and the leaders of the future, in both public and private sector organisations.

For further information on our coaching and facilitation services, contact our client liaison officer, Renate Lenze, at renate.lenze@DreamTeamCoaches.com

B True or false?

1 The people at the top of any organisation generally have an easy life.
2 Managers will become better and faster at doing their jobs.
3 Dream Team Coaches will improve their customers' profitability.
4 A coach will attend presentations to customers with the team.
5 Dream Team Coaches doesn't work with state-run organisations.

DEVELOPING PEOPLE

C You are Brian Owen, Mediaco's HR director. Complete this email to Renate Lenze to get further details about Dream Team Coaching's programmes by choosing the correct phrase to fill each gap.

I'd be grateful if you could	I am writing with reference to
we've realised that we urgently need	and roughly how many
I'm particularly interested to know	please don't hesitate to contact me
I look forward to hearing about	it would also be extremely useful
due to	

Send to: renate.lenze@DreamTeamCoaches.com
Subject: Enquiry about programmes
Date: 13 July 20___

Dear Ms Lenze

(1) _____ your web advertisement about your coaching and facilitation services. I am head of Human Resources at Mediaco, a mid-size media company with 170 employees, based in Bath.

(2) _____ the rapid growth of the company in a short space of time (3) _____ to develop our senior staff to ensure continued success and to manage our growing number of employees more effectively.

(4) _____ give me a few more details about your coaching sessions. (5) _____ where and how your coaching sessions are delivered, what sort of timetable this involves, (6) _____ executives you coach in a group. (7) _____ to have an idea of your prices.

(8) _____ your services in more detail, as soon as possible. (9) _____ if you need any more information.

Best regards,
Brian Owen

D You are Renate Lenze. Write a reply to Brian Owen's email.

- Thank him for making enquiries
- Explain that coaching can be delivered:
  - on a one-to-one or group basis
  - at the corporate coaching centre in Swindon, UK or in-company
  - by distance coaching via email / telephone / Internet downloads
- Costs vary – all inclusive, one-week residential group course £3,000
- Say that you have attached a company brochure showing programmes, costs and photos
  End suitably

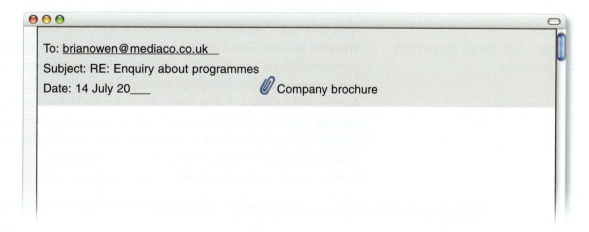

To: brianowen@mediaco.co.uk
Subject: RE: Enquiry about programmes
Date: 14 July 20___   📎 Company brochure

WRITING RESOURCE
14 Local partners

Business reports LifeCycles, a bike producer in the US, wants to expand into China. Alice Conway, the CEO, has called a meeting to devise an advertising campaign for their product range.

A Read the follow-up report to the meeting and insert the correct word from the box below.

| the | few | this | a | the | several | some of |

LifeCycles advertising campaign

Summary
Alice Conway, CEO of LifeCycles, asked the marketing team to attend a meeting to decide on a powerful marketing strategy for the LifeCycles range to be launched in China. She asked the team to come up with (1) _____ marketing ideas to present at (2) _____ meeting. The following short report, describes the Chinese market background, the current level of competition and the final agreed marketing strategy for the product.

Introduction
The following points were considered:
Local market
Competitive environment
Product range
Product range image
Product range marketing strategy

Local market
China's teenagers are extremely brand conscious and are attracted to local, Korean, Japanese and Western brands. Shopping for fashion, hanging out in malls and coffee bars, as well as punk music are (3) _____ the main interests of young Chinese people. There is also a strong interest in digital products such as music, Internet, cell phones and gaming systems, and these are likely to become one of the most marketing and advertising channels over the next (4) _____ years. Although China is dubbed 'the Kingdom of Bicycles', cycling is seen as a way of getting around instead of a competitive sport, or fashionable pastime.

Competitive environment
Although most basic bicycles are manufactured in China, (5) _____ high-end market is very limited. There is little domestic competition at present.

Product range
Silent Dragon bicycle
Blazing Saddles racing bike

Product range image
There is (6) _____ growing interest in raising the level of professionalism in Chinese cycle racing. Therefore, it was decided that the 'competitive spirit' would be the main focus of the brand image.

Product range marketing strategy
Whilst the foldable Silent Dragon bicycle will be advertised via mobile phone, the Blazing Saddles racing bike should be promoted in co-operation with cycle racing teams through sponsorship deals.

Conclusion
Analysis of the Chinese cycling trends shows that the high-end market is still relatively small. Current local competition from other cycle producers is currently still minimal, so there is an excellent opportunity for LifeCycles to combine with local producers and cycling teams to give (7) _____ highly successful established American brand a Chinese edge.

LOCAL PARTNERS

B You are a member of Sharp Edge Cycles marketing team. Write a follow-up report for Aarit Motala, the CEO of Dua. Use the notes you made from the meeting on page 59.

C Aarit Motala writes an email to Sharp Edge Cycles to confirm that he will use them as the exclusive local distributor. The sentences in the email have been mixed up. Put them in the correct order.

Finally, once again, many thanks for all your energy and hard work.

Dear Amit, Shalina and Ira,

Secondly, I'm keen to get this project underway as soon as possible, so I'd be grateful if you could start organising the marketing campaign immediately.

Could you also send me a progress report by the end of next month?

Aarit Motala

Therefore, I'm pleased to confirm that I would be happy to sign an exclusive, five-year distribution contract with Sharp Edge Cycles.

Firstly, let me congratulate you on our successful meeting two days ago.

I look forward to a strong and profitable partnership between our companies in the near future.

I was very impressed with your imaginative suggestions for marketing our Dua cycle range.

Kindest regards,

I'm extremely pleased with the outcomes we arrived at, and am confident that with your expert local knowledge, Dua Cycles will be a success in India.

WRITING RESOURCE
15 Getting away from it!

Press releases

A Read this press release about the opening of The Royal in Sharm El-Sheikh.

Sharm El-Sheikh
PRESS RELEASE

Today in Sharm El-Sheikh, the five-star hotel, The Royal, was reopened after a two-year refurbishment project costing over $20m. One of the hotel's main investors, Funsani Abbas, cut the cord at the lavish opening ceremony, which was attended by celebrity guests from all over the world.

In his opening speech, Mr Abbas (1) announced that the refurbishment would put the hotel back on the international luxury tourism map. (2) 'We already have bookings from a large number of world famous celebrities,' he proudly stated.

(3) He went on to say that it was not difficult to see why. 'The hotel is first class and situated in some of the best surroundings a holidaymaker could expect. Located on the southern-most tip of the Sinai Peninsula, Sharm is actually a series of bays lying between mountain ranges. Whether you are keen on diving, water sports or just sunning yourself on the beach, it's one of the most idyllic vacation spots in the world.'

(4) He added that at all hours of the day and night, Sharm's legendary promenade, which stretches from one end of the bay to the other, was one of the country's most romantic strolling spots. 'When the sun sets, Sharm comes to life with its thousands of lights reflected in the still, black waters of the sea.' (5) However, for diving enthusiasts, he continued, the real attraction lay beneath the surface of the crystal blue waters of the Red Sea. He added that it had some of the world's most spectacular coral and marine life.

(6) He boasted, 'the exquisite guest rooms, as well as the hotel's unrivalled 18-hole golf course, club house and spa will provide the ultimate in restfulness and pampering.'

(7) 'I am extremely proud to be the owner of one of the finest hotels in the world!' he concluded.

B Look at the phrases (1–7) above. Turn the direct speech sentences into reported speech sentences and vice versa.

1 Mr Abbas announced, '_____.'

2 He proudly stated that _____.

3 He went on to say '_____.'

4 He added, '_____.'

5 'However, for diving enthusiasts,' he continued, '_____.'

6 He boasted that _____.

7 He concluded that _____.

C Complete the text about Tanzania, using the words in the box below.

| very successful   astounding   most picturesque   extremely diverse |
| greatest concentration   second deepest   perfect place |

Tanzania is still one of the (1) _____ countries in the world and is most certainly the (2) _____ to attract the luxury tourism market. Safari tourism is already proving (3) _____. Home to the exotic islands of Zanzibar and Pemba, Tanzania has an (4) _____ range of flora and fauna. It has an (5) _____ number of natural features; the Ngorongoro Crater is believed to have the (6) _____ of animal species; Lake Tanganyika is the longest and (7) _____ lake in the world; Lake Victoria is the second largest lake in the world and Mount Kilimanjaro is the highest mountain in Africa!

D Using the press release in A as a model and the information on Tanzania in C, write a press release for the opening of the Katabaro Hotel. Include the features you decided on for the Katabaro Hotel from the meeting on page 89.

Student B Material

2 Dream teams

Communication

Student B

1 Listen to Student A telling you about a challenge they face. Make sure you listen actively and can summarise at the end.
2 Tell Student A about a recent success at work or at your institution (e.g. good results / a successful project / promotion).

Business across cultures

Student A

You feel the main problem is that people do not communicate about their projects. They need to represent their work well to other parts of the company, so people are well informed. You feel the answer is to make sure the project managers are good and influential communicators. (You are a *seller*.)

3 Independence

Reading and speaking

> Dear Kao and Frank,
>
> I'm coming to your seminar next month. As requested, I'm sending you a little information about myself.
>
> I currently have a good packaging design job and have worked there for four years. I have a degree in product design and I am learning web design at a very quick pace.
>
> My dream is to have my own creative design agency. Initially, I'd like to concentrate on web design to build up the company profile.
>
> My main concerns are:
>
> Do I risk going freelance when I already have a stable job?
>
> With only six months' web experience, is it wise to go into business now?
>
> I'm looking forward to the seminar and hope I'll get some useful tips.
>
> Best regards,
>
> Brent Caulway

Communication

1 You are in charge of a marketing team. Student A is a very good member of the team and he / she has asked to see you about working freelance from abroad. You are not in favour of this as it means it will be difficult to maintain team work and team spirit. However, you are prepared to listen as you would like to keep Student A working for the company in one way or another.
2 Student A wants to do a job share with another colleague. He / she has asked to see you to discuss this option. You are not in favour of job shares as they usually create more communication problems. However, you want to keep your team together if possible.

STUDENT B MATERIAL

2 Dream teams

Student B

You feel that the main problem is that people do not set up proper project management processes. As a result, there are projects going on with unclear objectives, no tracking of progress and no reporting of results. For you the only way forward is to introduce project management software throughout the company. (You are a *controller*.)

4 Are you being served?

Student B

1 You are the boss of Student A. You are aware that there have been problems with one member of Student A's team. Listen to the situation and proposal. Discuss whether this is the best solution.

2 You want to speak to a customer (Student A) about a delivery. There are two issues: firstly, that there has been storm damage at one of your warehouses and some stock has to be replaced. This means a delay in delivery. In addition, the product line has been discontinued. You want to propose an upgrade for the customer, at the same price but delivery two weeks late.

Business Scenario 1 Mediaco

Student A

You are Stella Wilmot, CEO of Mediaco. You chair the meeting.
- Start by summing up the findings of the questionnaire.
- Ask the HR Director and the consultant for their views.
- Put forward your opinions how to improve morale (see notes below).

Regular staff meetings: You like the idea of regular staff meetings as you think this will increase communication between the different teams. These would discuss the financial results for the month, and the status of various projects.

Flexible working hours: You are not keen on this as you think that all staff should be on site at the same time.

Management courses: You like this idea but you are concerned it would be too expensive. You'd like to suggest the idea of experienced managers mentoring the new managers.
Be prepared to discuss the other options.

6 The right look

Student B

ZARA

Design and production

Zara does not employ star designers but often unknowns, many of whom are recruited directly from top design schools.
In a typical year, Zara launches about 11,000 new items.
An entirely new Zara garment takes about five weeks from design to delivery.

Advertising and discounts

Zara spends just 0.3 per cent of sales on advertising, compared with the 3–4 per cent typically spent by rivals.
'We try to avoid discounts,' says José María Castellano Ríos, Inditex's deputy chairman.

Plans for growth

Inditex has only 16 shops in the US, the world's biggest market.
Mr Castellano says that over the next four years, Inditex (Zara's parent company) plans to double in size to some 4,000 shops with sales of more than €10 billion.

STUDENT B MATERIAL

Business scenario 3 Katabaro Hotel

Discussing a budget

Student A

You are Mr Macha of the Katabaro Hotel. You chair the meeting.
- Tell everyone that Mr Madani has agreed to invest $3,000,000 for a 40 per cent share in the hotel.
- Explain the purpose and process of the meeting.
- Give everyone a chance to express their views (see notes below).
- At the end of the meeting, summarise the decisions and action points.

Your views: **Business travel**: Tourism is growing rapidly in Tanzania. Therefore, you would like to eliminate items relating to business travel. **The travel agent and safari service** would be extremely profitable.

2 Dream teams

Business across cultures

Student C

You feel the main problem is that everybody works inside their own project and fights for their own resources but does not really feel part of a bigger group. As a result, people are not motivated to do things for the company, but more for their own promotion inside projects. You think the answer is that people need to work across different functions and project groups so that they get an insight into how other functions work. (You are a *negotiator*.)

7 Brand strategy

Information exchange

Student A

1 Ask your partner questions to complete the table below.

The company	
Main business	
Reputation	
Gross profit	
Origin of shirts that make the biggest profits	
Workers' pay and conditions at foreign manufacturers	
Recent media coverage	

2 Use the following information to answer Student B's questions. The information is not in any logical order.
- Levi-Strauss, for example, usually blends a small percentage of organic cotton in with traditional cotton
- Many customers have enquired about the availability of organic cotton shirts
- It is responsible for releasing toxic chemicals into the environment
- Traditional cotton shirts
- There is no need to include the organic cotton percentage on clothing labels
- They are far more expensive than traditional cotton shirts

STUDENT B MATERIAL

Business scenario 1 Mediaco

Role play

Student B

You are the HR Director, Brian Owen.

- **Flexible working hours:** You think that this will give employees greater freedom to work by themselves and reduce absenteeism and lateness.
- **Six-monthly appraisals:** You think these are a good idea but only if they are used as an opportunity to give positive and negative feedback. If employees reach their goals, they should be given additional responsibility.
- **Team-building events:** In your experience, these are a waste of time as most employees don't take them seriously. You would prefer to see regular meetings between the different teams to boost morale, motivate people and discuss any problems.
- Be prepared to discuss the other options.

8 The hard sell

Communication

Student B

1 Get feedback from Student A on one of the following topics:
- progress in learning (language, business, management skill)
- progress in career (new jobs, opportunities)
- challenge they face at work (deadlines, personalities, conflicts, etc.)

Follow the process and use the language above.

2 Reverse roles and give Student A feedback on one of the topics.

Business across cultures

Student B

1 Read the information below. Group each point under one of the following headings.
work   status and titles   ceremonies   dining   gender   time   personalities

- Rituals are very common and formal ceremonies with food and speeches will be considered more important than daily work. Hours may be lost while employees go through the rituals.
- Once the ice is broken, they may ask quite private questions. This is their way of showing that a foreigner is accepted
- Eating, drinking and socialising are very important as Malaysians like to conduct business with people they know and trust.
- Muslim women may not want to shake hands with men.
- There is no obvious sense of urgency. Time is just a framework, not something to be mastered and controlled.
- An expat should show proper respect for titles and status as this demonstrates respect for the local culture.
- In times of crisis, employees will look to the organisation for support. For example, employees expect their employers to allow them time off to attend funerals.

2 Exchange the information with Student A to build a picture of Malaysia.
3 Use this information to brainstorm an advertisement for your product.

2 Dream teams

Business across cultures

Student D

You feel the main problem is that there is no real innovation. People are starting projects which duplicate the work of other projects. A project is only worth doing if it makes a difference. The company needs to encourage 'out of the box' thinking. (You are a *creator*.)

103

STUDENT B MATERIAL

Business scenario 2 Dua

Speaking

Team A

Use the information below to give your presentation on the cycling culture in India.

Attitudes
- For many years, the status-conscious viewed the bicycle as an inferior mode of transport.
- These days, leisure cycling is viewed more favourably and is becoming quite fashionable. It is also being incorporated into fitness regimes.
- People only cycle in India's major cities if they have no alternative. The roads and traffic are hazardous and there are no cycle lanes.

Recent developments
- *Mountain biking* – This is an increasingly appealing leisure activity for the age 18–35 market.
- *Tour cycling* - Lance Armstrong's Tour de France victories generated interest in tour cycling, but this is not as popular as mountain biking. Although there are bike tours available to foreign tourists, there is no similar service targeting domestic tourists.
- *BMX (bike races on rough tracks)* – This has attracted a small niche of Indian teenagers following a revival of this alternative sport in the US.
- Like elsewhere in the world, leisure cyclists in India are beginning to upgrade to ultra-light cycles.

Competition: Although many high-end bicycles are manufactured in India, the range offered on the Indian market is very limited.

Promotion
- The All India Cycle Manufacturers Association is trying to promote cycling as an eco-friendly alternative to driving.
- The Himachal Pradesh Government organised a high-profile mountain biking rally, MTB Himachal 2006: The Himalayan Challenge, with the objective of promoting the sport. This is the only large mountain biking competition in India.

Market share of high-end bicycles: 40 per cent.

Market share predictions: This segment will grow to nearly 70 per cent of the market by 2010.

Business Scenario 1 Mediaco

Role play

Student C

You are an outside consultant, Serena Tomkins.

- **Team building events:** You are a big fan of these as you think it gives employees the chance to have fun. You have some ideas that you would like to suggest: paintballing, rock-climbing and go-kart racing. All of these activities make employees feel as part of a team and build leadership skills.

- **Regular staff meetings:** You think that these don't work as the focus is usually on financial results. They don't improve communication among staff.
- **Management courses:** You think these are a good idea but only if the company holds regular review sessions to ensure that managers put the skills they have learnt into practice.
- Be prepared to discuss the other options.

STUDENT B MATERIAL

6 The right look

Information exchange

Student C

H&M

Design and production

H&M hires star designers, like Stella McCartney.
In a typical year H&M launches 2000–4000 new items.
Production cycles are much longer than at Zara. (You don't have exact figures.)

Advertising and discounts

H&M typically spends 3 to 4 per cent of sales on advertising.
Discounts are now very common, especially in its US department stores.

Plans for growth

H&M currently has 76 stores in the US.
H&M has modest plans for expansion over the next four years. (You don't have exact figures.)

Business scenario 2 Dua

Meeting

Student A

You are Aarit Motala.

You have decided to launch the following products:

- Mountain bike: Rapidly expanding market. Great potential and little competition.
- BMX bike: A 'small niche in India' is actually quite a large market.
- Tour bike: Indian youth is heavily influenced by US trends.
- Dua sportswear: The clothing range will be a form of marketing for the bikes.

You want Dua to represent the alternative sports lifestyle for young Indians and these four products fit that image. You believe Dua can promote leisure cycling in India to create an even larger market. In this meeting you want to decide on four marketing strategies (one for each product).

Use these notes to help you chair the meeting.

- Tell them which products you have decided to launch on the Indian market and why.
- Explain the reason for the meeting.
- Ask each person to put forward their suggestions.
- Discuss the options.
- Create an outline of the four marketing strategies that will make up the final marketing campaign.
- Summarise decisions and action points.

9 A thriving economy

Speaking

Student A

You can see that the Chinese economy is booming and the stock market is rising fast. You are interested in investing in China, but you need to check some things first. Ask Student B questions about:

- the recent history of trading in the Chinese stock market
- the current state of the stock market, including some concrete figures
- any danger signs that the stock market may be overheating
- the Chinese government's policy on interest rates
- the liquidity of the market – if it is easy to buy and sell when you want
- any likely government policies which could affect the investment climate

STUDENT B MATERIAL

7 Brand strategy

Information exchange — *Student B*

1 Use the following information to answer Student A's questions. The information is not in any logical order.
   - Bangladesh
   - A national newspaper accused it of lacking corporate social responsibility
   - Well known for its stylish yet low-cost shirts
   - 7 per cent to 25 per cent depending on where the shirts are manufactured
   - The company has no information about the workers who produce the shirts
   - The sale of shirts in 15 stores

2 Ask your partner questions to complete the table below.

The product	
Types of shirts that the company sells	
Criticisms of the traditional cotton industry	
Demand for organic cotton shirts	
The cost of 100 per cent organic cotton shirts	
How other companies manufacture 'organic' cotton shirts	
Legal requirements relating to labels on organic cotton clothing	

Communication — *Student B*

1 Attend an interview with Student A for a management post in his / her company. The job is as a financial controller and you have ten years' experience of working in accounting and control. You have stopped work for five years for family reasons and are now looking to get back to work. You haven't sent a CV, so you will need to tell Student A about your experience and competence for the job.

2 Interview Student A for a work placement (internship) in your company. You take on one or two interns every year. Your company is a well-established medium-sized engineering firm, which manufactures electrical goods mainly for export. You are looking for a bright intern who can help out in administration, order processing and general office work.

2 Dream teams

Business across cultures — *Student E*

You believe the main problem is a lack of structure and organisation. You need to make the whole business more results-focused. This means having strong managers within a clear structure. You don't think these managers need to be controlled (e.g. by a project management software system) but they should be very structured in their approach. (You are an *organiser*.)

STUDENT B MATERIAL

Business scenario 2 Dua

Speaking

Team B

Use the information below to give your presentation on India's young high-end market.

Population aged between 18 and 35: Equal to the total population of the US.

Average purchasing power: Rs 6.90 lakh or $15,000 per annum.

Interests: Health and fitness, coffee bars, shopping malls, cinema, rock and pop music, computer games. Interest in outdoor recreation and alternative sports, such as BMX (bike races on rough tracks), climbing and outdoor survival, is beginning to emerge.

Aspirations: To own top-of-the-range motorcycles and cars, to have a good career, and to travel or work abroad.

Role models and heroes: Microsoft Chairman, Bill Gates; Indian national cricket team captain, Sachin Tendulkar; MTV India video jockey, Cyrus Broacha.

Shopping behaviour

- Prefer to shop online.
- Follow American trends and style.
- Extremely brand conscious. Attracted to big foreign brands.
- Quality, style and image are more important than the pricing.

Youth and media

Young people spend little time watching TV and reading. They spend most of their time on mobile phones and the Internet.

Examples of recent advertising approaches

- 24-year-old Chad Kagy, the world's top BMX competitor, performed at Pepsi's Mountain Dew market launch in India.
- TI Cycles, India's leading bike manufacturer, organized a 24 km cycle rally in Chennai that attracted thousands of cyclists.
- Chevrolet SRV and Coca-Cola India used the Internet to promote their latest ad campaigns and get feedback on their new launches.

Meeting

Student B

You are Amit Koduri.

Mr Motala has decided to launch the mountain bike, the BMX bike, the tour bike, and the Dua sportswear.

During the meeting, you will be asked to suggest strategies for marketing these products to the age 18–35 high-end market in India.

Your suggestions

- Deliver a health message: Adopt and promote a healthy lifestyle. Try to persuade the government to introduce exclusive cycle zones in and around cities for leisure cyclists.
- Organise events: Set up cycling clubs at schools and universities. Popularise leisure cycling through events at weekend resorts. Organise cycle rallies and competitions.
- Co-operate with outdoor recreation and adventure tour companies: Support the establishment of organised bike tours and cycling holidays targeting domestic tourists.

STUDENT B MATERIAL

9 A thriving economy

Speaking

Student B

Use the following information to answer Student A's questions.

- There was a big collapse in the mainland stock in 2001 and lasted nearly five years – confidence in the stock market was low.
- China now in the middle of a stock market fever.
- Market rose 130 per cent in 2006.
- Thousands of investors are signing up every day to open brokerage accounts.
- Shanghai stock exchange is worried that record trading volumes could destabilise its electronic trading system.
- There are warning signs that the market is now overstretched – Chinese companies listed on the Shanghai market have valuations twice as high as the same companies listed on the Hong Kong market.
- Interest rates on bank deposits very low (2 per cent); much of this money could flow into the stock market, increasing share prices to unrealistic levels.
- The demand for shares exceeds supply, but the government is planning new listings to try to cool the investment climate. This could bring prices down.
- There's a possibility that a capital gains tax for equity investments could be introduced. This could start an exodus from the market and a collapse of prices.

Business scenario 3 Katabaro Hotel

Negotiation

Student A

You are Mr Macha, owner of the Katabaro Hotel. You are very keen to persuade Mr Madani to finance the redevelopment of the hotel. You have to avoid giving him a large share of the business but, at the same time, convince him to invest a large sum of money.

During the meeting, find out:

- What role Mr Madani would play in the business. You want him to become personally involved as an advisor, but you want to remain decision-maker and leader.
- What kind of experience Mr Madani has in the tourism industry.
- About his involvement with your competitors. There are unpleasant rumours that he's going to buy the Flamingo Hotel in Dar es Salaam and upgrade it to a five-star hotel.

Negotiate the following:

- The investment amount. You require $4,850,000. Refer to the table on page 89 for the breakdown of costs. (Do not discuss the breakdown in detail during this meeting.)
- Mr Madani's share in the business. You will propose a 25 per cent share in the business, but, if persuaded, you would accept 38 per cent.

Stress the market potential in Tanzania.

- Tourism has been growing steadily for over ten years.
- Tanzania is famous for its attractions (natural, cultural, historic and archaeological).
- The Ministry of Tourism has just commissioned a $70 million Tourism Infrastructure Project, funded by the World Bank.

Emphasise your ability to rebuild the business.

- Your staff are experienced, have excellent organisational skills and are creative.
- None of them has strong IT skills, but they could undertake training.

STUDENT B MATERIAL

Business scenario 3 Katabaro Hotel

Discussing a budget

Student B

You are the hotel manager.
- People expect **health and beauty spas** and **fitness centres** at five-star hotels.
- **Beautiful gardens** and a **ballroom** would extend the hotel's range of services (e.g. wedding receptions and garden parties).
- The hotel's **classic image** needs to be maintained.

10 Foreign investment

Information exchange

Student B

	Brazil	India
Population		1 billion
Political climate		Long lasting democracy, with encouragement of business of economic crisis
GDP growth rate	3.1%	
GDP per capita	$8600	
Unemployment		7.8%
Inflation rate		5.3%
Population below poverty line	31%	
Mobile phones users		69.2m
Internet users		60m
Retail sector		Among most fragmented in world – combined market share of top five retailers less than 2%
Legal issues	Foreign ownership possible	
Infrastructure		Very poor roads – 40% of perishable food rots during transportation
Consumers	Growing middle class	

Communication

Student B

You have arranged a meeting with Student A to try and persuade him / her to invest in your country. Use the checklist below to help you present your country.

- economy
- political climate
- resources
- education level
- geography
- values and attitudes
- new trends / fashions

Make sure you ask all six question types during the meeting to find out about Student A's investment project.

Business scenario 2 Dua

Meeting

Student C

You are Shalina Dama.

Mr Motala has decided to launch the mountain bike, the BMX bike, the tour bike, and the Dua sportswear. During the meeting, you will be asked to suggest strategies for marketing these products to the age 18–35 high-end market in India.

Your suggestions

- Team up with car manufacturers: Innovate with car manufacturers to ensure that leisure cyclists can carry their bicycles in / on their cars without difficulty.
- Provide sponsorship through music events, leisure cycling events and student festivals.
- Celebrity endorsements: Get stars such as Kulbir Kaur, the silver medallist in the 2005 national mountain biking championship, to support Dua bikes.

STUDENT B MATERIAL

Business scenario 3 Katabaro Hotel

Negotiation

Student B

You are Saudi investor, Ibrahim Madani. You are very keen to invest in this hotel because it has huge potential. Naturally, you want to spend as little as possible on the investment for a considerable share in the business.

During the meeting, find out:

- What the market potential is. You've heard that tourism is suffering due to poor infrastructure.
- What skills Mr Macha and his team have to rebuild the business. You are a strong believer in electronic marketing systems as it increases competitive ability.

Negotiate the following:

- The investment amount. You would consider investing up to $3,500,000. Refer to the table on page 89 for a breakdown of costs. You think some of Mr Macha's proposed investments are not urgent and could be postponed. (Do not discuss the breakdown in detail during this meeting.)
- Your share in the business. You want a 45 per cent share in the business but you could be negotiated down to 40 per cent.

During the meeting be prepared to discuss:

- Your involvement in the business. You would provide an experienced business manager to act on your behalf in decision-making processes.
- Your investment experience. You have invested in 15 hotel operators. You have contacts in the travel industry who could facilitate further tourism in Tanzania.
- Your own investment portfolio in competing hotels in Dar es Salaam. You may buy the Flamingo Hotel to upgrade it to a five-star hotel. If Mr Macha objects, explain that co-operation as well as competition between the hotels could make Dar es Salaam a thriving conference destination.

11 The bottom line

Communication

Student A

You represent Movula. You charge for medical translations by the word – €0.25 per word and you have a minimum charge of €30, however short the document is. You offer a fast 24-hour turn-around service at twice this rate. Your bargaining position is:

- Keep the Movula name as translation provider. You do not want to become just a department of Medcare.
- Work directly with the end customer. You find that this way you can better understand the needs of your customers. You do not want to work through an intermediary at Medcare.
- Maximum commission to Medcare – €0.05 per word (20 per cent).
- Additional services – you are willing to discuss more services but you want to keep control yourself.

You are willing to negotiate about all these points. A contract with Medcare would be a real step forward for your company. However, you want to keep your independence.

Business scenario 3 Katabaro Hotel

Discussing a budget

Student C

You are Mr Madani.

- Tourists are not as profitable as **corporate events**. Therefore, you would like to eliminate the health and beauty spa and travel agent and safari service.
- The hotel needs to be **modernised** and brought up-to-date.

STUDENT B MATERIAL

Business scenario 2 Dua

Meeting

Student D

You are Ira Sumon.

Mr Motala has decided to launch the mountain bike, the BMX bike, the tour bike, and the Dua sportswear.

During the meeting, you will be asked to suggest strategies for marketing these products to the age 18–35 high-end market in India.

Your suggestions

- Market online or via mobile phones.
- Use product placement: Bollywood films, the Indian equivalent of Hollywood, are seen in over 13,000 cinema halls. Cricket is extremely popular in India so many brands have featured on cricketers' bats.

11 The bottom line

Communication

Student B

You represent Medcare. You are the number one supplier of medical services throughout the country and have contacts in every hospital and medical centre. You think a translation service will add value to the services you already offer and with an increased number of foreigners in your country, you know that this service is in demand. Your bargaining position is:

- Integrate Movula into Medcare and offer the service under the Medcare name. You don't want to buy Movula but keep it as an outsourced business. You think the Medcare name will help to sell the service.
- You propose that the translation requests are serviced by your customer help desks (24-hour telephone service). They will agree terms with the customer, according to quantity and speed of the translation and then email the document to Movula.
- You want a 40 per cent commission to cover commercial and administrative support.
- Additional services – you would like to offer your customers additional language support services, such as interpreting and instant mobile text translation for specialist terms.

You are willing to negotiate about all these points. You want to get Movula's trust and involvement in this project.

12 Escaping poverty

Communication

Student B

You work in finance in a large company. Your colleague in sales has approached you for a cash sum (approx €2,500) in order to 'wine and dine' a potential new customer. You know this customer is a major defence contractor and there is going to be a tender for a large contract. You don't like doing business in this sector. You also do not approve of this type of 'petty corruption'.

You might be willing to approve a small sum for one dinner out – €200 – but you think it's wrong to do more.

Your company does not have a clear policy on this type of issue.

Business scenario 3 Katabaro Hotel

Discussing a budget

Student D

You are Mr Madani's business manager.

- Both business clients and tourists could use the **tennis courts** and **outdoor pool**.
- The hotel's **classic image** needs to be maintained. A fitness centre would ruin that.
- In the past, dances and functions were held in the **ballroom** and **gardens**. It would be great if that could happen again.

AUDIO SCRIPT

1 Leadership

1.1 *Interviewer:* What characteristics do people need to become good leaders?

James Bartley: Well, we've all come across leaders with charisma, that magnetic quality that attracts other people. These individuals are visionary – they have a strong set of ideas and a strategic vision about how things can be different in the future, and how things can be improved. And they're inspiring – people listen to them and want to follow them. And they are often audacious – they do things that were previously thought very difficult or impossible.

Interviewer: But these charismatic individuals are few and far between. I mean, can all people become leaders?

James Bartley: You're right. Not all people are natural leaders. But yes, it is possible to take people who don't have these qualities and develop them into competent leaders.

1.2 *Interviewer:* So, how do you go about developing people into competent leaders?

James Bartley: Well, one approach is encouraging them to use a leadership style called task-focused leadership, also known as management by results or management by objectives.

Interviewer: Right.

James Bartley: With this leadership style, the organisation is clear about the tasks it has to achieve, and the individuals are clear about what they have to achieve. Organisations often use incentives like performance-related pay to promote high performance and to get motivated employees.

Interviewer: And are there any downsides to using this approach?

James Bartley: The main danger is that, although people are given an objective and they then work towards it, it doesn't actually connect to their inner motivations – so they're not really motivated deep down.

Interviewer: So how do you take care of these motivational issues?

James Bartley: Well, you need to move on from task-focused leadership and start treating people as individuals. This is where something called action-centred leadership comes in. With action-centred leadership leaders concentrate on the whole package: the task, the person, and the team or group that the person is in.

Interviewer: Right, I see. But where does the strategic vision come in that you were talking about at the beginning?

James Bartley: Well, the big strategic question for both the organisation and leaders is where the tasks come from – how you decide in the first place what tasks your team is going to undertake. In fact, it might be described as the difference between leadership and management. Management is organising the staff and making sure everything is done. Leadership is about defining what there is to be done and then inspiring people about why they should do it.

1.3
1 I wonder if we could think about this. Maybe we could look at a number of options and see what we think.
2 It's important to be clear. The process must be validated by the control staff and then reviewed on a two-month basis.
3 Why don't we just take a break? Let me know when you're ready to get together again and we'll see how far we can get.
4 There are two points. First, we have to analyse the results and then we have to decide whether to invest or not.
5 What do you think we should do? Have you thought about any options?
6 *A:* So, if I understand you correctly, you feel we should build up a bigger stake?

   B: Yes, that's right. I mean it's going to be difficult to really have any impact on the market otherwise, don't you think?

   A: I'm not sure I understand why you say that?
7 I'm afraid I can't say any more. It's a difficult issue and we need to weigh up the pros and cons.

1.4 Invesco Investment was unbelievable. Everything was so competitive. People competed about getting the most clients, about who earned the most. You even competed to see who the last person to leave the office was! And I'm not just talking about Monday to Friday. It was often the same at the weekend. The culture was very macho. There were hardly any women there. For us, it was alien, an alien world where, if you wanted to succeed, you had to play their game and compete on their terms. The senior partners were all men and they ran the firm like it was their own kingdom. They all had offices on the top floor – you know these beautiful oak-panelled offices with leather arm chairs. The problem was they were a long way from the reality of what was going on with the workers. The managers would organise these team-bonding events a few times a year. We would all go somewhere remote and climb a mountain or raft down a raging river. Their personalities were really suited to these things. They loved the competition between teams and individuals and they thrived on winning.

Of course, they'd say that this type of culture was enormously successful – bottom line results were always excellent and we were constantly reminded where Invesco was in the league of investment banks – never far from the top.

Markhams Derivatives was a very different experience. The managers who ran the Singapore office were professional managers, recruited for their ability to manage results and people. Of course, some were better than others, but I would say that, on the whole, they had built a very professional culture where people did their jobs to the best of their ability, whatever their background or gender.

There were a lot of processes which the managers monitored. For example, you had a performance review every six months where you discussed your progress with your boss. I used to sometimes think they were just going through the motions. I'm not sure if they really believed in it. But these systems did mean that everybody felt the culture was quite fair – you know – treated people equally. Maybe it was lacking a bit of spark because that team spirit wasn't there, and the results were maybe not so spectacular. But, it was a solid, well-managed company and less based on personality.

2 Dream teams

2.1 *Helen Clarke:* So, how've things been going with the team recently, Bob? I hear you've been having a few problems.

Bob Fisher: Yes, as you know, this was a new project, so we had to form a new team. Although some of the team members get on reasonably well together, the team as a whole seems a bit unmotivated. Some people work very hard and contribute a great deal but others are causing a few problems.

Helen Clarke: I see. Well let's look at each team member in turn and you can tell me what your main concerns are. How's Nadine getting on?

Bob Fisher: Nadine's a very important member of the team. She spends a lot of time listening to other team members and always provides them with the information they need. And she's very good at reducing friction and conflict between team members.

Helen Clarke: Well, no problem there. How about Janet?

Bob Fisher: Janet works very hard and she's always the first to arrive in the morning and the last to leave in the evening. My concern is that she just spends all day working on her own. In fact, she's a bit of a loner. She doesn't really understand that she needs to work as part of a team.

Helen Clarke: Umm. That's more worrying. She needs to realise that you value working as part of a team just as much as individual performance. And Karen?

Bob Fisher: Karen's very enthusiastic but she's absolutely hopeless with time. She always seems to have last-minute panics when she has to get something done. This affects the rest of the team who've worked hard to meet their deadlines.

Helen Clarke: Oh dear. How about Oliver? I gather he's the least experienced of the team?

Bob Fisher: True, but what he lacks in experience he makes up for with new ideas. He's got a great imagination. He's very creative and he's a huge asset to the team.

Helen Clarke: Well that's good. And finally James. How about him?

Bob Fisher: At the start of the project he was very reliable and efficient. But recently, he seems to have lost interest and he's missed a few days off work.

Helen Clarke: Well, that needs to be addressed. Well Bob, I can see why you've been concerned. It sounds like you need to get them working together more – they need to gel as a team. Have you ever considered organising a team building course?

Bob Fisher: Well to be honest, no, but I ...

2.2 A: Hello Mr Blake, how are things?

B: Not too bad, thanks. In fact, we're off on holiday next week. We can't wait.

A: I'm sure. Where are you going?

B: We're trying Greece this year.

A: That should be lovely. Anyway, what can I do for you?

B: Well, we've been thinking about an upgrade.

A: OK, what sort of job do you have to do?

B: Well, it's pretty straightforward. Up and down. But it's a big area.

A: What are you currently using?

B: It's a rotary model. The Hayman 225. Not bad. But it's a bit slow.

A: Yes, you're right. In their day, they were one of the best, but there have been lots of improvements since then.

B: I agree. It's done very well but it's now probably time to trade it in.

A: So, you're looking for something a bit more powerful?

B: I think so. I wondered whether we might try a sit-on model.

A: That's certainly a possibility. Let me just make sure I've got the picture. You've got an area of ...?

B: I suppose around 300 square metres.

A: And fairly flat?

B: Yes, it's not too bad but ...

2.3 A: Hi everyone. My name's Ludmilla Dementieva and I've been with Manthis for just a few months. I have a strong background in the sciences and I worked at the Government Bioscience Laboratories in Russia, where I'm from, for many years. Here, I've been appointed Scientific Director and will be in charge of anti-viral products. My job is to make sure that everything works well and that we respect quality standards at all times.

B: Hello everybody. My name is José Borges and I'm from Brazil. I've worked here for three years and for the past six months I have worked as Marketing Vice-President for Brazil. I guess I'm the sort of guy who likes to promote new ideas and products. I've always been on the commercial side

AUDIO SCRIPT

and I think we have a great opportunity with this vaccine. So I'm really looking forward to working with you all.

C: Good morning everyone. I think most of you know me. For those of you who don't, my name's Lena Malmstrom and I'm in charge of Public Affairs at a corporate level. In my job, a lot of my time is spent working with people in the biotechnology field. I have to ensure we are in line with current legislation and public opinion. I'm originally from Sweden but I've been based in our head office here in Vienna for the last two years. In my opinion, the success of these projects is always related to the people. I like working in teams and I'm sure we can build a really strong team here. I think the launch strategy will be crucial to the success of this product and therefore for our company.

D: I'm Karl Berger. I also work here in the head office, although I'm originally from Salzburg which is also in the north of Austria. I'm responsible for European Sales, so I look after the distribution and sales of all our range of products in Europe – that really means France, Germany, Scandinavia, and of course, Austria. It's the sort of job that requires tight schedules and very clear processes! I think this launch is going to be a great opportunity for Manthis but also a big challenge.

E: My name is Chen Meiling. I'm from Singapore. I work in our regional office there and I'm responsible for market research in the South East Asian region. My job involves not only researching the market but also coming up with new approaches. As you probably know, Manthis has targeted our region as having great sales potential and this vaccine could really establish us in the market. This is my first trip to Europe and I'm looking forward to working with you on this project.

3 Independence

3.1 1 I used to be a journalist, but when I had children I discovered I was good at telling stories, as my children really enjoyed them. So I decided to become a children's book writer. I suppose I have a natural talent as I didn't follow any particular training. You never know what's going to sell and what isn't, so my income is very irregular and unpredictable. I would say that's the main downside to being a writer. But the biggest advantage is the flexibility. I can use my time as I want. I would never go back to being a salaried employee, even if I was offered double my current income! I think my success comes from self-discipline – using time efficiently is certainly an issue for some people. I sit down every morning at 9 a.m. and I don't stop until I've written a thousand words. If I carry on being motivated and inspired, I'll continue to write a book a year.

2 In my last job I was a manager in a call centre, but four years ago I was made redundant. If I hadn't lost my job, I'd still be there. As I was already 56, I didn't think I had much chance of finding work in another company, so I decided to retrain as an independent financial advisor. I went on a two-week training course and now I visit people in their homes selling them financial products such as life insurance. I like the independence this gives me. The secret of success? Word of mouth – I find new clients through personal recommendations from existing clients, so I must be doing something right! Any disadvantages? Well, when the economy is doing badly, people cut back on buying financial products, and my income goes down. And then there's the problem of dealing with your admin and paperwork, but I'm reasonably organised about that.

3 I'm an IT specialist. I design computer systems for large engineering companies. I went freelance about seven years ago – I'd done a degree in computer science at university and I'd worked in an IT services company for twenty years but then I decided to strike out on my own. It was quite difficult in the beginning. I had to do a lot of networking and make a lot of contacts. This is still the most difficult part of my job. But if you want to succeed, you have to keep in touch with potential clients – and be patient because they may eventually offer you a contract! I guess the main disadvantage is the investment. You have to spend a lot of your own money on equipment, which you're always having to update. But it's worth it because of the variety that this kind of work offers – no two projects are the same.

4 I'm a plumber. I trained in a technical college after I left school at 16. My dad was a plumber and I didn't want to do anything else. Like him, I've always been self-employed. The worst thing about my job is that customers can be very difficult to deal with – they're always changing their minds. The best thing is the money. Plumbers have a reputation for earning a lot of money, and some of them do. I do quite well. I have a house in Spain, for example. My brother became a teacher, and I'm earning more than him. Of course, one issue is that you have to keep on top of your finances and your tax situation – it's crucial to get a decent accountant. The key to success is doing an accurate estimate for each job, and sticking to it – customers get very annoyed if it ends up costing more than what you estimated at the beginning.

3.2 1 A: Have you got a minute?

B: Sure. Go ahead.

A: You remember we talked about my role during my last review?

B: Aha.

A: As I said then, when I joined BLK I understood my role was going to be in property assessment and surveying.

B: Yes, I explained …

A: I know, but I wanted to make two points about my role. Firstly, my qualifications are in surveying and I think I am being wasted in my current role. Secondly, I wondered whether we could review our current working practice. I mean, a surveyor goes out and meets the vendor or agent and then views the property. He then passes on a file to me and I write a report. I don't mind writing the report but I could do it all. I have good contacts in the area and I'd like to be more 'out there' meeting the agents. It's important that we get to hear of opportunities as soon as possible. I could keep my ears open and build up good relationships with the agents. Then, as I said, I could also do some of the survey work. My training has prepared this for me so …

B: Excuse me, Katja. But I guess this means you want more money!

2 A: Sally, just before we finish, can we take a look at the terms for next year?

B: I suppose so. Don't tell me. You want to put your prices up?

A: Well, could we start with our service?

B: Of course. As you know, we're very happy. The customer-facing training in particular has made a significant difference.

A: That's good news, and we can see the progress as well. I don't know if you've done any benchmarking on your competitors in this area?

B: Well, benchmarking is an on-going process of ours. We think we're improving.

A: I'm sure you are. And we're pleased to be part of that. It seems to be a good change from just selling on price.

B: Absolutely, that's our strategy and I can see where you're going! So when did we last review your prices?

A: It was more than two years ago.

3.3 1 I used to work for a large cement company, owned by the state. There was a strong hierarchy. The top men were all party members and they had the power. They would have their meetings and we would see their chauffeurs waiting outside to drive them to some other important meeting. We didn't see them very often. They didn't get involved in the dirty business of making cement. I was a shift supervisor and it was my job to make sure we produced on time and met our customer orders. It wasn't easy, as the machinery was always breaking down.

Three years ago we were bought by a French company and since then, things have changed a lot. Yes, there are the big bosses with the chauffeurs back in Paris, but I've met the managers here and they are very good. They give us very clear targets and support us in achieving them. I've been promoted to Operations Manager and I think they will leave the site for me to manage soon. The company has invested a lot in new equipment and also training.

2 For many years I worked as a designer in a small fashion house. I wasn't paid very well but they were a nice group of people. Then they went bankrupt, and I was made redundant so I decided to go freelance. I now work with some of the top fashion houses – they are my clients. It's not easy as there are some real 'prima donnas' in the fashion industry – people who take themselves too seriously. Personally I'm not at all status conscious but I have to recognise that some of the people I work with are. Some of them are very ambitious and try to make their mark by bossing around poor freelancers like me. It's not just the men either. Often the women are worse. The power seems to go their heads!

3.4 For me, work is all about relationships. That's why I go to work. I couldn't stand working from home. Who would I talk to? The dog I suppose. When I arrive at work, I have coffee with my assistant, Debbie. We talk about the weekend, our kids, you know, that sort of thing. A couple of times a week the whole team has an informal meeting. It could be just standing around the coffee machine and catching up on things. In purchasing, it's our job to build partnerships with our vendors. Of course the decision to choose one company or another is based on price, delivery etc. But in the end the critical question is, *Can we work together?* So I see our partners a lot. I'll call in or invite them over and in some cases we'll see each other socially in the evenings.

4 Are you being served?

4.1 *Interviewer:* With consumers more likely to complain when faced with poor service, the pressure is on both the public and private sectors to perform well and meet rising and changing customer demands. However, the public sector in particular is in the spotlight for not delivering what we want as consumers. Its critics are calling for it to adopt private sector methods. With me in the studio today is Laura Wright, a management consultant who regularly works with both the public and private sector. Laura, can state-run organisations copy the methods of private sector companies?

Laura Wright: To a certain extent, yes. There's a great deal that public sector organisations can learn from private sector methods.

Interviewer: Could you give us some examples?

Laura Wright: Of course. Let's look at the National Health Service here in the UK. It's adopted private sector methods in supply chain management. For those listeners not familiar with this, supply chain management is the way that an organisation obtains and manages the supplies that it needs in order to run its operations. DHL, the German company which is usually associated with delivery services, is managing the supply chain for the NHS by applying its commercial experience and logistics know-how. So, they source the high quality goods, manage contracts with suppliers, and take care of inventory and distribution. Through this, the NHS has reduced costs and increased efficiency. Now, clinical staff can spend less time in the stock room and more time on patient care. So we know that adopting certain private sector methods can improve inefficient services, but problems occur when some state-run services are completely transformed into private sector services.

Interviewer: So you're saying that not all industries benefit from privatisation and free market competition?

Laura Wright: That's right. Services which provide social benefits tend not to thrive under private ownership. In these industries you often have a monopoly situation, which means that there's no room for competition or choice – there is one provider who can charge what they like. The most straightforward way of ensuring fair prices and safe standards is through state provision – the state provides the services itself.

Interviewer: Right. So are there any industries which have been privatised that perhaps would have been better left in the state's hands?

Laura Wright: Oh, yes. A classic example of this is the privatisation of the UK railways, which actually resulted in a series of private monopolies. For instance, if you are travelling from London to Manchester by train, you can't choose how to get there – there are no rival companies offering alternative services to the same destination. So the trains are running later and later, and fares are rising faster than ever. In an attempt to improve the situation for passengers, the government tried to introduce competition but the rail industry is – by its very nature – monopolised. Unfortunately, the government's intervention has fragmented management control, created a further decline in quality, and produced unreliable and unsafe systems. Then there's the water industry, which has been a total failure for similar reasons …

Interviewer: I see. So, can you give an example of a successful privatisation?

Laura Wright: Yes, in fact, I can. The privatisation of telecoms, for instance, is seen as a successful transformation by consumers all over the world. Latin America is becoming an explosive market for telecoms, in particular, Brazil and Argentina. In 1998, the Brazilian government, which was trying to gain popularity before the elections, sold off Telebras, the state-run phone company, because it wanted to create serious competition in the telecommunications field. When Telebras was state run, customers applying for a phone line had to pay thousands of dollars in start-up fees and wait for years for the service while the paperwork was being processed. Now getting a line takes less than a week. Not only has privatisation improved services but it has contributed towards greater economic stability and has had a favourable impact on the Latin America stock exchange.

4.2 A: Pablo, how are you?

B: Fine, thank you Carrie. And you?

A: Great. So what can I do for you?

B: Well, Carrie, I wanted to talk to you about the project.

A: Fine. How's it going?

B: Well, that's why I'm calling. There are some problems. In fact, there are two big problems.

A: Really?

B: Yes I'm worried. The first concerns one of the team, Martine Casals, and the other is more technical. You will remember that we asked Martine to join the team as a financial process expert?

A: Yes, I do. We needed someone to set up good cost control systems.

B: That's right. Unfortunately, she has proved to be the wrong person. I think she has a few personal problems at the moment and she's been upsetting the rest of the team.

A: I see. But can she do her job?

B: That's difficult to say but she's certainly not delivering at the moment. I'd like to make a proposal. I'd like to take her off the project and move her back into her old job. I have spoken to her old boss and that seems possible.

A: Right. You're the one on the ground. If you think that's best, let's go with that. How are you going to replace her?

B: Well, just before we come to that. Can I tell you about the other issue because I think we could solve them together?

A: Shoot.

B: So, it concerns the project management tool we are using. As you know it's PRO-GOAL and I think we can upgrade it to include a financial control module …

4.3 *Regula Tschudin:* So Marco, can you tell me what you like about your current job?

Marco Pestalozzi: I really like my job and I have some interesting projects. At the moment, I am working on a study of obesity in children. It's very important work.

Regula Tschudin: I'm sure. If you join us, you would be attached to our Central Marketing Department and be advising them on food safety issues. You would be doing less research than you do in your current job and writing more summaries of reports.

Marco Pestalozzi: I realise that. I think a change will be good for me. To be honest, the FSC is very bureaucratic and slow.

Regula Tschudin: Yes, I can imagine. Certainly we like to think we are not so bureaucratic. We give our people a lot of independence and expect a lot from them in return. I think you would find this a very different place to work. There are a lot of commercial pressures and we have very tight financial targets and budgets.

Marco Pestalozzi: I like the idea that it will be very different and I am used to working under quite strict budget constraints. What is really frustrating is that we wait so long for approval for our projects and then when we finish them we wait even longer for any feedback or action – in fact, often we don't get any at all.

Regula Tschudin: Yes, that must be frustrating. Do you usually work in a team?

Marco Pestalozzi: Not really. Of course, I am part of a department and I report to the manager but usually I work alone on projects.

Regula Tschudin: It'll be very different here as you'd be joining a dynamic marketing team and we will be looking for your contribution to that team.

5 Entering new markets

5.1 1 This approach involves opening your own facilities or subsidiaries in a new market. The good thing about it is that all the profits you make are yours to keep, well apart from the tax paid in the country! Of course, it has its downsides. It's an enormous gamble – you might lose vast amounts of money if you misjudge things. But, who knows, one day, you might open a plant in China!

2 This method is better than having an export agent in the country as the key advantage is that it allows you to get to know the market better. A disadvantage is that it can be expensive. If you want to enter a market this way, you'll need your own export manager and you have to decide whether to send someone out there or recruit someone locally. The good thing with a local person is that they know the local market and the business culture.

3 And this is another way of getting into a new market: the advantage is you don't have to make a massive investment. This is an arrangement that we have used in some markets where earlier sales were promising. You've got to find good local partners and make sure you get a good lawyer for the contract. The only bad thing about this is that the local guys might steal your idea and then make the product by themselves without telling you!

5.2 1 Thank you for inviting me to this beautiful city and giving me the opportunity to talk to you. I will be updating you on recent developments in our new product pipeline and also looking forward to the next three years of development. Now, as you can see on this first slide, there are two main thrusts to our development plans. On the one hand …

… So this next slide shows you the specific results we have had in the first area …

… As you can see, there have been some quite dramatic breakthroughs. Now I'd like you to look at some more results, here we can see the …

2 Thank you for inviting me to this beautiful city. I don't know if any of you have been to my part of the world – that's Scotland. No? Well I can understand why you would want to stay here! Now, I've come with a lot of results to show you from our latest research projects, but I've also put them on these handouts, so you can look at the detail later. What I'd really like to do is find out whether these projects fit in with your needs and that we are going in the right direction. So the first one, as you probably know is on a new innovation in infant food formula. Now does this excite you? I mean, are you waiting for something like this? How is this going to help you?

5.3 A: Arvind, can you tell us the secret of doing business in India?

B: Well, I think there are some cultural realities which are critical if you want to be successful in India. Coming from the West, you need to adapt to the Indian working day. The standard nine to five is not so different but generally we work six days with Sundays off. Some businesses give employees every other Saturday off, or make a shorter work day on Saturday.

A: Some people have a stereotype of India as a country which suffers from a lot of delays. Is that true?

B: I think it's true if you're dealing with the public sector. Government bureaucracy is well known and means things move at a slower pace. In the private sector, I think you'll find things happen at a fast pace, maybe even faster than the West. However, one thing which can lead to communication breakdown is that we don't like to say no. So it may be that an Indian agrees to do something or says 'I'll try' and in fact it's not realistic, so this can later lead to disappointment.

A: What about Indian companies? How do they work?

B: It's important that foreigners understand our attitude towards hierarchy. It's part of our culture and very much influences working life. We show respect to senior people and often there is a formal protocol for doing business, which may seem a little old-fashioned to some Westerners. Employees are often treated a bit like children and therefore may not be encouraged to take initiative. They will look to the boss to give the go-ahead and also approval for their work.

A: And what about the family?

B: Yes, that's key to understanding how we do business. Many Indian companies are family owned and the key jobs are only given to family members. Trust is very important in business and in India it's based on long-term relationships. So a foreign business person must give time to develop these relationships and understand that many doors will open and many obstacles will be removed, once you've won the trust of your partner.

6 The right look

6.1 So, thanks for giving up some of your time today to listen to me. I know this is a busy time of the month, so I won't keep you long. Now, I guess you've heard the rumours that we're going to be reorganising the sales and marketing function. In fact, in some markets, we've already done so. But, before we do anything here, I just wanted to take you through the arguments. This is a very successful market and that is largely down to your commitment and competence, so we want to show how we feel this change will enhance your results.

At the moment, you report direct to your local market head, José Antonio, and he's been doing a fantastic job. He's now moving to a new post and in the future you'll be reporting to the Regional Market Head. The key reason for this change is that we need to maximise sales of some of our regional and global brands. We feel they're not achieving the sort of results we could expect.

Moving on, you've been doing a great job in your own local market so we want to use some of that expertise in other areas of the region. This'll mean putting together regional rather than local marketing plans. I can see some of you are looking worried. Please don't. You will still work on your sales forecasts locally but these will be integrated into a regional plan.

We also believe that you can contribute a lot to enhancing our regional results. We'll be organising the region on a project basis and we expect you to lead some of these projects. We need to make sure your local best practice is exported to some of the other markets.

I guess you'll be wondering how your pay will be affected by these changes. Currently you have some of your pay linked to achievement of your local targets. In the new structure it will be linked to regional results, but this is an opportunity for you to really influence these results.

6.2 *Dolores:* So what clothes should I bring when I come to the UK?

Kate: Well, for a start, there's the weather to think of. You really need two wardrobes – one for the winter and the other for the summer. You'll need some smart clothes for the office, of course.

Dolores: What do you mean by 'smart'?

Kate: Well you know, conservative colours – blacks, greys – skirts, not too short mind and some blouses and maybe a trouser suit.

Dolores: It sounds a bit boring.

Kate: I guess it is. But some companies have started to dress down a bit – you know go a little bit more casual. The men get it wrong sometimes but I think women still dress smartly. In some companies you may even have a dress-down or casual Friday when employees can wear what they want. Of course, this all depends on who you're going to be meeting.

Dolores: What do you mean?

Kate: Well, are you going to have much customer contact?

Dolores: A bit.

Kate: Then, I'd play it safe! Dark colours!

Dolores: Okay, I think I'll have to do some shopping. What about outside work?

Kate: That's the funny thing. A lot of people dress up in the evenings now.

Dolores: That's okay. So do I.

7 Brand strategy

7.1 1 Obviously local brands are built with a much greater insight into what people want and need. I remember a funny situation a few years ago when global mobile-phone companies in China really made fun of the handsets offered by TCL, a Chinese manufacturer. The designs were not to Western taste, you see? But the Chinese loved them – you know, they were flashy with diamonds and things. Now TCL has passed Siemens and Samsung to become China's third-largest handset vendor after Motorola and Nokia. Ironically, Motorola itself started copying those handsets – the ones they had scorned! TCL had a far better understanding of Chinese tastes.

2 Well, when it comes to buying food, I prefer to buy local. I tend to go to my local farmers' market, not just because I believe importing and transporting food is harming the environment, but because I relish the experience. I've found farmers' markets in virtually every country I've been to. I used to go to the local souk while living in Saudi Arabia. Half the fun of it is just going in and looking around ... You meet a lot of really wonderful people and you get to support local producers. It's just not the same when you go to a big supermarket to pick up your Philadelphia cream cheese or Del Monte canned vegetables – even if they are organic! It's anonymous and it's nowhere near as enjoyable!

3 *A:* Without a doubt, global brands are infinitely superior. I always buy big brand PCs – that's by far the most sensible thing to do. And I've never encountered a local PC maker who can provide after-sales support as efficiently as a large company. They can't afford to!

B: Hah, you must be joking! I bought my PC at a local computer store that sells its own brands and they are very well-made. If there's a problem, the vendor comes and fixes it at once. In contrast, the last time I called one of these global brands, they contacted a local repair centre who took two days to call me and then it didn't have the component in stock so I had to wait another week. Can you believe it? I could've fixed it myself in ten minutes. But, of course, that would've affected my warranty ...

4 I always try to shop with a clear conscience whatever the brand or product. I don't like brands which use child labour to produce goods at low cost and then sell them at inflated prices in order to make more profit. Generally, people won't stand for global players exploiting employees. However, they turn a blind eye when local companies act in the same way. Big brands are under considerably more pressure to act responsibly. But, essentially, it's the same for both local and global brands: do what you do, but do it well and in an ethical way. Then customers will respect you and reward you with their custom.

7.2 A: Did you have any problems finding us?

B: No, it was fine. I left in plenty of time.

A: Good, would you like a coffee?

B: No I'm fine, thanks.

A: Okay, could you start by telling me something about yourself?

B: Well, I'm 28. I was born in Canada but brought up in the UK. My parents moved here when I was five. I've done all my education here except for a year which I spent in the States.

A: Interesting. Where were you?

B: I was in Miami on a university exchange.

A: And did you like it there?

B: I liked the people. I don't think I could live in Miami though.

A: Why's that?

B: It's just very different.

A: So, what made you go into marketing?

B: Well I studied business and economics at university and it was the marketing side which interested me most.

A: So what have you learnt so far?

B: Umm ... What do you mean?

A: I mean in your two jobs so far, what have you learned about marketing. You know, what are the key factors?

B: I see. I guess the main thing is the consumer, the end customer. I think if you understand and can reach them, you've cracked it.

A: Really. And in our business, how do you think we reach our customers?

B: I'm not sure but, looking at your website, I suppose you do a lot of indirect stuff – you know PR events, sponsorship – that sort of thing?

A: You're right. We do that but actually our sales operation is the key. Marketing identifies the targets and also prepares the ground but it's our account managers who really make the difference. Have you had any sales experience?

B: No, I haven't.

A: So, what do you think you could bring to us?

B: Well, I'm quite analytical. I think I'm good at problem-solving and I also have good communication skills. I hope my experience at Lazenbys will be of interest to you. I've been working on some new marketing tools which I mentioned in my CV.

A: Yes, we saw that. So why do you want to leave Lazenbys?

B: I think it's time to move on. I think I'm ready for a new challenge.

A: Fair enough. Is there anything you'd like to ask us?

B: Yes, I'd like to find out a bit more about the job – perhaps you could tell me what a typical day is like?

7.3 A: Mr Anholt, you work as a consultant to numerous governments, including Britain's. I suppose not everybody is in favour of nation branding?

B: You're right. At first there's often outrage. People say: 'You're treating nations like nothing more than products in the global supermarket!' But in fact, most big countries already have brands – gut associations that people make when they hear a country's name. Japan? Technology, expensive ... Britain? Posh, boring, old fashioned. Switzerland? Clean and hygienic. Sweden? Switzerland with sex appeal. My job is to make sure these associations are a help, not a hindrance. This is fundamentally not a marketing trick. It's national identity in the service of enhanced competitiveness.

7.4 A: How does nation branding help developing countries?

B: I think it helps a lot. The reality is that many emerging countries are fighting against a reputation – a brand image – which prevents real economic development from getting started.

A: What do you mean exactly?

B: Well, if a country is perceived as war-torn, famine-ridden, poverty-stricken, corrupt and utterly dependent on foreign aid, nobody is very likely to think of investing there, buying its products, going on holidays or going to work there. Sooner or later, the country's economy needs to get started – and that's where its negative brand gets in the way.

A: So, you have to change the image?

B: Brand strategy isn't about pretending everything's fine when it isn't, and it certainly isn't about switching off the supply of aid. But it is about helping tourists, investors and consumers learn about the good things that are going on there, to broaden and deepen their understanding of the country. It's about telling the story of the talent and the opportunity that the country has got, and giving it a chance to prosper in the global marketplace.

A: And are these stories being told?

B: Many developing countries are progressing faster than the eye can see, or certainly faster than their reputation can keep up with. There have been big improvements in the skills, the infrastructure, the government and the business environment in many of the 'transition' economies. If left to the natural course of events, these countries' reputations could take decades to catch up.

8 The hard sell

8.1 *Interviewer:* Welcome to Business Update. This morning I'm going to be talking to Antonio González of AG Advertising about reaching the Hispanic market. Good morning Antonio ... Now, you majored in Hispanic marketing at DePaul University and your agency deals exclusively with the Hispanic market. Why is the Hispanic market so important?

Antonio González: Well, this is the biggest niche market since the baby boomers of post-war US – the generation of children who grew up with completely different expectations, attitudes and tastes from their parents. The Hispanic market is worth about $700 billion, and is expected to grow to $1 trillion over the next few years. Their disposable personal income is greater than that of any other minority group in the United States.

Interviewer: So how do companies reach this market? Can you give us some examples?

Antonio González: Sure. Sprint and Verizon, two wireless carriers, have used a range of tactics. One very simple example – Verizon's English slogan was 'It's the network' but that doesn't translate very well into Spanish, so they came up with *conectividad total*, or 'total connectivity'. You can't simply translate slogans into Spanish – that's a pitfall many advertisers get into.

Interviewer: Right ...

Antonio González: Then there's Movida Communications Inc., which provides wireless voice and data services and targets the Hispanic market. The company's customer service motto is: 'For English, press two.' Anyway, there are more effective ways of gaining customer loyalty. The language is only a small part of it. Verizon has used community events to form 'emotional connections' with customers. For example, it has served as an official sponsor of World Cup soccer. And it also organised adult soccer tournaments in cities with large Latino populations.

Interviewer: I see ... So they're using a kind of grassroots tactic ...

Antonio González: Exactly. Sprint uses music and entertainment to establish similar bonds with its customers. Its live Spanish-language television – Sprint TV En Vivo – was the first in the United States. And the Sprint Music Store stocks more than 20,000 Latin-related songs. What's more, the company is the title sponsor of the 2007 US tour of the Latin rock group Maná, which attracted more than 12 million people in 32 countries on its last global tour.

8.2 *Interviewer:* One thing I'd really like know is – Does it make sense to have a 'Hispanic market'? I mean it groups together people from different backgrounds and cultures. After all, what does a lawyer from Argentina, raised in a middle-class neighbourhood in Buenos Aires, for instance, have in common with a factory worker from Mexico? Besides, does a Hispanic born in the US share many similarities with a newly arrived Hispanic immigrant?

Antonio González: You're right – that's why advertisers are changing the way they advertise to this market. Most money spent on Hispanic advertising targets individuals born outside the United States, yet the majority of Hispanics in the US were born here. Many are fluent in English and Spanish, and identify strongly with both American and Latino cultures. Advertisers are becoming more aware of this and are changing their approach. They try to show universal human themes that appeal to viewers regardless of language or culture.

Interviewer: In that case, why not just use mass marketing campaigns to reach out to Hispanics?

Antonio González: Well, this group is not very visible in mainstream advertising. How many Latino faces do you see?

Interviewer: That's true ...

Antonio González: The answer is probably to treat this group as a 'fusion' market, this is a term we use for bilingual and bicultural markets. Actually, a good example of advertising for the fusion market is the bilingual ad Toyota ran during the Super Bowl to promote its 2007 Camry Hybrid vehicle. You know, where a father speaks to his son in Spanish and English, reflecting the car's ability to switch from gas to electric power. I've no doubt we'll see more examples of this type of advertising in the future.

Interviewer: Indeed. Many people are convinced that Latino culture will eventually become the new mainstream popular culture. If that's the case, your experience in the Hispanic market is sure to give you a head start.

Antonio González: Well, I certainly hope so.

Interviewer: Well, thank you for joining us this morning and giving us an interesting insight into targeting the Hispanic market.

8.3 A: So Bill, how do you think things have gone so far, this year?

B: Pretty well, I think.

A: Good, let's have a look at your targets. I seem to remember there were two main ones. Yes, the first was to take a more active role in project work. Do you feel you are doing that?

B: Yes, I do. I've been making quite an effort. As you know, I've been working on the 2020 project and I feel I've made more of a contribution. I don't know. What do you think?

A: Well, from what I hear, it's going well and Anna seems pleased with its progress and the fact that everybody's getting on well together. So, I'm pleased about that and I can see you've made a real effort.

B: Great. I feel much more involved now and I really care about each project I work on.

A: Good. So, the other target was in terms of your time management. You went on that course and we agreed that you needed to get better at prioritising. So how's that been going?

B: To be honest, not very well. The course was fine but it's easy in theory. In practice, I just seem to have too many things to do.

A: I understand. I think we all do. But it's stressful for you and your colleagues if you are always struggling with your deadlines.

B: I know, I know. But it's difficult to change. Some days I feel I've got nowhere. In fact some days I feel I've gone backwards.

A: What's stopping you from prioritising?

B: I do try. I make a list but then other things come up and they're not on the list. I don't know. It's just really difficult and I know it's no good for Anna and the rest of the team.

A: So what are you going to do?

B: I wondered whether I could have a coach for a few months. I've heard that some people have one. What do you think?

8.4 1 In Iran, they have recently tried to ban advertisements for imported goods. It's all part of a campaign against foreign cultural influence. There have been lots of attempts to ban icons of Western culture such as Barbie dolls and Coca-Cola. In fact, this has tended to make them even more popular – especially with the young. A couple of years ago, ads for Castrol oil showing the face of the football star David Beckham, with the slogan 'Makes your bike go like Beckham' were blacked out on the orders of the authorities and TV commercials showing his bare legs were withdrawn.

2 Here in France we have a long tradition of trying to protect our culture from Anglo-Saxon influence. The Académie Française rules on language issues and tries to protect the French language from English words such as *le weekend* and *le jogging*. We also try to limit the number of American films shown in French cinemas – again we are trying to protect our own film industry. But I'm not sure that the impact of these measures is very great.

3 In most parts of Africa, they have their own brands or African versions of the brands which we have. They can't afford the prices we pay so this way, the products they sell are cheaper. Very often they buy in smaller quantities and adapt the product to their taste. Milo, the drink made by Nestlé, is a good example. In Ghana it is mixed with hot or cold water instead of milk. In Australia, where it started, they always drink it as a milk drink. In Africa they have been developing their products and adapting ours for years.

9 A thriving economy

9.1 *Interviewer:* Do you think China's going to continue growing the way it has been doing?

Economist: It's very tempting to think it will. China currently exports nearly $1,000 billion a year of manufactured goods, and is about to overtake Germany to become the world's third largest economy. And foreign investment is literally pouring into the country. But there could be trouble ahead, but it's more because of politics than economics.

Interviewer: What do you mean exactly? Can you give me some examples?

Economist: Well, take the private sector. From the outside people imagine there's a booming capitalist sector, thriving under the guidance of the government. But the reality can be quite different. Private companies are still expected to work closely with provincial governments and state-owned enterprises. Basically, the government still hasn't decided if it's in favour of a truly free market, so private entrepreneurs are never sure where they stand. But things are changing all the time. For now multinationals remain very attractive to the Chinese for a variety of reasons: including the fact that they are mostly foreign and therefore do not pose a threat to the political status quo.

Interviewer: So how is all this likely to affect the economy?

Economist: Well, continued high growth can only come from an expansion of a locally based private sector. This should eventually lead to the rise of large Chinese companies which are genuinely global. A good example of this is Lenovo, which bought IBM's PC business. This may be a sign of things to come but for now all the other big Chinese companies are still state owned.

9.2 A: Okay, look let's start. I think you've all seen the memo which I sent round yesterday, so you'll know why we're having this meeting. Basically, one of our employees has gone to the press and accused us of discrimination. Now, this sort of thing can soon get out of hand so I've called this meeting to talk through the issue and to decide on how we're going to respond. Is everybody clear about that? Now, I know you all have a busy day ahead of you so I'd like to structure this carefully. We'll start by hearing from Helen. She's going to tell us what the employee is complaining about. Then I'd like to consider our options – in other words, decide on our response – and then finally we should be able to agree an action plan. Right, let's start with you Helen.

B: Thanks. Well, we've been contacted by the *Daily Herald*, asking us to confirm or deny the story told to them by Josh Reynolds. He's a packer on the finished product line and is accusing us of discrimination against men. He's saying that he and some of his colleagues are going to lose their jobs in the current round of restructuring because they're men. In other words, we favour our female employees.

A: Okay, so I think we all understand the picture. Let's now talk about the options. Helen, what's your feeling?

B: Well, we've already denied this story, but of course that won't stop the press from publishing it. I think we need to put out a press release which stresses our equal opportunities policy …

A: Let's try to bring this together then. So, we're going to take the following actions. Firstly, Helen is going to issue a press release which stresses our equal opportunities policy. Secondly, Peter is going to call a factory meeting in which we communicate to all the staff our trust in them and the quality of their work and finally, Max is going to contact our lawyers to make sure we're ready to fight any case for wrongful dismissal. Okay. Let's stop there and we'll monitor developments and report back at our weekly meeting next Monday.

9.3 A: Tom, you've been doing business with China since the 70s. What sort of problems do you come across?

B: At the root of most problems is miscommunication. Often suppliers will agree to terms, for the sake of being agreeable – you know, they like to say 'yes'. Every detail needs to be clarified. Another problem is not knowing the right people – in China it's really important to build good relationships.

A: So you feel the success of the business can be directly linked to the quality of continued relationships with Chinese vendors?

B: That's right. The vendors in China have a tremendous amount of loyalty to the people they work with. There may be horror stories about the Chinese leaving Westerners high and dry, but if we keep our word, they keep theirs. A lot of Westerners go into Asia and expect Asia to act like the West. At the end of the day, if you act like this you won't succeed. Eat the food, enjoy the people, read the books – you have to get to know the culture.

10 Foreign investment

10.1 *Interviewer:* What are the main things a company should be concerned about when planning an investment in a foreign country?

Richard Parker: Well, you need to look at things from two angles. First, what are the positive points, which may encourage a company to invest in a country? This would include things such as the state of the local economy – GDP, inflation rates, labour costs and the size of the domestic and neighbouring markets. You also need to take into account the skill levels of the labour force and the industrial relations climate – is there a history of industrial unrest and strikes, for example? Finally, there are financial and regulatory aspects – the stability of the currency, exchange control regulations if any, and whether there're any government incentives on offer for inward investment.

Interviewer: And what about the negative things – the so-called risk factors? Where do they come into the equation?

Richard Parker: The first thing to consider is political stability. This doesn't mean that the country has to be a fully fledged democracy, only that it's relatively stable and not likely to descend into chaos. Related to that is the issue of security and safety. Then there's the government attitude to foreign investment. Do they encourage or discourage it? Do they insist on a local partner? Can you remit profits out of the country?

Interviewer: And are there certain parts of the world which are high risk for investment?

Richard Parker: The risks of investment in certain parts of Africa are well known, but closer to home I'd say to invest in Russia can also be risky. There's still some corruption and money laundering going on and central government and local legislation keep changing. One particular sector where companies have had their fingers burnt is the oil and gas industry. Russia has huge reserves and in the confusion of the 1990s the foreign oil giants were able to move in and take controlling interests in some of the large exploration projects. But the political climate has changed, and the Government now wants to have control of its natural resources so it can get the full benefit from them, especially with the oil price being so high.

Interviewer: So would you recommend companies invest in Russia?

Richard Parker: So long as they weigh up all the risks and go in for the long term, I would say yes, depending on the product or service they're offering. The potential market is huge and it has a lot to offer. But you have to be able to live with the risk of things not working out quite as planned, and you really need some local help.

AUDIO SCRIPT

10.2
1. A: I will be visiting St Petersburg next week actually.
   B: That's good. Can we make sure we all know what the next steps are?
2. A: Really, there are lots of opportunities.
   B: I see that, but don't you think that's a difficult market to break into?
   A: No, no more than anywhere else. Of course it's different and we need to adapt our products and especially our distribution.
3. A: So, I have drawn up a shortlist of agents we could use.
   B: What exactly do you mean by agents? I mean, are they going to be our distributors?
   A: Well, yes. In some cases they could do this as well …
4. A: Well I've been working incredibly hard to find these people and you've got to remember that it's a massive country.
   B: So, you're really feeling pretty stretched?
   A: You can say that again. I haven't been home for a full weekend in months.
5. A: Let's see where we've got to. We have agreed to go ahead with the Moscow company. Is that right?
   B: Absolutely. I have already talked to …
6. A: I have been spending a lot of time in Russia recently and I think there's lots of potential.
   B: Could you elaborate on that a little? You know, what have you seen that brings you to this conclusion?
   A: Well mainly that consumers are now looking to upgrade …

11 The bottom line

11.1 Hello, everybody. Well, I've worked out the budget for our conference in September.

As you can see, there are five main items on the budget.

Well, let's start with the first item: the conference venue. As you know, the conference will be for 2,000 people, so I've looked at venues of an appropriate size. The Charlotte Hotel, right in the heart of downtown Chicago, is certainly our best option. I think it's completely in line with the atmosphere we want to create. However, it doesn't come cheap at $9,000 for two days.

Moving on! The next item is promotion and invitations. By putting advertisements in local journals and magazines, such as *The Journal of Business* and *Chicago Business in Print*, we'll reach our target audience. This will cost in the region of $100 per ad and I reckon we'll need eight of them, at the most.

With regard to nice, glossy posters, we'll need about 50, so at $5 each they'll set us back $250. We can send them to places like the Chamber of Commerce and the Chicago Business Forum.

As for invitations, we'll send them to everyone on our mailing list. That's currently 3,000. A local printer does very good ones. Unfortunately, he's not prepared to provide sponsorship, but he's offered us a special deal. Together with envelopes and postage, they will be 65 cents each. We're sending 3,000 so that'll come to $1,950.

So, the subtotal for promotions and invitations will be $3,000 at most.

The third item: our guest speakers. What a line up this year! Angela Perkins, who spoke at the Annual Women's Leadership Exchange in Chicago last year, will be our first speaker. And, contrary to our expectations, we've managed to convince Simon Chapman and Lily Chang to speak. And thanks to Ben here and his powers of persuasion, we've got Mario Castello, which is great timing as his book's being published in August. Anyway, this is all beside the point.

Our speakers' fees will be $3,000 per person maximum. We had expected Angela Perkins to ask for more … So that adds up to $12,000 for four speakers.

I haven't included speakers' travel expenses on account of the fact they're all Chicago based.

So, item number four: handouts. By this, I mean programmes and simple evaluation forms. We could get a local printer to donate these in exchange for advertising. By doing that, we'd save a considerable sum of money because the best quote I've had works out at about $2 per guest, which would amount to $4,000.

And, finally, item five, which is insurance. For this type of event we're looking at about $2,000.

So, according to my calculations, that all works out at $30,000. And, all going well, with the attendance fees we certainly won't be running at a loss. So, let's go through that again step by step and hear what you've got to say about it.

11.2
1. Well, it's difficult but I suppose we could offer you better payment terms so long as you can guarantee to make orders on a monthly basis.
2. Perhaps we could consider a discount, provided that you put in an order straight away.
3. We'll be happy to accept a smaller order if you keep to a minimum order quantity.
4. What would you think if we offered you an exclusive deal on condition that you promise to promote our products across your market?

11.3
1. A: Well, it's difficult but I suppose we could offer you better payment terms so long as you can guarantee to make orders on a monthly basis.
   B: I'm afraid we're not in a position to do that.
2. A: Perhaps we could consider a discount, provided that you put in an order straight away.

AUDIO SCRIPT

    B: That would be difficult at the moment, but maybe next week.

  3 *A:* We'll be happy to accept a smaller order if you keep to a minimum order quantity.

    B: Yes, that sounds fine.

  4 *A:* What would you think if we offered you an exclusive deal on condition that you promise to promote our products across your market?

    B: I think we could accept that as long as you can support us with promotional material.

11.4 *Interviewer:* What should people take into account when doing business in Brazil?

Maria Fernandes: A key point to consider when doing business in Brazil is that business is seen as any other sort of social interaction. For example, if you call up a business partner in Brazil, be prepared to chat first and then talk business second. Whether it is asking about their children or chatting about the latest news or soccer results, don't get straight to the point. This is something Brazilians find quite aggressive.

Interviewer: I see. I've heard that coffee breaks are a way of life. Is this true?

Maria Fernandes: Oh yes, expect to be interrupted! And you had better like strong, dark coffee. You won't find milky coffees in Brazil! Coffee will be offered to you when you arrive, and several times during the day.

Interviewer: How do you address each other? Do you use first names?

Maria Fernandes: Only use a first name if you are invited to do so. When meeting someone for the first time, address them formally. The American way of using first names in the workplace is quite disconcerting to Brazilians. We are accustomed to very defined social status and ways of addressing each other. It is a good idea to keep your distance, linguistically speaking. At least at the beginning.

Interviewer: What about attitudes towards time?

Maria Fernandes: The perception of time and the concept of punctuality are very different in Brazil, but I insist, it has nothing to do with Brazilians being lazy. It just means that their working day doesn't follow the same rigid structure. When scheduling meetings, allow for some degree of lateness. In the US, punctuality and time-keeping are both very important. In Brazil, we are happy to do many things at the same time, so interruptions and diversions are far more common.

12 Escaping poverty

12.1 *Interviewer:* We all know that the global economy is racing ahead. China, India, and many other developing nations are growing very fast, and their booming economies are pulling millions of people out of poverty. But about half the world's population still lives on less than $2 a day. Here in the studio today is Sanjay Chakraborty, a specialist in poverty reduction from the organisation 'Power Over Poverty'. Good morning, Sanjay. Thank you for coming along today. Now, getting rid of global poverty is the most important economic and social challenge of our time. From your point of view, how can this be achieved?

Sanjay Chakraborty: Well, obviously, there is foreign aid. More than a trillion dollars of international aid, that's a thousand billion dollars, has been handed out in the last 50 years, but I would say that the results are hard to see.

Interviewer: Aha.

Sanjay Chakraborty: A more effective approach, in my opinion, is to encourage entrepreneurial activity among the poor, but of course, that requires finance, and traditional banks have not been willing to lend to poor people.

Interviewer: Ah, yes. As the famous economist Milton Friedman once said: the poor stay poor, not because they're lazy but because they have no access to capital.

Sanjay Chakraborty: That's right. And this has hindered progress in the developing world. In recognition of this fact, something called 'microfinance' has emerged to give poor people access to the precious capital they need to invest in their own projects or start up their own enterprises.

Interviewer: How and when did this start?

Sanjay Chakraborty: It was in the mid-1970s in Bangladesh. An academic called Muhammad Yunus had the idea of lending money to the very poor, particularly women. He set up a bank and called it the Grameen Bank Project, and it now has six million borrowers in over 64,000 villages. And 96 per cent of the customers are women.

Interviewer: 96 per cent? Why's that?

Sanjay Chakraborty: Because studies have shown that women are more likely to reinvest their earnings in the business and in their families, and they are more willing to be accountable. As families cross the poverty line and their businesses grow, the rest of their communities reap the rewards. Jobs are created, knowledge is shared, and women are recognised as valuable members of their communities.

12.2 *Interviewer:* So, how does microfinance work?

Sanjay Chakraborty: Well, clients do not need collateral in order to receive loans. This allows people who would not usually qualify with traditional financial institutions to receive credit.

Interviewer: Wow. Does the bank make a profit? I mean it doesn't sound very profitable or secure.

Sanjay Chakraborty: Yes, the Grameen Bank has made a profit in every year of its existence except three. And the repayment rate for loans is 98 per cent. This is serious business, not charity. In fact, the repayment rates in many microfinance programmes often exceed those related to big business. Large banks and investors are increasingly viewing microfinance as a good opportunity because of the high loan repayment rates, and they have figured out that there is enormous market potential in the large population of 'unbanked' poor, particularly in India.

Interviewer: So, has the approach taken off in other parts of the world?

Sanjay Chakraborty: Yes, there is an abundance of microfinance lending institutions which have sprung up throughout Asia, Latin America, Africa, Eastern Europe, and elsewhere in the developing world, and even in poor communities in the developed world.

Interviewer: Aha.

Sanjay Chakraborty: They come in all shapes and sizes: from small co-operatives that just take care of a few villages to giant companies spanning a nation. These institutions altogether have over 94 million customers.

Interviewer: I see. So is microfinance the solution to beating global poverty?

Sanjay Chakraborty: Microfinance alone will not stamp out global poverty, but it is having a significant impact. To illustrate this, a World Bank study showed that, in Bangladesh, Grameen Bank clients are escaping poverty at the rate of 10,000 per month.

Interviewer: Well, that's quite impressive and …

12.3
1 Yes. You're right. The loan was crucial in helping us to start a business and build up a future for our family.
2 It's not fair I'm in so much debt when the banks make huge profits.
3 A self-help group system means that a group works together to make an enterprise succeed.
4 I think that women in particular will benefit from the service for a long time to come.
5 I give you my word that everyone in the village will have access to a phone by the end of the year.
6 Not only that, but the bank runs several telephone and energy companies as well.
7 I admit that a lot of the money given in aid has been spent unwisely.
8 It's not true that poor people have a lower repayment rate for loans.
9 The repayment rate for loans is 98 per cent. Really, 98 per cent.
10 You must register your application by 1 December, or it'll be too late.

12.4 *Sean:* It's not my fault, you know.

Helen: Well, it certainly isn't ours! Mastertons is your client and you introduced them to us. You're responsible for the contract and that includes payment. They've only been with us for six months and they've caused too many problems already!

Sean: OK, but it's your company that provides technical support and Mastertons aren't happy with the support they've received.

Helen: Sean, this is not going anywhere. Let's see where we are and where we can go. So, we know that Mastertons have refused to pay for technical support. Why exactly have they said this?

Sean: Basically, they say they're not paying for something they haven't received.

Helen: They haven't received the support because they haven't implemented the software fully. But, more to the point, we have a contract with fixed payment terms. They have to pay!

Sean: But Mastertons is one of my best clients. I can't afford to upset them.

Helen: Upset them! How do you think we feel about this? I'm sorry but they've got to pay up.

Sean: Well, I think you'll have to go to court to get the money.

Helen: So, that's what we'll do. I'd like you to get that moving. Maybe they'll pay up when they see we mean business.

Sean: And meanwhile I will have lost a lot of other business with Mastertons and the prospect of any more in the future.

Helen: So what do you suggest?

Sean: Well, I think we need to make them an offer – you know – something positive. We need to find something in all our interests.

Helen: Like what?

Sean: Perhaps we can agree to forego payment on the support, on the basis that they buy one of your off-the-peg packages.

12.5 The thing about corruption is that it really undermines everybody's belief in a fair society. It undermines the rule of law and means that people don't trust official authorities. Some people avoid paying taxes because they can't see any benefit from paying them. Corruption also affects the political system as people no longer believe that politicians can do anything for them. So, many people don't vote because they don't believe in the system. In the business world, corruption affects competition. Businesses that play by the rules don't necessarily succeed. This means they cannot create wealth for the country. People believe they can only create wealth for themselves by paying bribes. Corruption also results in the inefficient allocation of resources – very often the people who get the resources are the last ones who need them. Unfortunately, the poor get poorer and the rich get richer.

ANSWER KEY

1 LEADERSHIP

Vocabulary and listening

1.1

B 1 visionary 2 charismatic 3 intimidating 4 authoritarian 5 inspiring 6 subservient

C 1 charismatic visionary inspiring audacious
2 People can learn how to become competent leaders.

1.2

D 1 Task-focused leadership, also known as management by results or management by objectives.
2 When both the organisation and individuals are clear about the tasks they have to achieve.
3 Using incentives like performance-related pay doesn't motivate people deep-down.
4 Action-centred leadership. It is better because it thinks about the individual in their social and team situation within the organisation.
5 Management is about organising the staff to make sure things get done, whereas leadership is about defining what there is to be done and inspiring people about why they should do it well.

Reading and speaking

B 1e 2d 3g 4b 5f 6c 7a

C 1 T
2 F If a worker cares enough to share criticism, the least you can do is listen.
3 F Leaders shouldn't do every job themselves.
4 T
5 F Leaders should learn about time management and goal setting.
6 T

Grammar

A Use the article to check your answers.

B 1 be trying / try 2 worry 3 be given 4 have known

C 1 permission
2 deduction
3 past habits
4 lack of obligation
5 obligation
6 possibility
7 lack of ability

Communication

A 1b 2b 3b 4a 5a 6a 7b

 1.3

B 1 complex
2 active listening
3 emotional
4 direct
5 giving advice
6 impersonal
7 formal

Business across cultures

A **Invesco Investment**: male-orientated competitive personality-driven results-orientated hierarchical long hours
Markhams Derivatives: impersonal fair managing results process-driven

1.4

B Use the audio script to check your answers.

C Imaginative: creative innovative
Hands-on: concrete pragmatic practical
Professional: qualified expert
Truthful: open frank honest
Caring: supportive nurturing

ANSWER KEY

2 DREAM TEAMS

Vocabulary and speaking

C 1 independence
2 commitment
3 communication
4 creativity
5 time management
6 conflict avoidance
7 performance

Listening and speaking

 2.1

A 1 Nadine: Conflict avoidance
Janet: Independence
Karen: Time management
Oliver: Creativity
James: Commitment
2 Nadine and Oliver

B 1 get 2 friction 3 loner 4 panics 5 asset 6 gel

Reading and vocabulary

C 1 breaking down barriers
2 sceptical
3 engrossed in
4 get the pulse going
5 gimmick
6 whipping the group into a frenzy
7 breaking the ice

Vocabulary

A 1 Possible answer: Try to find new business

B 1 pull 2 be 3 cut 4 think 5 face 6 pull 7 touch 8 take 9 have 10 go

C 1g 2f 3e 4a 5b 6j 7c 8i 9d 10h

D 1 touch base with you 2 pulls their weight 3 took on board
4 has a lot on her plate / is rushed off her feet 5 has gone through the roof

Communication

 2.2

A 1 A lawnmower
2 By asking questions.

B Use the audio script to check your answers.

Business across cultures

A 1d 2a 3e 4c 5b

B 1b 2e 3d 4c 5a

D

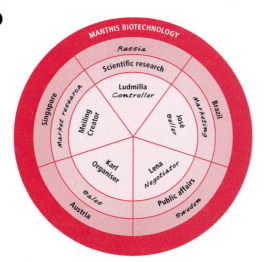

E 1b 2d 3c 4e 5a

ANSWER KEY

3 INDEPENDENCE

Listening and speaking

3.1

B

	Freelance job	Training	Main advantage	Main disadvantage	Secret of success
1	Writer of children's books	None	Flexibility	Irregular and unpredictable income	Self-discipline
2	Independent Financial Advisor	Two-week training course	Independence	Income relies on how the economy is doing	Word of mouth and recommendations
3	IT Specialist	Degree	Variety	Investment	Keep in touch with clients and patience
4	Plumber	Technical college	Money	Difficult customers	Accurate estimates

Reading and speaking

B

1a Never let clients think that you have cash flow problems. There is also a risk that the word will spread. Clients can cost you a great deal of time and money by not paying their debts so make sure you have a good system in place to manage this aspect of your business. Try to do a credit check to find out about the financial status and reliability of a potential customer.

2b Agencies often have a clause in their contracts which would prevent you from approaching the customer for new work in the future.

3b If you have a reliable, experienced and capable team, delegate as much as possible. You can't do everything! Working every weekend will only lead to burn-out.

4a Always act in the best interests of your clients. You will gain a reputation for honesty, integrity and professionalism.

5a Gain confidence by meeting a few people who also arrive early before it gets crowded.

6b In the long term, you cannot compete on price alone. Market (and gain a reputation for) your quality, service and value for money. However, consider reducing your rates for clients who have a limited budget but are likely to require ongoing work.

Score
5–6 → You may have the ability to set up your own business. Nonetheless, do not give up your job until you are sure that there is a market for your skills as a freelancer.
0–4 → Do not rush to leave your job – It might be risky! Remember that working for someone else has its benefits ...

C **Possible answers:** flexible, organised, reliable, trustworthy, punctual, confident, energetic, driven, decisive, patient, motivated

Grammar

A
1 something that didn't actually happen
2 an imagined or hypothetical situation
3 something that you usually do
4 a possible event in the future

B
1 third conditional
2 second conditional
3 zero conditional
4 first conditional

C
1 look
2 will steal
3 would be
4 would have started
5 am offered

D
1 fact
2 strong recommendation
3 prediction
4 past regret
5 unreal future situation

ANSWER KEY

Communication

3.2

B

	Katja	Phil
1	Her manager	Client
2	Push	Pull

C Use the audio script to check your answers.

Business across cultures

C A person's need for **power** can be one of two types – personal and institutional. Those who need personal power want to direct others, and this need often is perceived as undesirable. Persons who need institutional power want to organise the efforts of others to further the goals of the organisation. Managers with a high need for institutional power tend to be more effective than those with a high need for personal power.

People with a high need for **achievement** seek to excel and tend to avoid both low-risk and high-risk situations. Achievers avoid low-risk situations because the easily attained success is not a genuine achievement. Achievers need regular feedback in order to monitor the progress of their achievements. They prefer either to work alone or with other high achievers.

3.3

E
1 T
2 F They didn't get involved.
3 F They didn't see the managers very often.
4 T
5 T
6 T
7 T
8 T
9 F She works with them. They are her clients.
10 T
11 F They treat freelancers badly.

F Use the audio script to check your answers.

H 1 Community spirit
2 Quality
3 Money
4 Size

3.4 **J** colleagues   suppliers   investors

4 ARE YOU BEING SERVED?

Listening and speaking

4.1

C 1 F It is only managing the supply chain for the NHS.
2 F They spend less time in the stock room and more time on patient care.
3 T
4 F There are no rival companies offering alternative services to the same destination.
5 T
6 F They have dramatically improved. It used to be very expensive and customers had to wait years to be connected.

Grammar

A 1 that public sector organisations can learn from private sector methods. (defining)
2 that an organisation obtains and manages the supplies (defining) that it needs in order to run its operations (defining)
3 which provide social benefits (defining)
4 which was trying to gain popularity before the elections (non-defining)

B Possible answers:
1 are controlled / run / managed by the government
2 work in the private sector
3 that there is no competition / that they can charge whatever they like for a product or service, etc.
4 has been kept in the public sector / is usually in the public sector / hasn't been privatised, etc.
5 is a genuine market / is in the public sector in many countries, etc.

129

ANSWER KEY

Reading and vocabulary

B 1a 2d 3e 4c 5b

C 1 People are more likely to complain when faced with poor service.
2 There is a greater awareness of consumer rights and people are more confident about speaking up for themselves when they experience poor customer service.
3 In implementing customer service initiatives, such as self-service systems and self-learning tools that organise and present customer information.
4 Lack of budgets and failure to understand the importance of customer service.

Communication

4.2

A 1 A member of the team isn't right for the job. He also wants to discuss the project management tool they are using.

B Use the audio script to check your answers.

Business across cultures

4.3

B

FSC	BBN
Working on study of obesity in children	Advise Central Marketing Department on food safety issues
Bureaucratic and slow	Less research and more report writing
Wait a long time for approval and feedback on projects	Give people a lot of independence
Works alone on projects	Lots of commercial pressures
	Tight financial targets and budgets
	Work as part of a dynamic team

E 1 person culture
2 role culture
3 power culture
4 task culture

F 1 Task culture 2 Role culture 3 Person culture 4 Power culture

REVIEW AND DEVELOPMENT 1–4

Vocabulary

Leadership characteristics

A

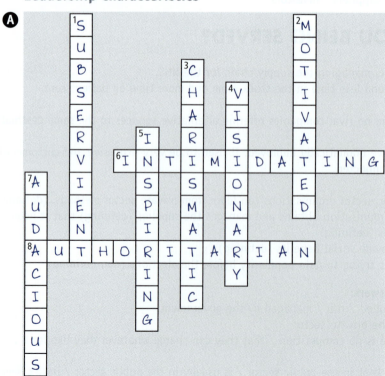

ANSWER KEY

Grammar

Modals

A 1 would   2 could   3 must   4 shouldn't   5 must

B 1 past habits   2 prediction   3 deduction   4 advice   5 obligation

Vocabulary

Idioms

A
1 The programme did not have enough viewers, so the TV company <u>pulled</u> the plug on it.
2 I wanted to finish the proposal by this evening, but I've been rushed off my <u>feet</u> all day.
3 OK, let's stop talking about secondary issues and <u>cut</u> to the chase.
4 We've ignored the problems for a long time, but now we need to <u>face</u> the music.
5 The department is overstaffed: half the people there are not pulling their <u>weight</u>.
6 She was very quick to <u>take</u> the new situation on board.
7 I've been meaning to call you, but I've <u>had</u> a lot on my plate recently.
8 I need to touch <u>base</u> with the US office and let them know how things are going.

Grammar

Conditionals

A 1b   2c   3a   4f   5d   6e

B 1 third   2 zero   3 first   4 third   5 second   6 zero

Grammar

Relative clauses

A
1 The drug <u>that</u> was invented last year will save thousands of lives.
2 The City is the leading financial centre in London, <u>where</u> you'll find hundreds of international banks.
3 Paul Bishop was a company executive <u>who</u> was shot in mysterious circumstances last year.
4 The privatisation of the post office, <u>which</u> has not been discussed much in the media, could be next.
5 The candidate <u>whose</u> CV was outstanding was offered the job.

Vocabulary

Verb-noun combinations

A 1c   2e   3d   4b   5a

B
1 exceeding quotas
2 implement safety measures
3 delivered fresh goods
4 resources were deployed
5 has faced / has been facing criticism

Communication

Model answers

A
1 I'm afraid I'm not sure about this.
2 I really feel we need to review the system.
3 So, have you thought about the next step?
4 I thought the performance was fantastic.
5 Hi, you must be Geoff. How's life treating you?

B
1 What sort of work do you do?
2 Really! (show interest)
3 So, a big part of your job is food safety?
4 I see.
5 OK, so if I understand you, there are two main issues: firstly demanding legislation and secondly, team management.

C Push

131

ANSWER KEY

5 ENTERING NEW MARKETS

Vocabulary and listening

 5.1

A 1f 2c 3d 4e 5a 6b

C 1 Direct investment 2 Direct export 3 Licensing

D

	Method	Advantage	Disadvantage
1	Direct Investment	All the profit is yours to keep, apart from tax paid in the country	Big gamble
2	Direct export	Get to know the market better	Expensive
3	Licensing	Don't have to make a big massive investment	Local partners might steal your idea

E Use the audio script to check your answers.

Reading and speaking

C The order and answers are as follows:
  d JCB was involved in a joint venture with an Indian company, Escorts. JCB ended its partnership as it likes to be in charge.
  a India's regulation of foreign investment is becoming less severe as the Indian government has made it easier for foreign companies to have full control over their operations there.
  c India still regulates foreign investment in industries such as telecommunications, agriculture, retailing and insurance.
  e In TVS's collaboration with Suzuki, there were gains in both directions. TVS gained expertise and Suzuki could get into the market.
  b TVS did not gain as much from its joint venture with Suzuki as it had hoped because Suzuki wanted to keep its technology for itself.

Grammar

A 1 the the
2 a The
3 the the the a a

B 1 A
2 several
3 both
4 any
5 little
6 this
7 Another
8 other
9 enough
10 neither

C

Singular count	Plural count	Uncount
a	several	little
another	both	this*
neither	any	enough
	other	

*This can also be used with a singular count noun.

D 1 both of, neither of, all of
2 Many of, A few of
3 All of, Neither of

Communication

5.2

C The second presentation engages the audience better.

D Use the audio script to check your answers.

ANSWER KEY

Business across cultures

A 1 c There is no official religion in India. India is a pluralist society and all religions have equal status, although Hinduism is the dominant religion.
2   Hindu   80.5 per cent
    Muslim   13.4 per cent
    Christian   2.5 per cent
    Sikh   1.9 per cent
    Buddhist, Jain, Parsi   1.8 per cent
3 b When Indians are in conversation or receiving instructions, they often shake their head from side to side, which to most Westerners looks like they are indicating disagreement; but they are simply indicating they are listening and understand what you say.
4 c There are over 400m cows in India, mostly in the countryside but some in the towns. Food for them is so scarce that they are sent to graze and eat what they can find. The fact they are left alone to wander along the street is because they are considered sacred by Hindus.
5 c The bindi that women wear is traditionally a sign of a married woman, but among young women in urban India it is now a fashion statement, and many different designs and colours can be found. It is also something only worn by Hindus, so to some extent all three options are true.

B 2 Tax holidays, more control over infrastructure like water and power, and less regulation.
3 It's close to the market and there are many highly educated people there.

🔊 5.3   **E** Time   Agreement   Seniority   Hierarchy   Family   Relationships

F Use the audio script to check your answers.

6 THE RIGHT LOOK

Reading and speaking

B 1 It studies the demands of customers in its stores.
2 It doesn't create demand for new trends using fashion shows.
3 It delivers at lightning speed (very quickly).
4 Inditex.
5 The designers are in daily contact with store managers.
6 They cut the fabric in-house and then send it to independently owned firms for sewing.
7 Because most designs are quickly replaced with new ones.

Vocabulary

A 1e 2c 3f 4a 5b 6d 7i 8j 9g 10h

B 1 replenishment of stock
2 Fabric
3 a cluster
4 bestselling items
5 Garments
6 conveyor belts
7 warehouses
8 in-house

Grammar

B 1 is set
2 is sent
3 can be bought
4 is worn

B **Model answer**
What happens first is that a stunning outfit is worn at a special event by a celebrity – a pop star or an actor. Next, a team of designers is sent to copy and distribute the design at lightning speed. After that, the production process is rapidly set in motion, controlled by Zara's head office in Spain. After as little as five weeks, the outfit can be bought at Zara outlets all over the world.

ANSWER KEY

Communication

🎧 6.1

A

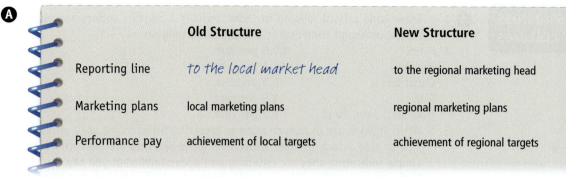

	Old Structure	New Structure
Reporting line	to the local market head	to the regional marketing head
Marketing plans	local marketing plans	regional marketing plans
Performance pay	achievement of local targets	achievement of regional targets

B Use the audio script to check your answers.

D Use the audio script to check your answers.

Business across cultures

🎧 6.2

7 BRAND STRATEGY

Reading and speaking

B 1 in limbo 2 tarnish 3 iconic 4 trimmed 5 triggered thoughts of 6 leverage
7 Re-orchestrating

C 1 Piano
2 President and CEO of Steinway & Sons
3 Mid-level piano
4 Entry-level piano
5 Major area of future growth

Listening

🎧 7.1

A 1 Market relevance
2 Community
3 Quality and standards
4 Social responsibility

B 1 F Global mobile-phone companies made fun of the handsets offered by TCL, a Chinese manufacturer.
2 F They have different tastes.
3 F She also relishes the experience.
4 T
5 T
6 F It would have affected his warranty.
7 T
8 F Both local and global brands should act with integrity.

Grammar

A 1–3 much, by far, a great deal
4–5 a little, slightly
6 just
7 nearly
8 nowhere near

B Local brands are being compared with global ones in terms of the manufacturers' insight into the market. TCL is being compared with companies such as Siemens and Samsung in terms of understanding consumers' tastes. Supermarket shopping is being compared with shopping at farmers' markets and souks.
Model answers
1 Local brands are built with a much greater insight into what people want and need than brands produced by global companies.
2 TCL had a far better understanding of Chinese tastes than global mobile-phone companies (such as Siemens and Samsung).
3 Supermarket shopping is nowhere near as enjoyable as shopping locally.

ANSWER KEY

communication

🔊 7.2

B 1 Marketing job.
2 A business and economics degree. He's had two jobs but doesn't have any sales experience.
3 He is analytical, good at problem-solving and has good communication skills.

C Use the audio script to check your answers.

D He asks what a typical day is like.

business across cultures

🔊 7.3

🔊 7.4

A 1 Because they think that nations are being treated in the same way as products.
2 He mentions Japan (technology, expensive), Britain (posh, boring, old fashioned), Switzerland (clean and hygienic) and Sweden (Switzerland with sex appeal).

D 1 It has an impressive market share in the US and manufactures high quality goods.

F 1 If the country has a bad image, countries won't want to invest there.
2 It is about informing people about good things going on in a country to broaden and deepen their understanding of the country.
3 Yes. There have been big improvements in the skills, the infrastructure, the government and the business environment.

8 THE HARD SELL

Reading and speaking

A 1c 2a 3b 4d

B 1 It has become one long advert.
2 They can get the reach they wouldn't be able to get elsewhere.
3 Bond films appeal to both the young and old. The ratio of men to women is 60:40.
4 It won't be too long before interactive television and mobile technology link up.

Listening

🔊 8.1

🔊 8.2

C 1 It is worth about $700 billion.
2 The slogan 'It's the network' and the motto 'For English, press two'.
3 Community events, sponsoring sporting and music events, and organising adult soccer tournaments.

D 1 They are becoming aware that Hispanics are not one homogenous group.
2 In their advertising, they try to show universal human themes that appeal to viewers regardless of language or culture.
3 Hispanics are not visible in mainstream advertising.
4 The fusion market represents Hispanics who relate to both American and Latino cultures. Antonio mentions the Toyota ad in which a father speaks to his son in Spanish and English.

Grammar

A 1 certainty
2 doubt
3 probability
4 possibility
5 probability
6 certainty

B 1 definitely / certainly / inevitably
2 I have no / There's no
3 (absolutely) certain / sure / positive / convinced
4 sure to / bound to / certain to

communication

🔊 8.3

B

	Targets	Progress	Further action?
1	Take a more active role in project work	Anna is pleased with the progress and everyone is getting on well together.	None mentioned
2	Time management	The course was fine but feels he has too much to do.	A coach

135

ANSWER KEY

Business across cultures

 8.4

C She got the feedback from asking Bill a series of questions and then expanding on his answer. The first target got affirmative feedback and the second received development feedback.

D Use the audio script to check your answers.

E

Market	How they resist globalisation	Impact
Iran	Ban advertisements for imported goods	Makes these brands more popular
France	Protect culture from Anglo-Saxon influence	Impact not very great
Africa	Have their own brands or adapt international brands	Makes it cheaper for consumers

REVIEW AND DEVELOPMENT 5–8

Vocabulary

Market entry

A 1 construct
2 end
3 absolutely
4 raise
5 Inner
6 experiments
7 result

Grammar

Determiners and quantifiers

A 1 Neither
2 little
3 less
4 either
5 Many of
6 few of
7 Few

Vocabulary

Production, distribution and delivery

A Store large quantities of goods in a warehouse.
Carry out production in small batches.
Place an order for 1,000 components.
Ship the finished products to the customer.
Replenish stock quickly
Develop a prototype according to specifications.

Grammar

The passive

A Model answers
1 First, an order for a customised tool is placed.
2 Then 'quality and production planning' is done.
3 After that, the prototype is developed based on the customer's specifications.
4 Next, a trial on the prototype is carried out to ensure that …
5 Then a production trial run is done to confirm that …
6 After that, mass production is carried out.
7 Next, the tools are inspected for any irregularities.
8 Finally, the tools are packed and shipped to the customer.

Vocabulary

A 1 iconic   2 extended   3 billboard   4 niche   5 Sponsorship   6 Telemarketing   7 placement
8 fusion

ANSWER KEY

Grammar

Making comparisons

A Model answers
Brand B is much more reliable than Brand A.
Brand B is slightly better value for money than Brand A.
Brand A's running costs are marginally more expensive than Brand B's.
Brand A is just as stylish as Brand B.
Brand A is nowhere near as easy to maintain as Brand B.
Brand A's customer service is infinitely more satisfactory than Brand B's.
Brand B's CO_2 emissions are considerably higher than Brand A's.
Brand B is a little safer than Brand A.

Grammar

Making predictions

A

Certainty	Probability	Possibility	Doubt
I'm certain that … I've no doubt that … … is / are bound to …	… is / are likely … should …	There's a good chance that … may / might / could …	I doubt … … is / are unlikely …

B Model answers
1 are likely
2 I've no doubt
3 should
4 I doubt
5 are bound
6 could
7 it's likely

Communication

A 1d 2b 3f 4e 5a 6c

B 1 faced 2 contribute 3 background 4 career 5 finding 6 join 7 add

C
1 Could you tell me about your targets?
2 I can see you have made a big effort.
3 I feel I am going backwards.
4 What is getting in your way?
5 How is it going?
6 I think I am on the right track.
7 I am finding it very difficult.

9 A THRIVING ECONOMY

Reading and vocabulary

B
1 Hangzhou is the capital of Zhejiang province, south-west of Shanghai. It is famous for its lake and its tea, and its sense of refinement.
2 Shenzhen is in the south of China, in Guangdong province close to Hong Kong. It owes its economic success to the proximity of Hong Kong and to the heavy investment by Hong Kong and Taiwanese entrepreneurs in the region.
3 Because it was neglected by Beijing.
4 1988.
5 Private entrepreneurs now face few restrictions if they start a new company, unless it is in one of the heavily regulated sectors such as telecoms, finance or media.
6 The political climate and access to finance.
7 From friends and family or underground banks.

C
1 to pin down   3 thriving   5 hanging over   7 corridors of power
2 flourished   4 founded   6 port of call   8 spectacular

D
1 founded   3 flourished   5 corridors of power   7 hanging over
2 port of call 4 spectacular   6 pin down   8 thriving

137

ANSWER KEY

Listening and speaking

 9.1

A
1 Not given. It exports just under $1,000 billion of manufactured goods. Nothing is mentioned about imports of raw materials.
2 F It is still just behind Germany, but will soon overtake it.
3 T
4 T
5 T
6 Not given. Nothing is mentioned about exactly how big Lenovo is.
7 F It can only come from an expansion of a locally based private sector.
8 NG There should be a rise of genuinely global companies, but for the moment they are still state owned.

Grammar

A

Cause	Effect
because due to because of owing to as as a result of since on account of	therefore so consequently as a result lead to cause result in

B
1 Due to / Because of / Owing to / As a result of / On account of
2 therefore / consequently / as a result
3 Because / Since / As
4 lead to / cause / result in

C 1 result of   2 reason for   3 result of

Communication

 9.2

A/B Use the audio script to check your answers.

Business across cultures

 9.3

A
1 He mentions relationships, loyalty and understanding.
2 For the sake of being agreeable.

C 1f   2b   3c   4e   5d   6a

10 FOREIGN INVESTMENT

Reading and speaking

B
1 The total amount of FDI worldwide in 2006.
2 New investment to expand a company's activities in that country.
3 The US.
4 A result of mergers and acquisitions.
5 $70m.
6 Brazil, Russia, India and China.

Vocabulary and listening

10.1

B 1e   2d   3j   4c   5f   6a   7b   8h   9i   10g

C the state of the local economy – GDP, inflation rates, labour costs and the size of the domestic and neighbouring markets.
skill levels of the labour force
the industrial relations climate
financial and regulatory aspects – the stability of the currency, exchange control regulations if any
whether there're any government incentives on offer for inward investment
political stability
security and safety
government attitude to foreign investment – do they encourage or discourage it? Do they insist on a local partner? Can you remit profits out of the country?

D Russia is mentioned as a high-risk country. He does recommend investing in Russia because the potential market is huge and it has a lot to offer. However, they need to weigh up all the risks and invest in the long term.

E 1g   2i   3d   4j   5c   6h   7k   8e   9f   10b   11a

ANSWER KEY

Grammar

A 1 This factor ...
2 These ...
3 This problem ...

B 1 The two angles are the positive and negative aspects of investing in a country. The first is introduced by *First*, and the second by the interviewer, who says: *And **what about** the negative things ...*
2 Positive angle: *things such as ..., also, Finally*
Negative angle: *The first thing ..., Related to that ..., Then*

Communication

A 1b 2c 3d 4f 5a 6e

 10.2

B 1f 2d 3a 4b 5e 6c

Business across cultures

A

Advantages	Disadvantages
rich natural resources	*high unemployment*
annual growth	high inflation
100 per cent literacy	lack of industrial equipment
infrastructure	government influence
proximity to Europe	
nuclear power	

11 THE BOTTOM LINE

Reading

C 1 Cash flow
2 Investment
3 Inventory
4 Promotional expenditure
5 Premises
6 Overheads
7 Skills
8 Staffing levels
9 Staff input

Listening and speaking

A

Equal to $	Approximately $	More than $	Less than $
To work out at $	To be in the region of $	To be just over $	To be just under $
To come to $	To be approximately $	To exceed $	To be just short of $
To cost $	To be $ at most		To be almost $
To add up to $	To be $ maximum		
To total $	To be around $		
To amount to $			
To set us back $			

139

ANSWER KEY

11.1 B
C

	Two-day professional motivation conference				
	1	2	3	4	Notes
	Budget item	Unit cost	No. units	Estimated cost	Charlotte Hotel. Downtown Chicago. Right atmosphere.
1	Conference venue (two days)	$9,000	1	$9,000	
2	Promotion / Invitations				~
	Advertising in journals	$100	8	$800	Send to the Journal of Business and Chicago Business, for example
	Posters	$ 5	50	$ 250	Send to Chamber of Commerce and Chicago Business Forum
	Invitations / Postage	$ 0.65	3,000	$ 1,950	Send to everyone on the mailing list. A local printer offered a special deal
	Subtotal	~	~	$ 3,000	~
3	Guest speakers			~	Angela Perkins who spoke at the Annual Women's Leadership Exchange Simon Chapman and Lily Chang. Mario Castello whose book's being published in August
	Fees	$3,000	4	$ 12,000	Thought Angela Perkins would ask for more
	Subtotal	~	~	$ 12,000	~
4	Handouts	$ 2	2,000	$ 4,000	Programmes / Evaluation forms. Could get a company to donate the copying in exchange for advertising
5	Insurance	$ 2,000	1	$ 2,000	~
			Total	$ 30,000	~

Grammar

A in line with the atmosphere we want to create   thanks to Ben here and his powers of persuasion
As for invitations
on account of the fact they're all Chicago based
contrary to our expectations   According to my calculations

B 1d   2c   3a   4e   5b

C 1 As for / In terms of / With regard to   2 according to / depending on   3 except for / apart from
4 In view of   5 Thanks to   6 in spite of   7 as well as / in addition to

D Model answers
by no means: *not at all, not by any means, not in any way*
at the most: *maximum, not more, tops, at the (very)*
beside the point: *irrelevant, off the subject, by the way*

Communication

 11.2

A 1 a discount ... provided that ... place your first order today
2 better payment terms ... so long as ... guarantee regular orders
3 an exclusive deal ... on condition that ... promote the products nationally
4 a smaller order ... if ... order a minimum quantity

ANSWER KEY

11.3 **B** 1d 2b 3a 4c

B 1 It stifles economic growth.
2 Economic progress occurs when the bureaucrats sleep.
3 Business transactions are done through a despachante (middleman).
4 Some businesses keep some transactions and records off the books.

11.4 **D** time   negotiation   breaks   titles

E 1 Be prepared to chat first and talk business second.
2 Only use first names if invited to do so.
3 Allow for a degree of lateness.

F 1c 2b 3d 4e 5a

12 ESCAPING POVERTY

B 1 tariff 4 hinder / impede 7 accountable
2 collateral 5 an abundance 8 extortionate
3 volatility 6 emigrate 9 antiquated

B 1 They are hard to see.
2 Because they have no access to capital.
3 Microfinance.
4 In the mid-1970s in Bangladesh.
5 Women are more likely to reinvest their earnings in the business and in their families.

C 1 In microfinance, customers do not need collateral in order to receive a loan.
2 The rates in microfinance programmes often exceed those related to big business.
3 Because of the high loan repayment rates, and the enormous market potential in the large population of 'unbanked' poor.
4 Throughout the developing world, and even in poor communities in the developed world.

D

Proportion of world's population that live on less than $2 a day: *more than half*
Amount of international aid given to developing countries in the last 50 years: *more than a trillion dollars*
In relation to Grameen Bank:
Number of borrowers: *6 million*
Percentage of women borrowers: *96 per cent*
Rate of repayment of loans: *98 per cent*
Number of customers using this form of finance worldwide: *94 million*
Rate at which clients are escaping poverty: *10,000 per month*

A 1 He stressed that traditional banks had not been willing to lend to poor people.
2 He agreed that microfinance had emerged as a new approach to lending money.
3 He said that women were more likely to reinvest their earnings in the business.

12.3 **B** 1 replied 2 complains 3 explained 4 predicted 5 promises
6 added 7 confessed 8 denies 9 emphasised 10 warned

C 1 She replied that the loan had been crucial in helping them to start a business and build up a future for their family.
2 He complains that it isn't fair he is in so much debt when the banks make huge profits.
3 She explained that a self-help group system meant that a group worked together to make an enterprise succeed.
4 He predicted that women in particular would benefit from the service for a long time to come.
5 She promises that everyone in the village will have access to a phone by the end of the year.
6 He added that the bank ran several telephone and energy companies as well.
7 She confessed that a lot of the money given in aid had been spent unwisely.
8 He denies that poor people have a lower repayment rate for loans.
9 She emphasised that the repayment rate for loans was 98 per cent.
10 He warned us that we had to register our application by 1 December, or it'd be too late.

ANSWER KEY

D 1 He asked how and when this had started.
2 He asked how microfinance worked.
3 He asked whether / if microfinance was the solution to beating global poverty.

Communication

 12.4

B 1 The conflict is about who is responsible, Masterstons being unhappy and not paying for technical support.
2 She says Masterstons have to pay as they signed a contract with fixed payment terms.
3 He can't afford to upset them as they are his best client.
4 Take them to court to get the money.
5 Make them an offer.

C Use the audio script to check your answers.

Business across cultures

 12.5

C 1 People don't trust official authorities any more.
2 People no longer believe that politicians can do anything for them, so they don't vote.
3 Business people cannot create wealth for the country. They can only create wealth for themselves by paying bribes which leads to inefficient allocation of resources.

REVIEW AND DEVELOPMENT 9–12

Vocabulary

A thriving economy

A 1 port   3 pin down   5 found   7 flourish
2 thriving   4 spectacular   6 corridors   8 hang over

```
M P F L O U R I S H E L A M
Y I O P E C N Z P W J N C U
I T H R I V I N G D E E S L
S P E C T A C U L A R R B T
P E S T O A U V F L P U M H
I S N J T R O K O D U D C A
N R I Y H F R K U Z U Y E N
D P Q O X B U I N V Y N T G
O X A C U A Y Q D P D A A O
W U L P L H A N G O V E R V
N S F C C P L Q U I R I X E
R E S T R I C T I O N S G R
P I N E Q U A L I T Y M E L
```

Grammar

Cause and effect

A 1b due to
2c due to / because of / owing to / as a result of
3d because / as
4a because / as
5g so
6e therefore / consequently / as a result
7h results in
8f therefore / consequently / as a result

Vocabulary

Foreign investment

A 1 money laundering   2 come into the equation   3 weigh up   4 inflation

Grammar

Referring and sequencing

A 1 These include   2 This is   3 First   Then   Finally

Vocabulary

Boosting the bottom line

A 1 economic downturn   5 expenditure
2 revenue   6 stretch
3 plummet   7 overheads
4 lay off

142

ANSWER KEY

B to dampen down   to bring down   to cut back on   to minimise   to cut

Grammar

Prepositions

A
1 in line with
2 In terms of
3 in view of
4 With regard to
5 besides the point

Vocabulary

Escaping poverty

A
1 Strict tariffs <u>prevent</u> the free flow of goods between countries.
2 The educated <u>emigrate</u> for better opportunities abroad.
3 Extortionate world interest rates <u>force</u> third world countries to maintain impossible interest payments.
4 Poor infrastructure <u>hinders</u> development and progress.
5 Due to antiquated emergency mechanisms, the third world <u>suffers</u> more when natural disasters occur.
6 Awkward geographic features <u>slow</u> the spread of new technology.
7 An abundance of natural resources <u>brings about</u> market volatility.
8 Entrepreneurs <u>require</u> collateral to get a business loan.
9 Lack of accountability <u>encourages</u> corruption.

Grammar

Reported speech

A
1 He argued that there was no evidence that microfinance …
2 He promised that he would arrive on time for the meeting.
3 He complained that he hadn't received the report.
4 He admitted that he was capable of making mistakes and that he had invested in the wrong equipment.
5 He asked me whether poverty strengthened corruption.
6 He informed us that our company was too small to invest in.
7 He predicted that, by 2050, China, India, Brazil and Russia would probably be larger …

Communication

A 1e 2f 3a 4h 5c 6d 7b 8g

B Model answers
1 Could you go over that again?
2 So, you're worried about the budget?
3 Could you tell me more about the budget?
4 Don't you think we should limit travel this year?
5 Does everyone agree that we should cut the budget?
6 What steps do we need to take?

C
Anna: So we have proposed our new prices. What do you think?
Matt: I'm afraid we can't agree to them.
Anna: I'm sorry to hear that. Would you consider them if we offered a quantity discount?
Matt: Perhaps. Provided the discount is across the full range of products.
Anna: That will be difficult as you do not buy some of the products in the right quantity.
Matt: Well, that may be so. But we can't go any further without an across the board discount.
Anna: We can't really agree to that but we could offer you a significant discount on your five main product categories.
Matt: That sounds interesting. What sort of discount?
Anna: Well, as long as you can guarantee minimum orders, we could offer a 15 per cent discount linked to early payment.
Matt: That could be interesting for us. Can you put this in writing?

D
1 difficulty
2 sticking point
3 propose
4 middle way
5 shared interest
6 option
7 answer
8 offer

143

ANSWER KEY

13 DEVELOPING PEOPLE

Email exchange

B 1 F They are under enormous pressure.
2 T
3 T
4 F They will coach the team before a presentation.
5 F They work with both public and private sector organisations.

C 1 I am writing with reference to
2 Due to
3 we've realised that we urgently need
4 I'd be grateful if you could
5 I'm particularly interested to know
6 and roughly how many
7 It would also be extremely useful
8 I look forward to hearing about
9 Please don't hesitate to contact me

D Model answer

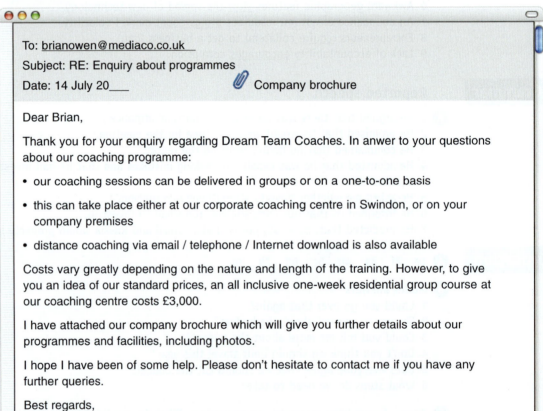

To: brianowen@mediaco.co.uk
Subject: RE: Enquiry about programmes
Date: 14 July 20___   Company brochure

Dear Brian,

Thank you for your enquiry regarding Dream Team Coaches. In anwer to your questions about our coaching programme:

- our coaching sessions can be delivered in groups or on a one-to-one basis
- this can take place either at our corporate coaching centre in Swindon, or on your company premises
- distance coaching via email / telephone / Internet download is also available

Costs vary greatly depending on the nature and length of the training. However, to give you an idea of our standard prices, an all inclusive one-week residential group course at our coaching centre costs £3,000.

I have attached our company brochure which will give you further details about our programmes and facilities, including photos.

I hope I have been of some help. Please don't hesitate to contact me if you have any further queries.

Best regards,

Renate Lenze

14 LOCAL PARTNERS

Business reports

C 1 several 2 the 3 some of 4 few 5 the 6 a 7 this

B Model answer

Dua Cycle Range advertising campaign

Summary
Aarit Motala, CEO of Dua, asked the Sharp Edge Cycles marketing team to attend a meeting to decide on a powerful marketing strategy for the Dua cycle product range to be launched in India. He asked the team to come up with a variety of original marketing ideas to present at the meeting. The following short report describes the Indian market background, the current level of competition and the final agreed marketing strategy for each product.

Introduction
The following points were considered:
Local market
Competitive environment
Product range
Product range image
Product range marketing strategy

Local market
Young Indians prefer to shop online, are extremely brand conscious and are attracted to big foreign brands. Health and fitness, music, coffee bars and shopping malls are some of their main interests. Although there has so far only been one big mountain biking rally organised in India, leisure cycling has started to become quite fashionable in India and is seen as an eco-friendly alternative to driving.

Competitive environment
Although many high-end bicycles are manufactured in India, the range offered on the Indian market is very limited.

Product range
Mountain bike
BMX bike
Tour bike
Dua sportswear range

Product range image
Due to the growing trend towards health and fitness and outdoor pursuits, it was decided that the emerging Indian youth alternative sports lifestyle would be the main focus of the brand image.

Product range marketing strategy
Whilst the mountain bike will be advertised via mobile phones, the tour bike should be promoted in co-operation with cycling holiday industry. Whereas the BMX bike would be best promoted through Bollywood product placement, sponsorship of student cultural and sporting events would be the most appropriate method of promotion for the sportswear range.

Conclusion
Analysis of the Indian cycling trends for the last few years shows that whilst this market is still relatively small, interest in cycling is on the increase. Dua is a highly successful established European brand which will be well received by the Indian youth market who have an appetite for quality foreign brands.

c

Dear Amit, Shalina and Ira,

Firstly, let me congratulate you on our successful meeting two days ago. I was very impressed with your imaginative suggestions for marketing our Dua cycle range. I'm extremely pleased with the outcomes we arrived at, and am confident that with your expert local knowledge, Dua Cycles will be a success in India. Therefore, I'm pleased to confirm that I would be happy to sign an exclusive, five-year distribution contract with Sharp Edge Cycles.

Secondly, I'm keen to get this project underway as soon as possible, so I'd be grateful if you could start organising the marketing campaign immediately. Could you also send me a progress report by the end of next month?

Finally, once again, many thanks for all your energy and hard work. I look forward to a strong and profitable partnership between our companies in the near future.

Kindest regards,

Aarit Motala

15 GETTING AWAY FROM IT!

Press releases

B 1 Mr Abbas announced, 'The refurbishment will put the hotel back on the international luxury tourism map.'
2 He proudly stated that they already had bookings from a large number of world famous celebrities.
3 He went on to say 'it is not difficult to see why'.
4 He added, 'at all hours of the day and night, Sharm's legendary promenade, which stretches from one end of the bay to the other, is one of the country's most romantic strolling spots'.
5 'However, for diving enthusiasts', he continued, 'the real attraction lies beneath the surface of the crystal blue waters of the Red Sea.
6 He boasted that the exquisite guest rooms, as well as the hotel's unrivalled 18-hole golf course, club house and spa would provide the ultimate in restfulness and pampering.
7 He concluded that he was extremely proud to be the owner of one of the finest hotels in the world.

C 1 most picturesque
2 perfect place
3 very successful
4 extremely diverse
5 astounding
6 greatest concentration
7 second deepest

D Model answer

Katabaro hotel
PRESS RELEASE

Today in Dar es Salaam, the spectacularly refurbished five-star Katabaro hotel, once regarded as one of the most classically luxurious hotels in the world, was reopened after a one-year refurbishment project costing over $4m. Investor Ibrahim Madani and owner Mr Macha were joined by a large number of world famous guests to reopen the hotel.

In his opening speech, Mr Madani announced, 'We already have bookings from a large number of high profile guests, including minor royalty and world famous business tycoons.'

He went on to say that it was easy to see why. 'The hotel is first class and situated in some of the most breathtaking scenery a holiday maker could wish for!' Home to the exotic islands of Zanzibar and Pemba, and with an exciting and diverse wild animal population, the luxury safari industry was already very profitable for the region. 'What is more, I don't think any other country can provide such a high number of astounding natural features!', he boasted. 'Tanzania is home to the largest crater in the world. For divers and anglers, Lake Tanganyika, the longest and second deepest lake in the world, is a paradise, with over 350 species of fish.' Whether you are keen on water sports or just enjoying the wonderful relaxation of the hotel's health and beauty spa and romance of its legendary giant ballroom, Tanzania is one of the most idyllic vacation spots in the world.'

'I am extremely happy to be the owner of one of the finest hotels in the world!', he proudly stated.

COMMUNICATION

COMMUNICATION

The communication section is designed to develop your skills in key areas such as presenting and negotiating. The foundation for all good communication is to establish a two-way channel with both parties making sure the message comes across. We need to use language to achieve this two-way communication – language for questions, checking, giving feedback and forming clear messages. The first module prepares the foundation and then module two and three applies best practice to presenting, interviewing, meeting and negotiating. By the end of the course, you will have practised and applied a clear set of guidelines for effective communication.

Units 1–4 establish some basic guidelines for good communication.

UNIT 1 PROFILING YOUR OWN COMMUNICATION STYLE

A key factor in developing your effectiveness as a communicator is to be aware of how your currently communicate and identify areas you would like to develop. Communication styles are influenced by culture, personality and business situations.

Some cultures are more direct (they say 'no' more easily) than others. Some people are quite indirect, avoiding any possibility of conflict. In some situations, we may decide to force the issues more directly onto the table.
In terms of complexity, some professions often feel the need to communicate complex ideas in a complex way. However, we all need to be able to simplify our message with some audiences.

Formality is also demanded more in some cultures than others. We need to be aware of how to address our business partners – are titles important or not. Sometimes the rituals of communication (e.g. drinking tea together before a meeting) are just as important as the business message.

Individuals and cultures vary a lot in terms of how much emotion they show when they communicate. We see this not only in what we say but also in our body language – for example how close we stand and whether we touch each other.

Finally, asking questions is closely linked with active listening. It is a different way of communicating – it shows that you are interested and you want to engage in two-way communication.

UNIT 2 ACTIVE LISTENING

Active listening means trying to put yourself in the shoes of your partner and trying to really understand their position. Most of the time, we stop listening when we think we know what someone is going to say or we lose interest in what they are saying. We develop these bad habits in our own language and then transfer them when we speak English. When using English we need to be very careful that we really understand each other. One way to make sure of this is to use active listening techniques. This means showing that you are interested, that you understand, and then proving that you have understood. You can prove that you have understood by summarising or putting your understanding into different words. This also helps to develop the conversation as it indicates you are ready to move on to another point.

UNIT 3 INFLUENCING

Influencing is a key skill which we use every day at work. We sometimes need to persuade a colleague to work late or we need to convince a supplier to deliver earlier and in sales, we have to work hard to win new customers. We can do this by the power of our message and also the strength of our arguments – this is what we call a 'push approach' – presenting a strong argument in a forceful way. We can also do this by listening to them, by asking them the right questions in order to get them to consider your point of view – this is what we call a 'pull' approach. It is important to develop both techniques – pushing (for example making a very convincing presentation) and pulling (for example, sitting down together and asking a lot of questions). People are generally much more ready to accept a change if you show them first that you understand them. If you just present the arguments, they will often reject them or not put them into practice.

UNIT 4 GETTING YOUR MESSAGE ACROSS

In order to get your message across, sometimes it is a good idea to tell people what you are going to say, say it, and then tell them what you have said. When you are working internationally, with people who have different levels of English, it always helps to support their understanding as much as possible. If you say, 'I think we should increase prices', your partners have to react immediately. If you say, 'I would like to make a suggestion. Perhaps we should increase prices' you allow your partners more time to consider their reaction. You also make it clear that you are not ordering them or demanding something, and that you are just making a suggestion. Communication often breaks down because people misunderstand the intention of the speaker. This often happens when people criticise something and people take it personally. If the criticiser starts by saying, 'This is not personal, but I want to improve our process ...', we understand the intention better.

Units 5–6 focus on presentations and how you can connect with your audience.

UNIT 5 PRESENTATIONS: ENGAGING YOUR AUDIENCE 1

Presentations are often wrongly considered to be a one-way communication. However, if you don't make the communication two-way and connect with your audience, you won't know if you got your message across. You can engage with the audience by using certain expressions to show interest and get feedback but we can also engage through body language – making eye contact and not hiding behind slides.

At least 50 per cent of the message comes across through body language, so you can be very successful at presentations even if you are not fluent in English.

UNIT 6 PRESENTATIONS: ENGAGING YOUR AUDIENCE 2

Communication is always more successful when you put yourself in the shoes of the audience you are presenting to. Before you start a presentation, it is helpful to think about what your audience wants from you.
- What is their current situation – are they here because they want to be?
- What do they need to get from you – information, ideas, fun?
- What are they worried about – how can you show that you care?
- What recognition can you give to motivate them and to make them feel better about themselves?

Units 7–8 focus on how you can use questions to interview and give feedback.

UNIT 7 INTERVIEWING

Whether you are an interviewer or an interviewee, you will be more successful if you are prepared. This means thinking about the type of questions you will ask or answer.

Background
This has a very wide meaning; it could mean talking about your origins, your education, your family or your career.

Professional experience
It is important to identify which part of your experience is relevant to the new job.

Competencies
These include skills like communication and organisation, as well as behaviours like curiosity and courage.

Critical incidents
These include difficult situations or challenges you have faced.

Motives
It is helpful to think about the underlying reasons you want to leave a job and start a new one. You could be bored or not challenged enough, or you might want more money.

UNIT 8 FEEDBACK

It is often easier to give negative rather than positive feedback. We notice something goes wrong so we comment on it. People frequently take these criticisms personally. However, if you also notice and comment on what they do well (affirmative feedback), they will be much more willing to listen to feedback on areas they could improve (development feedback). Giving feedback often works better when you ask the person to reflect on their own performance and give feedback on themselves, rather than starting with your feedback to them. If they mention something which you have also noticed, you can reinforce this. If they are not aware of something which they do well or not so well, then you can often use questions to get them to think about it.

Units 9–12 continue to develop your skills in developing two-way communication.

UNIT 9 LEADING MEETINGS

Meetings often fail because of different expectations and objectives. In order to make them a success, you can follow the four Ps. Firstly, it is important you establish a clear way of dealing with expectations through good *preparation* before the meeting. It is also important you clearly state the *purpose* of the meeting so people know why it is taking place. A meeting should follow a transparent *process* so that all the participants know where the meeting is going and how it is going to get there. Finally, through clear roles and active participation, *people* contribute positively to the meeting.

UNIT 10 PARTICIPATING IN MEETINGS

Questions, rather than statements, are often a more powerful way of influencing people in a meeting. Clarifying questions not only make sure the meaning is clear to you, they also give participants a chance to ask for clarification. Reformulating questions shows that you have listened and want to understand. Showing interest encourages people to be positive. Leading questions push the discussion in a certain direction. It is frustrating if there is no clear outcome of a meeting so seeking agreement and suggesting action ensure that people feel the meeting has a concrete outcome and benefit.

UNIT 11 NEGOTIATIONS 1: BARGAINING

Negotiation is about reaching an agreement which satisfies both parties. Considerable time is often spent in business communication bargaining over something. In order to arrive at a successful conclusion, it is important to identify what you want to achieve and what points you would be willing to negotiate on. You often have to compromise or offer concessions so that both parties feel the agreement is fair. You may accept an offer or you may reject it for a new offer. Often an offer is linked to a condition so you may accept something on the condition that you get something else in return. Sometimes an offer is not in your best interests and you have to reject it.

UNIT 12 NEGOTIATIONS 2: HANDLING CONFLICT

Handling conflict with your colleagues or business partners requires special skills.

Firstly, you need to consider what is your and your partner's attitude towards conflict. Should it be avoided at all costs or can you benefit from bringing the conflict to the surface and dealing with it? Cultural and personal preferences vary a lot in this area.

Secondly, if you bring the conflict to the surface, there is the question of how you deal with it. It is important to analyse and identify the obstacle so that both parties are clear about the issue. Finding common ground and introducing different options are an effective way of resolving conflict.

BUSINESS ACROSS CULTURES

Business across Cultures aims to develop your understanding and competence to work with people from other cultures. Culture is like the glue which helps people to stick together. It can be a very positive dimension, providing a set of common values which support the success of a company or business. But, it can also be an obstacle which outsiders find very difficult to join and be part of. Our approach is to build understanding of these common values, beliefs, rules and behaviour – not only of other cultures but also of your own culture.

> **Units 1–4** explore working cultures and the people within them. The aim is to build a framework for understanding their key dimensions and influences.

UNIT 1 INTERNATIONAL LEADERSHIP

The biggest influence on the culture of a company is the leadership style of managers. Most people at work have a manager or a boss and the behaviour of this person will have a big effect on your day-to-day experience at work.

Leadership style will depend on the values which managers believe in and also the values which the organisation supports. Some of these key values are listed below.
- Family – do we see the company like a family, in which the employees should be looked after and cared for?
- Hierarchy – do we think it is important for people to know their position in relation to others, to show respect for more senior people?
- Results – what do we think is the purpose of the organisation? Is it to increase dividends for shareholders / to serve the community / to become No. 1 in the world?

UNIT 2 UNDERSTANDING THE TEAM

Culture is like an onion. At the centre, we have the individual, then the team, then the department (function), then the company and then the country. Behaviour in organisations is not just about culture. It is also about the individuals in the organisation. Many of the challenges people face at work are not only connected to clashes between different personalities but also clashes between different functions.

Personalities: It is more and more common to use psychometric profiles to increase understanding of yourself and your team. These profiles (e.g. Myers-Briggs or Belbin) are based on studying key dimensions of behaviour such as how you relate to others, how you make decisions and how you organise yourself. Understanding yourself better is a good starting point for understanding your colleagues.

Functions: Departments or functions (Marketing, R & D, Finance) often develop their own culture at work. Jargon (professional terminology) is one way in which people protect their culture from others. Using complex terms makes it difficult for others to join in and feel part of your culture. Certain types of people are attracted to certain functions – for example, you would not expect an introvert to work in field sales. This reinforces the cultural stereotype for a certain function.

UNIT 3 MOTIVATION AT WORK

Power, achievement and affiliation are key factors which motivate people at work. These factors apply across all cultures. However, cultural values will affect the importance people attach to each factor.

- **Masculinity / Femininity**
  Some cultures are more masculine than others. A masculine culture values assertiveness, achievement, and acquisition of wealth, as opposed to caring for others, social support and the quality of life. Masculine cultures often have very clear expectations of male and female roles in society. Feminine cultures focus more on quality of life issues such as helping others and sympathy for the unfortunate. They also prefer equality between men and women and have fewer defined roles for each other. (This concept was developed by Geert Hosftede. Go to http://www.geert-hofstede.com for more information.)

- **Power distance**
  High power distance cultures are characterised by a clear distance between one layer and the next in hierarchies. People know their position, managers keep their distance and there are clear status symbols which are attached to power, such as a big office on the top floor. In low power distance cultures there are smaller differences between layers and fewer layers. People respect what people do more than what position they hold. There are few signs of power and who holds it. (This concept was developed by Geert Hosftede. Go to http://www.geert-hofstede.com for more information.)

- **Context**
  In a high-context culture, people understand the message more from the environment that surrounds it rather than what is actually said. In other words, relationships, dress and rituals are very important in understanding what is going on. In low-context cultures, people rely mostly on what is said and less on the environment which surrounds it. In low-context cultures, people are usually quite direct, and they say 'no' which can bring offend people. Achievement will be seen as more important in low-context cultures, whereas affiliation plays a bigger role in high-context cultures. (This concept was developed by the anthropologist E.T. Hall. For more information, see his book, with Mildred Reed Hall, *Understanding Cultural Differences* published by Intercultural Press, 2000.)

UNIT 4 ORGANISATIONAL CULTURES

Sometimes organisational culture is more important than country culture in affecting behaviour at work. Companies develop their cultures over time and they are very dependent on factors such as size and industrial or commercial sector.

Charles Handy uses Greek gods to illustrate four types of organisational culture.

A **power culture** is like a web with a ruling spider. Those in the web are dependent on a central power source. Power and influence spread out from a central figure or group. In a *Zeus* organisation, power derives from the top person, and a personal relationship with that individual is more important than any formal title or position, e.g. small entrepreneurial companies and political groups.

A **role culture** is often referred to as a bureaucracy. It is controlled by procedures, role descriptions and authority definitions. Co-ordination is at the top. Your job position is central. An *Apollo* culture creates a highly structured and stable company. This means bureaucracy with precise job descriptions and usually with a single product e.g. large public companies and utilities.

A **task culture** is very much a small team approach with small organisations cooperating together to deliver a project. The emphasis is on results and getting things done. Individuals are empowered with discretion and control over their work. The *Athena* culture emphasises talent and youth and continuous team problem-solving e.g. consultancies.

In a **person culture** the individual is the central point. If there is a structure it exists only to serve the individuals within it. Employees have strong values about how they will work and can be very difficult to manage. A *Dionysus* organisation exists so that individuals can achieve their purposes, e.g. a university, medical practices or other professional groupings.

Units 5–8 look at more aspects of culture and give examples from country and company cultures.

UNIT 5 INDIA

In this unit we explore the difficulties foreigners may face when doing business in India.

We also explore the dimension of time. Some cultures consider time and its control very important. In these so-called monochronic cultures (e.g. Germany, UK, US) punctuality is a very important value. You are judged by your punctuality – arriving late is seen as a sign of either inefficiency or lack of respect. Working life is dominated by start times and finish times, structured agendas and almost an obsession with time-keeping. On the other hand, in polychronic cultures (e.g. India) time is not such an important resource. Finishing the topic and allowing everybody an opportunity to talk is much more important than finishing on time. In these cultures, people will be happy to do many things at the same time – for example, a business meeting won't be very structured, allowing for many more interruptions and diversions than would be possible in a monochronic culture. (This concept was developed by the anthropologist E.T. Hall. For more information, see his book, with Mildred Reed Hall, *Understanding Cultural Differences* published by Intercultural Press, 2000.)

UNIT 6 DRESS

Although some people think judging people on the clothes they wear is superficial, dress is an important part of culture and plays a bigger role than most people realise. In some cultures (especially Latin ones), appearance is considered very important, for both men and women. The Italians talk about 'bella figura' meaning the way you look tells you a lot about the person. On the other hand, dress plays a much smaller role in the US, where most people play safe when they dress for work. In cultures where appearance is more important, people will talk more about it and compliment each other on how they look.

UNIT 7 BRANDING NATIONS

Nation branding is a relatively new area of marketing and explores the brand image of countries. It is important when studying culture to distinguish between identity and culture. Companies talk about their 'corporate identity' – this is to do with their external image, their logo and other aspects of the company. It is not the same as corporate culture – which is the internal experience that people have when they work in a company. Similarly, country identity, as expressed and promoted through a national brand is not the same as the country culture. Tony Blair, the Prime Minister of the UK, tried to promote Britain as 'cool Britannia' by associating with British pop bands during the 1990s. Many British people did not recognise this image of Britain and it failed.

UNIT 8 GLOBAL MARKETING

This section explores a key concern for international businesses – to what extent you can market your products and services in the same way in different cultures. Globalisation on the surface seems to have created common needs and markets. People across the world buy the same brands of jeans, listen to similar music and use the Internet in the same way. However, you don't have to spend too long in a new culture to understand that many values and behaviour differ a lot. The global versus local debate is something marketers need to take into account when marketing their product or service in different countries. Some products can be sold in a similar way, especially technology and clothing products, but other products and services need to be adapted to the local market.

Units 9–12 explore three major cultures – China, Russia and Brazil. They also take a look at changes in Africa.

UNIT 9 CHINA

When doing business in China, it is important to be aware of some key values in Chinese culture. Guanxi is connected with building a strong network of people you can rely on. This is the biggest challenge for investors entering the Chinese market. Many will underestimate the importance of a good network. Working internationally means building networks across cultures and the skill of making and maintaining business relationships across big distances becomes the key. Westerners also find it hard to adapt to the importance of values such as humility, modesty and collective behaviour. Although Westerners believe politeness and courtesy are important, they also value frankness, transparency and individual performance. Often the clash in cultures is around the Westerners' need to push for resolution and closure, rather than allowing things to stay open and unresolved.

UNIT 10 RUSSIA

When investing abroad most companies only think about the financial and marketing issues. However, it is important to consider cultural differences too.

Climate: think about how climate affects your behaviour.

Geography: cultures need to adapt to different geographies. For example, Russia has a lot of space and perhaps this is one reason people form communities and look after each other.

Law: attitudes towards the law vary a lot from culture to culture.

More 'universal cultures' (e.g. Switzerland or Singapore) have a very strong sense of the law and the need to follow it, whereas in other cultures, the law is there to be avoided and people try to find a way around it.

UNIT 11 BRAZIL

This section on Brazil uncovers some key dimensions of cultural difference.

Task- versus person-orientation: Business is always about achieving results. However, in very task-oriented cultures, a focus on results dominates thinking and attitudes. In more person-oriented cultures, forming good relationships are more important in achieving results.

High and low context cultures: (See Unit 3, Business across cultures, page 151, for more on this topic.)

Universalist and particularist cultures: (See Unit 12, Business across cultures, page 153, for more on this topic.)

Emotional versus neutral cultures: In more emotional cultures (typically the Latin cultures), people are encouraged to show how they feel. This means that you can see more easily in their facial expressions what they are feeling. For emotional cultures, this is an honest and helpful way of communicating. In more neutral cultures, people are encouraged to hide what they are feeling. Showing what you feel, especially in business, is considered unhelpful and maybe even unprofessional. It is better in these cultures to keep emotion out of business.

Monochronic and polychronic cultures: (See Unit 5, Business across cultures, page 152, for more on this topic.)

UNIT 12 AFRICA

In universalist cultures, a lot of importance is attached to the law. The United States is often given as an example of a universalist culture and a symptom of this is the very high number of lawyers in this country. The law is quickly brought into play in the case of any dispute and it is even used to govern personal relationships at work where men must be careful in the way they treat women. However, this does not mean that there is no corruption in universalist cultures. Lawyers are employed to find ways around the law, as much as to follow the law.

In particularist cultures, people are less likely to look to the law for guidance on how to behave. They will use their instinct and traditions to tell them what is right and wrong. They will often be sceptical about the law, seeing it as something which is used to protect the powerful.

GRAMMAR OVERVIEW

UNIT 1 Modals

Modal verbs and phrasal modals have a number of uses. Here are the main ones.

N.B. Unless otherwise stated, the negatives are formed using *not* or *n't*, and mean the opposite.

- **Indicating ability:** *can, could, be able to*

  > He's really **been able to** make things happen in this company.

- **Indicating obligation, prohibition and lack of obligation:** *must, have to (don't have to), should, ought to, need to (don't need to or needn't)*

  > A leader **must** take command, establish rules, and determine values and principles.

Must and *have to* mean roughly the same, but their negatives are different. *Mustn't* is used to prohibit something, while *don't have to* means that there is no obligation.

  > You **don't have to** make a firm commitment, just give me an idea of your availability.

- **Predicting and indicating likelihood:** See page 160.
- **Indicating intentions:** *will, shall* (rarely), *be going to, may, might*

  > I **will** soon be asking everyone to come and discuss their personal development plan.

- **Deducing and making assumptions:** *may, might, could, would, must, can't* (not *can*)

  > Surely he **must** know how much everyone dislikes his style of leadership.

You use *can't* or *couldn't* (**not** *mustn't*), when you think something is definitely not the case.

  > He **can't** have learned much from that leadership course he went on.

- **Indicating possibility:** *may, might, can, could*

  > You **could** be creating more friction in the company by failing to delegate.

- **Asking for and giving permission:** *can, could, may, be allowed to*

  > You **can** use all the company's facilities to prepare your presentation.

- **Talking about past habits:** *would* (but not *wouldn't*), *used to* (*didn't use to*)

  > Leaders **didn't use to** be as accountable to their colleagues as they are now.

- **Giving advice and opinions:** *should, ought to, had better*

  > I think the management **ought to** be doing more to protect our pensions.

Note that modals and phrasal modals are often used together, for example, *A good leader* **should be able to** understand the strengths and weaknesses of her team.

Practice

1 Complete the sentences using the modals in the box below.

can't   have to   'd better   may   could

1 Good leaders _____ possess a combination of strategic vision and tactical skills.
2 _____ I just give you a few examples of what these skills involve?
3 I think you _____ try and upgrade your skills if you want to stay in the company.
4 Surely he _____ be the new human resources manager? He looks far too young!
5 The last manager _____ really make this place run smoothly – I'm sorry she's gone.

2 Match sentences 1–5 with the functions below.

obligation   deduction   ability   advice   permission

UNIT 3 Conditionals

You have learnt about the **zero**, **first**, **second** and **third conditionals**. These are typical, but you can use a much wider variety of tenses and modals to make different meanings, as the examples show.

Note that the main clause and the *if* clause can come in either order.

- **Facts and regular occurrences**

    *Customers **get** angry if the job **costs** more than you estimated.* (typical zero)
    *If a product **is** not available, you **can expect** a wait of up to five working days.*
    *People **find** it easier to work freelance if they **have had** training in time management.*

- **Possible events and situations**

    *If I **decide** to go freelance, I **will start** by decorating my study.* (typical 1st)
    *If a competitor **is speaking** at a meeting, **attend** the talk.*
    *If you**'ve finished** the basic website design, we **could launch** it next week.*

- **Hypothetical events and situations**

    *I **would miss** the flexibility if I **stopped** working freelance.* (typical 2nd)
    *I figured that if we **could sign up** two of the companies, then the business **would take off**.*
    *If things **were going** better with the business, I**'d be** able to take a holiday.*

- **Events and situations that were possible, but the opposite happened**

    *If I **hadn't had** children, I **wouldn't have become** a freelance writer.* (typical 3rd)
    *If I **had gone** freelance sooner, I **would be making** a lot more profit by now.*

Note that you can also say ***Had I gone** freelance sooner ...*

If collocations

There are some *if* clauses that people use very frequently.

if you don't mind ...	*if I were you ...*	*if you like ...*
if all else fails ...	*if I'd known ...*	*if it hadn't been for ...*

If all else fails, you can always go back to accountancy.
If it hadn't been for the insurance, we would have lost the entire business.

There are also some common verbless *if* clauses.

if so	*if not*	*if any*
if anything	*if at all*	*if in doubt*
if possible	*if at all possible*	*if necessary*

*Is Hapax going to fold? **If so**, it's a great opportunity for us to grab market share.*
*I answer the phone on the first ring **if possible**.*

Practice

Complete the sentences using the items in the box.

if in doubt	if not	if anything	if I were you	if any

1 I'm not expecting many orders today, _____ .
2 Do you do your tax self-assessment online? _____ , now is the time to switch.
3 _____ , I'd cut down on your travel expenses.
4 _____ , consult your independent financial adviser.
5 I don't think the falling dollar rate will affect us. _____ , it'll work in our favour.

UNIT 4 Relative clauses

Defining and non-defining relative clauses

- The information in defining relative clauses is essential to the meaning of the sentence, and can not be omitted. This is especially obvious when you are using a relative clause after a pronoun.

    > Be suspicious of **anyone who offers you 'the investment opportunity of a lifetime'**.

- The information in non-defining relative clauses is extra or non-essential.

    > He will soon relocate to Dublin, **where the company is setting up a small operation**.

- You can use *which* to introduce a comment on a whole clause rather than just a noun.

    > The privatisation of the railways was not a great success, **which many of its critics had predicted**.

Relative pronouns

- When they introduce relative clauses, the pronouns *who* and *whom* refer to a person, *that* refers to a person or thing, and *which* refers to a thing or situation.

- *Where* and *when* refer to place and time, and *whose* (+ noun) indicates possession.

    > We will identify those areas of the country **where consumer demands are being met**.
    > Those were the days **when no-one considered it feasible to privatise the railways**.
    > There are complaints from public sector workers **whose jobs have been privatised**.

Omission of the relative pronoun

- You must include *who/that/which* when it is the subject of the relative clause.

    > Civil servants are on strike in protest at moves towards privatisation **that could cost them their jobs**.

- When *who/that/which* is the object in a defining relative clause, you can often leave it out.

    > The solution **(that) we propose** is set out clearly in our privatisation report.

- When the verb in the relative clause is passive or continuous, both the relative pronoun and the auxiliary *be* are often unnecessary.

    > The economist **(who was) interviewed on Newsnight** has spoken out on rail safety issues.
    > New plans have been announced by one of the companies **(that are) bidding for the rail franchise**.

Practice

Underline the relative clauses, and state whether each is defining or non-defining. Insert commas where they have been wrongly omitted.

The Hapax Group which is a leading international transport company has submitted a bid for the new East Coast franchise. Hapax based in Perthshire currently operates the North Island franchise and also runs Trans Valley reputed to be Europe's smallest rail franchise. An executive said 'The East Coast franchise is the area's most important railway, and we have developed bold plans that will unlock the full potential of the network and attract passengers who have not previously benefitted from convenient rail links. We sincerely believe that we can deliver on our firm promise which is to make rail travel in the region even better and continuously improve performance.

UNIT 5 Determiners and quantifiers

Determiners

The and a(n)

You use *a(n)* before a singular count noun to talk about a person or thing when:
- you mention them for the first time
- you are giving an example of something that is one of many

> Until the late 1990s, foreign investors had to team up with **a local company**.

You usually use *the* before singular, plural and uncount nouns when:
- you mention something specific for a second time in a conversation.

> They made detailed plans for a partnership, but were forced to abandon **the project**.

- you and your hearer both know what you are referring to, like *the economy* or *the manager*

> There was concern about corruption in **the public sector**.
> They were slow to recognise **the potential** of this new market.

- the noun is followed by a defining relative clause or by *of*
- something is thought of as unique, like *the wind* or *the sun*

No article is needed before plural count nouns and uncount nouns when the meaning is general.

> **Joint ventures** remain mandatory in several sectors, such as **agriculture**.
> Franchising is when **exporters** sell **goods** through **intermediaries** such as **export agents**.

Other determiners

Determiners include *this, that, these* and *those*, as well as the possessives *my, his, our* etc.

> Many local companies and **their design teams** were involved in **this project**.

Many determiners can be grouped according to the quantity involved:

100% ────────────────────────────────────→ 0%

all, each, every	much, many, most, several	some, any	(a) few, (a) little	both, either		another	neither, no

Note that most determiners are also pronouns and can be used alone.

> Both companies gained from the partnership, but in the end **neither** wanted it to continue.

Quantifiers

- The determiners above (except *every*) are also quantifiers when followed by *of*. Other common quantifiers are *lots of, a lot of, plenty of, a bit of* and *none of*.

> **None of** these new regulations has come into force yet.

- Quantifiers are often followed by *the, this, my* etc + noun, or by a plural pronoun.

> The key to the future for **many of our small businesses** lies in access to technology.
> The country has several oilfields, but **few of them** have been fully developed.

Practice

Choose the correct determiner or quantifier.

1 In (all of / both / either) countries, foreign direct investment is increasing rapidly.
2 Joint ventures hold (several / another of / every) attractions for inward investors.
3 (A little / Every / No) company that wishes to grow has to plan its future strategically.
4 Let us now explore (much of / a few of / either of) the advantages of indirect export.
5 These rules ensure that (any / each of / no) company can fall under foreign control.

UNIT 6 The passive

Uses

- You often use the passive when you do not know who the agent is, when you do not want to say, or when it is obvious.

  > Liz Claiborne Inc. **was founded** in 1976 and **is based** in New York.

- When you are interested in the agent, you use *by*.

  > The business has been affected **by an industry-wide slowdown**.

- You can also use the passive to report what people in general say, believe or think. There are two main structures:

  1. *it* + passive verb + *that*

  > **It was rumoured that** the fashion house would off-load one of its prestige labels.
  > **It is expected that** as many as 400 jobs in the fashion industry will disappear.

  This structure is used with a wide range of verbs, for example *say, believe, think, allege, claim, consider, expect, feel, hope, report, be rumoured* and *suggest*.

  2. subject + passive verb + *to*-infinitive

  > **He is said to hate** the work of younger, flashier designers.
  > **The store is believed to be** the biggest retail fashion outlet in Ireland.

  You can use all forms of the infinitive after *to*.

  > Sales of M&S women's clothing **are thought to have surged** more than 20 per cent.

  This structure is less frequent and is not often used with *claim, feel, hope* or *suggest*.

Restrictions on the use of the passive

- You can use the passive only with transitive verbs (verbs that have an object).
- Intransitive verbs like *come, fall* and *sleep* have no passive.
- There are a few common transitive verbs that are rarely used in the passive, such as *get, let, have* and *like*.
- Link verbs like *be, seem* and *appear* have no passive.

Passive with *get*

- Sometimes you use *get* to form the passive instead of *be*.

  > Our production methods ensure that 90 per cent of our projects **get completed** on time.

Passive or adjective?

Some words, like *interested, surprised, disappointed, satisfied* and *bored* are the passive forms of the active verbs *interest, surprise* etc, but are now thought of as adjectives. This is because, unlike verbs, they can be modified by words like *very* or *quite*.

> I **am very interested** in finding out how M&S has come to lead the market in women's underwear.

Practice

Rewrite the sentences using the passive.

1. People hoped Burberry would reconsider plans to close its Welsh factory.
2. The newspapers reported that about 80 staff travelled to London to protest against the closure.
3. People claimed that Burberry had chosen to move manufacturing outside the UK because it was cheaper.
4. People widely believe that competition from the developing world is a threat to the British clothing industry.
5. Everyone expects the company to lose sales in Britain after the closure.

GRAMMAR OVERVIEW

UNIT 7 Making comparisons

- There is a wide range of modifiers you can use before comparative adjectives to emphasise the size of the difference between two things. Some more of these are *a great deal, vastly* and *rather*. The adjective sometimes modifies a noun.

  > *Skoda is **vastly more successful** since it changed its brand image 10 years ago.*
  > *The new Skoda models have **much more attractive styling** than the early ones.*

- You can also use *even* for emphasis.

  > *Sales figures are **even better** this year than last.*

- You can also use all these words before *less*, with the same meaning as *not as ... as*.

  > *Although owned by Volkswagen since 1991, Skodas are **far less expensive** than VWs.*

- The same words are often used before **adverbs** to emphasise the difference in the way things are done.

  > *The company marketed its products **a lot more efficiently** after the takeover.*

- When you use a **superlative**, you can use *by far*, or in informal language *far and away*.

  > ***By far the most popular** model in the Czech Republic was the Fabia.*

Sentence linkers and conjunctions

- When you make comparisons you can use sentence linkers like *however* and *in contrast*. You can also use conjunctions like *but, whereas, while, both ... and*, and *neither ... nor*.

  > ***While** brand snobs go on buying expensive VWs and Audis, smart people know they can get the same in an £11,000 Skoda.*
  > ***Both** Volkswagen **and** Skoda use the same engines, transmissions and electronics.*

- **Adjectives** like *same, similar* and *different* are also used in comparisons, as well as **prepositions** such as **(exactly) *like*** and ***unlike***.

  > ***Unlike** before, no-one would dream of selling a car now without emphasising the safety features.*

Practice

Complete the text using the words in the box. (Sometimes there is more than one possibility.)

| slightly | far and away | much | even | a lot | far | nowhere near | while | unlike | similar |

I compared the Kia Sportage with the new Hyundai Tucson, and at first the Kia seemed very (1) _____ , just with (2) _____ better styling. But the Kia's suspension is (3) _____ firmer, confirming claims that it is (4) _____ the best of any Korean vehicle to date. The Kia has (5) _____ more attractive upholstery than the Tucson, and (6) _____ the Tucson, the interior is available in black, which is (7) _____ more visually striking than grey. (8) _____ the Tucson is a very attractive car, I think the Kia is (9) _____ more impressive, especially as it is (10) _____ as expensive.

UNIT 8 Making predictions

- You typically use the modal *will* (*'ll*) or *will not* (*won't*) to make predictions. You can also use *be going to* when there is evidence in the present situation that something will happen.

  > *Internet advertising **is going to become** hugely popular as more and more people log on to shop.*

- To talk about what will probably or possibly happen, you use the modals *may*, *might* and *could* + infinitive. You can also use *should* when you are predicting that something will happen because it seems normal and logical.

  > *Word-of-mouth marketing **should offer** great opportunities for advertisers in the future.*

- You often use a **conditional** sentence to say what will happen in certain circumstances.

  > ***If** you **make** it easy for customers to complain, you**'ll** definitely **improve** your company image.*

- You can also *will*, *may*, *might* etc with the **continuous** and **passive** forms of the infinitive.

  > *No doubt **they'll be focusing** their efforts on a 'niche' component of a larger market.*
  > *The design of our website **could be completed** next week.*

- Or you can use the **past** form of the infinitive to predict that something will be finished by a certain time in the future.

  > *By the end of the course, you **will have learnt** a great deal about the Hispanic market.*

- You often use more than one prediction expression in the same sentence.

  > ***No doubt about it** – they**'re sure to find** ways of curbing the growth of Internet spam.*

Impersonal structures

- You can begin a sentence with *there* or *it* to make your prediction sound as if it is generally accepted rather than being just your own opinion.

  > ***There's little doubt that** product placement on computer and video games will take off.*
  > ***It's unlikely that** drugs companies will get the go-ahead to advertise on British TV.*
  > ***It's widely expected that** interactive television will link up with mobile technology.*

  Note that the *it* here is a 'dummy' *it*, not a pronoun. You could say *That mobile technology will link up with mobile technology **is widely expected**.*

- The use of *seem*, *appear* and *look* make your prediction more tentative.

  > ***It doesn't seem likely that** alcohol advertising will ever be banned completely.*

Practice

Match the two parts of the sentences.

1. Internet advertising is bound to
2. If you're selling holidays abroad,
3. The DoubleClick Advertising Service
4. I'm convinced that the quantity of spam
5. There's a strong possibility that we will

a. launch a youth marketing programme soon.
b. is expected to be available globally in 2007.
c. generate substantial income for DoubleClick.
d. a website will probably help your business.
e. will double by 2008 unless action is taken.

UNIT 9 Cause and effect

There are several ways of talking about causes and effects, or reasons and results.

Multi-word prepositions

You can use the multi-word prepositions *due to, because of, owing to, as a result of* and *on account of* to introduce a reason, while the rest of the sentence gives the result.

> **Owing to** its farsighted education policy, Singapore now has a highly skilled workforce.
> This tiny country is seen as an investment haven, partly **because of** its political stability.

Conjunctions

Because, as and *since* all introduce a subordinate clause that gives a reason. The main clause gives the result. Either of the two clauses can come first.

> **Because** Singapore lacks land and natural resources, its port is an economic boon.
> The country is a healthy climate for investors, **as** corruption is almost non-existent.

Sentence linkers

- You can link a reason with its result by using a sentence linker like *consequently, therefore, as a result* and *so*, often at the beginning of a sentence.

  > Singapore is a business-friendly, well-regulated economy. **As a result**, there are now thousands of foreign business people working there.

- Only *so* can be used after a comma.

  > Starting up a business in Singapore takes only six days, **so** it is an attractive prospect for entrepreneurs worldwide.

Verbs

You can use the verbs *cause, lead to* and *result in* to link the reason for something with its result, as well as less common verbs like *contribute to, spark off* and *bring about*.

> Low interest rates **contributed to** Singapore's vigorous growth in 2004–6.
> But competition from its neighbours is expected to **bring about** some economic changes.

Nouns

You can talk about reasons using nouns like *cause, reason* and *explanation*. You can talk about results using nouns like *effect, consequence, result* and *outcome*.

> One **explanation** for Singapore's economic success is that its investment laws are clear and fair.
> The port is facing severe competition from neighbouring Malaysia, and the **outcome** might be a slow-down in growth.

Practice

Complete the sentences using the words in the box.

| consequently | because of | result | since | sparked off |

1 It was foreign trade and investment that _____ Taiwan's economic growth 40 years ago.
2 _____ its conservative financial approach, Taiwan suffered little during the Asian financial crisis of 1997–9.
3 _____ Taiwan's economy remains export-oriented, it depends on an open world trading system.
4 Taiwan's per capita income level has risen steeply. _____ , demand for imported, high-quality consumer goods has increased.
5 Taiwan's transformation is the _____ of three decades of hard work and sound economic management.

UNIT 10 Referring and sequencing

Referring

- You can use *this*, or, less often, *these* or *that* to refer back to what you have just said or written. You can also use *this*, *these* or *such* followed by a noun. The noun gives a 'label' to what you have just said, and this helps to structure your argument.

  > More than 1,200 companies chose to invest in the UK last year, up 14 per cent from 2005. **This** makes it the best year ever for inward investment.
  >
  > Political stability will be a major challenge to the country's competitiveness. **This issue** will require serious attention if we are to gain investor confidence and FDI increases.
  >
  > We rely on investors looking at what a country can offer and taking the plunge. **Such decisions** are not made easily.

- To refer back to an action you have just mentioned, you can use the verb *do + so*.

  > We were advised to increase our investment in the Russian oil industry. But we are not thinking of **doing so** in the near future.

- You can also use *so* to refer back to a whole statement or series of statements.

  > The first thing for a potential investor to consider is political stability. It is not difficult to see why this should be **so**.

Sequencing

- You use words like *first(ly)*, *second(ly)* and *finally* to structure what you are saying, as well as a variety of words and phrases like *then*, *next*, and *another point is* …
- Or, you can use conjunctions like *when* and *after* to present events in a particular order.

  > **After** doing a thorough analysis of investment conditions, we opted for the UK.

- You can also use phrases like *there are three reasons* … and *the following* to show your reader how you are going to structure what you say next.
- This (incomplete) passage gives examples of both sequencing and referring.

  > **First and foremost**, multinational companies must adopt policies that protect both the local workers and the environment. However, the governments of the countries that **these companies** invest in should **also** encourage **such social and environment-friendly practices**. A government keen to ensure that FDI is truly pro-poor should implement **the following measures**. **For one thing**, it should promote education and worker training … **Another priority** is …

Practice

Complete the text using the words in the box.

| then | the initial step | such policies | when | this type |

(1) _____ towards promoting training and education is to put in place a well-administered scheme that links taxation and grants with good practice. In (2) _____ of scheme, firms would make an upfront tax payment of between one and two per cent based on their payroll. They would (3) _____ receive a grant back (4) _____ they had trained their workers. Brazil and Chile serve as good examples of the success of (5) _____ .

UNIT 11 Prepositions

- Prepositions – both single and multi-word – are normally followed by a noun group.

  *A team-building exercise can promote team spirit <u>during</u> **an economic downturn**.*
  *We will invite employees' reactions to the scheme <u>by means of</u> **a detailed questionnaire**.*

- Sometimes, however, prepositions are followed by a clause starting with the *-ing* form of a verb.

  *A team-building event is a good way <u>of</u> **encouraging** staff to develop skills that are relevant <u>to</u> **co-operating** with others <u>in</u> **achieving** shared goals.*
  *Careful planning of the budget takes the stress <u>out of</u> **looking** for money-saving deals at the last minute.*

- You often use *by* + *-ing* to talk about means or method.

  *<u>By</u> **using** a nearby venue, we can reduce the budget allocated to the event.*

The preposition *of*

- The most common preposition, *of*, is very different from other prepositions, and has a much wider range of uses. For example, you use it in quantifiers like *a bit of* and *plenty of* (see Unit 5). You also use it before an uncount noun to talk about quantities.

  two bits <u>of</u> **advice**   a piece <u>of</u> **software**   three sheets <u>of</u> **paper**

- You use it in descriptions, as in *problems of varying complexity* or *a man of twenty-two*. Or you can use it to say who or what performed an action, as in *the hard work of the manager* or *the growth of computer technology*. It is also used to talk about possession:

  *The budget is the responsibility <u>of</u> **the Finance Department**.*
  (The budget is the Finance Department's responsibility.)

Prepositions with nouns, verbs and adjectives

- Many nouns are typically associated with particular prepositions, such as **reason** <u>for</u>, **investment** <u>in</u>, **restriction** <u>on</u>, **promotion** <u>to</u>, **partnership** <u>with</u> and **trend** <u>towards</u>.

  *Hundreds of companies have grown up to profit from the current **trend** <u>towards</u> team-building events.*

- Verbs too are often followed by specific prepositions, such as **refer** <u>to</u>, **recover** <u>from</u>, **change** <u>into</u>, **apologise** <u>for</u>, **insist** <u>on</u> and **put** <u>forward</u>.

  *A meeting will be held to allow everyone to **put** <u>forward</u> their views on boosting morale.*

- Similarly, many adjectives collocate with particular prepositions, including **suitable** <u>for</u>, **different** <u>from</u>, **interested** <u>in</u>, **payable** <u>to</u>, **familiar** <u>with</u> and **good** <u>at</u>.

  *We need to find someone who's **good** <u>at</u> planning and budgeting for events like this.*

Practice

Match the two halves of the sentences.

1 I've looked   a in the future of the company.
2 Apparently a wide range   b with food and drink.
3 We can save money   c into the question of accommodation.
4 We can afford to be generous   d by locating the event nearer home.
5 This is an investment   e of evening entertainment is available.

UNIT 12 Reported speech

- When you report what someone said, you often take the tense of the reported verb 'back'. So, for example, present perfect changes to past perfect, the modal *will* becomes *would*, and *can* becomes *could*.

- In general, you take the tense back when the reporting verb is **past**, but not when it is **present**.

  > 'The tsunami of 2004 **has caused** widespread poverty.'
  > He **admitted** that the tsunami of 2004 **had caused** widespread poverty.
  > He **admits** that the tsunami of 2004 **has caused** widespread poverty.

- But when you are reporting a fact that is always true, or a situation that is still current, there is no need to change the tense even if the reporting verb is past.

  > *Natural disasters such as earthquakes **can cause** terrible poverty.'*
  > *He **stressed** that natural disasters such as earthquakes **can cause** terrible poverty.*

  Note there are no precise rules about taking the tense back, so these are only rough guidelines.

To-infinitive clauses

- The reporting verbs above are followed by *that* clauses. Some verbs, such as *offer* and *refuse*, are followed by a *to*-infinitive clause instead. Others, like *promise, agree* and *claim*, can be followed by either type of clause.

  > *They've agreed to raise the amount of resources in the hands of poor agriculturalists.*
  > *But others refuse to accept that resources for the rural poor should be geared towards farming.*

Mentioning the hearer

- You often mention your **hearer** or **reader** with some reporting verbs, with or without *to*. This table lists some of these verbs and the clauses they are followed by.

She	assured informed notified	me the boss etc	that ...	She	said explained admitted mentioned suggested remarked reported complained	to me to the boss etc	that ...
	encouraged invited ordered	me the boss etc	to ...				
	reminded told warned	me the boss etc	that ... or to ...				

> *They **notified** us **that** the funds had been earmarked for the building of a school.*
> *The speaker **encouraged** the village leaders **to promote** entrepreneurial activity.*
> *The writer **warns** his readers **that** today's workers need basic education to escape poverty.*

- With some reporting verbs, you do not usually mention the hearer. Some of these are *add, argue, demand, deny, reply, predict, confirm, refuse* and *offer*.

Practice

Underline the correct answers.

The speaker explained (1) <u>us / to us</u> that the agreed aim of development policy is to slash extreme poverty, (2) <u>saying / reminding</u> that programmes should focus on the rural poor. He (3) <u>mentioned / warned</u> that some rural projects have been very successful, and (4) <u>argued / told</u> that the way forward is to use sustainable methods: water control, better seeds, and land reform. He (5) <u>added / informed</u> that microfinance also contributes to reducing rural poverty.

ANSWER KEY

UNIT 1 Modals
1 have to; obligation
2 may; permission
3 'd better; advice
4 can't; deduction
5 could; ability

UNIT 3 Conditionals
1 if any
2 If not
3 If I were you
4 If in doubt
5 If anything

UNIT 4 Relative clauses
The Hapax Group, which is a leading international transport company, (non-defining) has submitted a bid for the new East Coast franchise. Hapax, based in Perthshire, (non-defining) currently operates the North Island franchise and also runs Trans Valley, reputed to be Europe's smallest rail franchise. (non-defining) An executive said 'The East Coast franchise is the area's most important railway, and we have developed bold plans that will unlock the full potential of the network (defining) and attract passengers who have not previously benefitted from convenient rail links. (defining) We sincerely believe that we can deliver on our firm promise, which is to make rail travel in the region even better and continuously improve performance. (non-defining)

UNIT 5 Determiners and quantifiers
1 both
2 several
3 Every
4 a few of
5 no

UNIT 6 The passive
1 It was hoped that Burberry would reconsider plans to close its Welsh factory.
2 It was reported that about 80 staff travelled to London to protest against the closure.
About 80 staff were reported to have travelled to London to protest against the closure.
3 It was claimed that Burberry had chosen to move manufacturing outside the UK because it was cheaper.
4 It is widely believed that competition from the developing world is a threat to the British clothing industry.
Competition from the developing world is widely believed to be a threat to the British clothing industry.
5 It is expected that the company will lose sales in Britain after the closure.
The company is expected to lose sales in Britain after the closure.

UNIT 7 Making comparisons
1 similar
2 slightly
3 a lot/much/far
4 far and away
5 far/much
6 unlike
7 much/a lot/far
8 While
9 even
10 nowhere near

UNIT 8 Making predictions
1c 2d 3b 4e 5a

UNIT 9 Cause and effect
1 sparked off
2 Because of
3 Since
4 Consequently
5 result

UNIT 10 Referring and sequencing
1 The initial step
2 this type
3 then
4 when
5 such policies

UNIT 11 Prepositions
1c 2e 3d 4b 5a

UNIT 12 Reported speech
1 to us
2 saying
3 mentioned
4 argued
5 added

GLOSSARY

absenteeism *n* the habit of not being at work when you should be, often without a good reason

abundance *n* a very large amount of something, often more than is needed

acquire *v* to obtain something, especially by buying or being given it

acquisition *n* **1** a company which is bought by another company **2** the process of buying or obtaining something

ad campaign (informal) *n* advertising campaign: a planned group of business activities that try to persuade people to buy a product or service

advert (Br Eng) *n* advertisement: a short film, radio article, or picture that is used to try to persuade people to buy a product or service

agenda *n* a list of things that people will discuss at a meeting

aid *n* money, food, medical supplies, etc. that is given by a government or other organisation to a country in a difficult situation

appoint *v* to choose someone for a particular job or responsibility

appraisal *n* a meeting between an employee and a manager to discuss how well the employee is doing their job, **appraise** *v*, **appraisee** *n* the person who is being appraised, **appraiser** *n* the manager who appraises someone

approach *n* a particular way of thinking about or doing something

asset *n* money or property that a person or company owns

away day *n* a day when a group of people who work together meet at a place which is not where they usually work in order to get to know each other better, talk about business activities and discuss future plans

bargaining *n* the activity of trying to persuade a person or company to give you a better price or make an agreement that is better for you, **bargain** *v*

beneficiary *n* a person or organisation that receives money or other advantages as a result of something

bid *n* **1** an offer to provide goods or services for a particular price **2** an offer to pay a particular amount of money for something, **bid** *v*

board *n* the group of people who are responsible for controlling and organising a company

bonus *n* extra money paid to an employee in addition to their usual salary

boom *n* a sudden increase in trade, profits, or other business activities

bottom line *n* the total amount of money that a company makes in a particular period of time after all costs and taxes have been paid

brand *n* a recognised name for a product or group of products made by one particular company

brand conscious *adj* only interested in buying products which have a particular brand

brand extension *n* the activity of increasing the range of products or services which have a particular brand

branding *n* using design, advertising etc. to name a particular product in order to make people recognise and remember it

brand strategy *n* a plan or method in business based on the use of brands

budget *n* **1** a plan to show how much money a company will need or be able to spend and how much it will earn **2** the amount of money a company or organisation has to spend on something

build relationships *v phr* to develop links with a person or organisation

bureaucracy *n* a system for controlling a country or organisation which involves a lot of complicated rules that must be carefully followed, **bureaucrat** *n* someone working in a bureaucracy, **bureaucratic** *adj* involving a lot of complicated rules and processes

campaign *n* a planned group of business activities which are intended to achieve something, especially activities that try to persuade people to buy a product or service

capital gains tax *n* a tax paid on profit from selling capital assets such as property

cash flow *n* the amount of money going into and coming out of a business as products or services are bought and sold

CEO (also **managing director**) *n* chief executive officer: the person with the most senior position in a company who has overall responsibility for managing the company

chain *n* a group of businesses, especially restaurants, hotels or shops, which all belong to the same company

colleague *n* a person who works for the same company as you

commission *n* **1** an extra amount of money earned in your job when you sell a product or get a new customer **2** an amount of money paid to a bank or other organisation when they provide a service

competency *n* an important skill needed for doing a particular job

competitive *adj* **1** always trying to be more successful than other people or organisations **2** offering goods or services at cheaper prices than other companies **3** involving competition

complain *v* to say that you are annoyed, unhappy or not satisfied with something

complex *adj* made up of many different but connected parts and therefore difficult to understand or deal with

compromise *n* when people agree to something that is not exactly what you want, **compromise** *v*

conference *n* a large meeting, usually lasting a few days, where people who do the same work come together to discuss their opinions

connotation *n* an idea that a word suggests in addition to its usual meaning

consensus *n* agreement between all the people involved

consultancy firm *n* a company that provides expert advice on a particular subject to other companies or organisations

consultant *n* an expert or professional person who gives advice on a particular subject

contractor *n* a person or company that is paid a particular amount to do work or provide goods for another company

GLOSSARY

corruption *n* dishonest or illegal behaviour, especially by people in positions of power

criticism *n* **1** the activity of giving a professional opinion about something or someone, **constructive criticism** *n* criticism that is intended to be helpful **2** comments that show you think something is bad or wrong

cross-border *adj* involving people or organisations from different countries

cross-functional *adj* involving people or organisations with different skills

CSR *n* corporate social responsibility: the belief that a company should consider the social and environmental effects its activities have on its employees and the surrounding community

culture *n* the set of ideas, beliefs, and ways of behaving of a particular group of people

customer service *n* the activity of providing customers with information and dealing with any problems or complaints that they have

debt *n* an amount of money owed to a person or company

delegate *v* to give part of your work or responsibilities to someone else

deliver *v* to provide what you have promised or are expected to provide

delivery *n* **1** the process of bringing goods or letters to a place **2** goods or letters brought to a place

demand *n* the amount of products or services that people want to buy from a company

discrimination *n* when a person is treated unfairly because of their race, religion, sex, etc.

distributor *n* a company or person that supplies products or services to different shops, companies or other organisations

domestic *adj* inside a particular country; not foreign or international

effectiveness *n* the quality of being successful and achieving the result that was intended

end consumer *n* the person who buys and uses the products or services sold by companies

enhance relationships *v phr* to improve links with a person or organisation

entrepreneur *n* a person who starts their own business, especially when this involves taking financial risks, **entrepreneurial** *adj*

equipment *n* tools, machines, or other things needed for a particular job or activity

equity *n* **1** the value of a company's shares **2** the value of a property after all debts have been paid

ethical *adj* **1** relating to principles about what is right or wrong **2** morally correct and acceptable

exhibition *n* an event in which a collection of the products or services offered by a particular company are shown to the public

expand *v* if a company expands, it grows by moving into new areas and selling more products or services

expansion *n* the process of making a company grow by moving into new areas and selling more products or services

expectation *n* the belief that something will or should happen in a particular way

exploit *v* to treat someone unfairly by not paying them enough for the work that they do

export *n* **1** the business of selling products to another country **2** a product that is sold to another country, **export** *v* to send products to another country in order to sell them there

facilitate *v* to make something possible or easier

facilitator *n* someone who helps a person or organisation do something more easily by giving advice and discussing any problems

FDI *n* foreign direct investment: money invested by a person or organisation from one country in the business of another country

feedback *n* comments about how well or badly a person has done something

firm *n* a company that sells products or services

flat *adj* a flat organisation is one in which there are very few levels of importance

flexibility *n* the ability to change easily according to what is needed in a situation

fluctuation *n* a frequent change in the amount, value, or level of something

forecast *n* a statement about what is likely to happen in the future

foreign *adj* relating to or dealing with other countries that are not your own

freelance *adj* earning money by selling your work or services to several different companies rather than being employed by one particular company, **freelance** *adv*, **freelance** *v* to earn money by selling your work or services to several different companies

freelancer *n* a person who sells their work or services to several different companies and is not employed by one particular company

fusion market *n* a combination of several languages, cultures and groups of people that a particular product is sold to

GDP *n* gross domestic product: the total value of all the goods and services produced by a country in one year

globalisation (US also **globalization**) *n* **1** when available goods and services gradually become similar in all parts of the world **2** the increase of trade around the world, especially by very large companies who produce and sell goods in many different countries

goal *n* something that you hope to do successfully in the future

gross profit *n* the difference between the price that goods are sold for and what it costs to produce them

growth *n* an increase in the success of a business or country's economy

hands-on *adj* a hands-on person is someone who becomes closely involved in organising something and making decisions

headhunting *n* the activity of trying to persuade someone to leave their job and work for a different company, **headhunt** *v*

head office *n* the main office of a company

hierarchical *adj* a hierarchical organisation is one in which people or things are arranged in order of importance

GLOSSARY

hierarchy *n* a system in which the people in an organisation are arranged in order of importance

high-context culture *n* a culture where communication is less explicit and being direct is seen as rude

high-end *adj* high-end goods are more expensive and better quality than other goods of the same type

hire *v* **1** to give someone a job **2** to pay money so that you can use something for a short time

holding company *n* a company that buys shares in other companies which it then controls

HQ *n* headquarters: the main offices of a company

HR *n* human resources: a company department that is responsible for employing and training people

hub *n* the most important place in which a particular activity takes place

image *n* **1** an idea or a picture in your mind of what something or someone is like **2** the way that something or someone is thought of by other people

implement *v* to make a system, idea, plan, etc. start to happen and work

import *v* to buy products from another country and bring them into your country

import *n* **1** a product brought into your country from another country **2** the process of buying products from another country and bringing them into your country

inflation *n* an increase in the price of goods and services, or the rate at which this happens

infrastructure *n* the basic systems and services, such as communication and transport, that a country or organisation needs in order to work effectively

innovation *n* **1** the introduction of new ideas or methods **2** a new idea or method that has been introduced

innovative *adj* original and using new ideas and methods

insurance *n* an arrangement with a company in which you pay them money and they pay you costs if, for example, you are ill, have an accident, or lose or damage something

integrate *v* to combine two or more things so that they work together more effectively

intermediary *n* a person or organisation that helps two or more organisations make business agreements, often by communicating information between them

intern (Am Eng) *n* a student who gets practical work experience in a job by doing it for a short time

internship (Am Eng) *n* a job that a student does in order to get practical work experience, or the period of time a student spends doing this job

interview *v* to ask someone questions in order to see if they would be suitable for a job, **interview** *n* a meeting in which someone asks another person questions to see if they would be suitable for a job

inventory (Am Eng) *n* **1** all the goods in a shop or other business: stock **2** a written list of all the things in a place

investment *n* the money that someone puts into a business in order to make a profit, or the act of doing this

know-how *n* knowledge and experience of how to do something

launch *v* to start a new activity or introduce a new product or service, **launch** *n*

law *n* **1** an official rule **2 the law** the system of official rules in a country or society

layer *n* a level or rank within a company or organisation

leadership *n* **1** the position of being in charge of an organisation **2** the qualities and skills of a leader

level *n* the position that someone has in a company or organisation, which shows how important they are

line manager *n* a manager who is one level higher than you and directly manages the work that you do

liquidity *n* **1** when a business has money or property that it can sell if it needs to pay out money **2** a situation in which it is easy for a business to buy or sell

loan *n* an amount of money that a person or business borrows, usually from a bank

localised (US also **localized**) *adj* only happening within a particular area

logistics *n* the practical arrangements needed to successfully organise something, especially if this involves moving products or equipment

low-context culture *n* a culture where communication is explicit and being direct is appreciated

maintain relationships *v phr* to continue to communicate and have links with a person or organisation

management *n* **1** the control and organisation of a company **2** the group of people who control and organise a company

manufacturer *n* a person or company that makes products in a factory, **manufacture** *v*, **manufacturing** *n* the business of making products in a factory

market *n* **1** a particular place or group of people that products are sold to **2** trade in a particular type of product

mass market *n* a large amount of many different types of customers

matrix *n* an arrangement of connected parts within a company or organisation

mean business *idiom* to be serious about achieving something

memo *n* memorandum: a written message sent by one person in an organisation to another

mentor *n* an experienced person who helps and advises someone with less experience in their job, **mentoring** *n* the use of a mentor to teach a less experienced person about their job

merge *v* if two companies merge or one company merges with another, they combine to form one bigger company.

merger *n* when two companies combine to form one bigger company

microfinance *n* the activity of providing loans and other financial services to people who are poor and would not normally be able to access loans

monochronic culture *n* a structured approach to time with a strong emphasis on punctuality and good organisation at work

monopoly *n* when one company has complete control over the supply of a particular product or service because it is the only company that provides it

morale *n* the amount of confidence and enthusiasm a person or group of people feel about their situation at a particular time

motto *n* a short sentence or phrase which expresses the aims and beliefs of a person or organisation

multinational *adj* a multinational company has offices and factories in many different countries,
multinational *n* a large company that has offices and factories in many different countries

natural resources *n* valuable substances such as oil and coal which exist in a country's land and sea and can be used to make money

negotiation *n* a formal discussion in which people or organisations try to reach an agreement

network *v* to meet and talk to people that could be useful to you in your work, **networking** *n*

niche market *n* a particular group of customers who want a specific product

operation *n* a planned business activity

organisation (US also **organization**) *n* **1** the way in which the different parts of something are arranged **2** a group of people with a shared purpose or interest who form a business, club, etc.

outsource *v* to arrange for a person or organisation outside a company to do work for that company, **outsourcing** *n*

overheads *n* the regular costs of running a business, such as rent, electricity, paying employees, etc.

paperwork *n* **1** all the official documents you need in order to be able to do something **2** the written work that is part of a job, such as producing reports, filling in forms, etc.

partner *n* **1** one of two or more people who own a company and share its profits **2** a business, organisation, or country that has an agreement or working relationship with another

partnership *n* **1** the state of being a partner in business **2** a company owned by two or more people who share the profits

patent *n* an official document that gives a person or company the exclusive legal right to make or sell a product for a particular period of time, **patent** *v*

per capita *adj* for each person

performance review session *n* a meeting with your manager in order to discuss how well you are doing your job

performance-related pay *n* pay which increases when you are successful in your job

perform *v* to do your job with a particular amount of success

personnel *n* (also **human resources**) **1** the company department that is responsible for employing and training people **2** the people who work for a company

plant *n* a large factory

player *n* a person, company, or country that influences a situation, especially in business or politics

plummet *v* to suddenly become much lower in amount

policy *n* a set of plans or actions agreed by a company or organisation

political climate *n* the general political situation and attitudes at a particular time

polychronic culture *n* an unstructured approach to time where more than one work task is dealt with at a time, and where timing is less important

potential *n* the possibility of developing or achieving something in the future

PR *n* public relations: **1** the relationship between an organisation and the public **2** the activity of creating a positive opinion among people about a company or product

premises *n* the building and land around it that a company owns or uses

press release *n* an official statement that a company or organisation gives to journalists

private sector *n* businesses and industries that are not owned or controlled by the government

procedure *n* a particular way of doing something, especially a correct way

procrastination *n* when you delay doing something that you should do, often because it is unpleasant or boring

product placement *n* when companies pay for their products to be used and shown in films and television programmes

production *n* the process of making products for sale, or the company department that is responsible for this

productivity *n* the rate at which a worker or company produces goods compared to how much time, work and money is needed to produce them

profit *n* money that a company makes by selling products or services and that is left after it has paid all its business costs and taxes

profitable *adj* making or likely to make money

project[1] *n* a planned piece of work with a particular aim

project[2] *v* to calculate what the size, cost, or amount of something will be in the future using information that is available now

project management *n* the planning and organisation of the work involved in a project

proliferation *n* a sudden increase in the number or amount of something

promotion *n* **1** a move to a more important job or a higher level in a company **2** business activities which try to help increase the sales of a product or service

proposal *n* a suggestion or plan

prosper *v* to be successful, especially by making money

rapport *n* a relationship in which people like and understand each other and can communicate very well

rate *n* **1** a measurement of the speed at which something happens or changes **2** a fixed amount of money that is charged or paid for something

receipt *n* a piece of paper that shows that goods or services have been paid for

regulation *n* **1** the control of an activity by official rules **2** an official rule which controls how things are done

GLOSSARY

repayment *n* **1** the process of paying back money that you have borrowed **2** an amount of money paid to the person or bank that you have borrowed money from

reporting line *n* a connected set of levels in an organisation which shows which person is in charge of another

reputation *n* an opinion people have about what someone or something is like, often based on what has happened in the past

research *v* to study something carefully in order to discover new information about it, **research** *n*

rights *n* the legal authority to do or use something

route *n* **1** a means of achieving something **2** a way which can be followed to get from one place to another

rule *n* an official instruction about what you must or must not do in a particular situation

scarcity value *n* an increase in the demand for, and price of a product because supplies of it are relatively low

schedule *n* a plan that shows events and activities and the time they will happen or be done, **ahead of/behind/on schedule** before/after/at the time that was planned for something to happen or be done

sector *n* a particular part of a business activity

self-employed *adj* working for yourself and not employed by a company

seminar *n* a meeting at which a group of people discuss a subject or have training

set up *phrasal v* to start a company or organisation

shareholder *n* a person who owns shares in a company or business

shift *n* a period of time during the day or night when a group of workers do a job

slogan *n* a short phrase used to advertise something

small player *n* a small company or organisation in a certain sector

SME *n* small and medium-sized enterprise: a company that has a small number of employees, usually less than 50, or a medium number of employees, usually less than 250

sponsorship *n* money given by a person or company to help pay for a particular event, especially as a way of advertising

standard *n* a level of quality

state-owned *adj* owned by the government of a country

stock *n* goods that are available for sale

stock exchange also **stock market** *n* **1** the place where people buy and sell shares in a company **2** the activities related to buying and selling shares in a company **3** the value of shares being bought and sold

strategy *n* a plan or method used to achieve a business aim

stress *n* worry caused by difficult situations, **stressed** *adj* worried

sublet *v* to allow someone to rent all or part of a building that you are renting from someone else

subordinate *n* a person who has a less important position in an organisation than someone else

subsidiary *n* a company which is owned or controlled by a larger company

supplier *n* a company or organisation that supplies a product or service

survey *n* an examination of opinions or behaviour made by asking people questions

takeover *n* a situation in which one company takes control of another company by buying the majority of its shares, **take over** *phrasal v* to take control of something

tap into *phrasal v* to make use of something for your own advantage

target *n* something that a person intends to achieve

tariff *n* a tax that is paid on goods entering or leaving a country

task *n* a piece of work

teambuilding (also **team building**) *n* organised activities which help a group of people to work more effectively as a team

team spirit *n* an enthusiastic attitude towards working with other people as a team

team up with *phrasal v* to work together with someone in order to achieve a particular aim

telecom service *n* telecommunications service: a service which makes it possible for signals, messages and pictures to be sent by telephone, radio or television

trade *n* **1** the buying and selling of goods and services **2** a particular area of business

trade fair (US also **trade show**) *n* a large event at which companies display and sell their products

trademark *n* a name, symbol or picture that a company uses for its products or services and that cannot be used by another company

trading *n* **1** the activity of buying and selling products or services **2** the activity of buying and selling shares in companies

unemployment *n* **1** the number of people that do not have a job **2** the state of not having a job, even though you are able and want to work

universalist *adj* a collective belief that what is good and true can be applied to every situation

up for sale *phrase* available to buy

word-of-mouth *n* informal communication consisting of spoken comments that people make to each other

workforce *n* all the people who work for a particular company

workplace *n* the offices, factory, etc. where people work

NOTES

NOTES

NOTES

NOTES

Title: Best Practice Intermediate
ISBN: 9781424000654

Photos sourced by Pictureresearch.co.uk

Illustrations by Melvyn Evans p 27, ODI p 15

Photo credits

The publishers would like to thank the following sources for permission to reproduce their copyright protected photographs:

Action Plus p 98tc (Bruno Van Loocke); Alamy pp 8bc (Douglas Pulsipher), 8bl (Kirsty McLaren), 22tcl (Bob Turner), 22bl (Bob Johns/expresspictures.co.uk), 22br (Justin Kase), 34tr (Roger Bamber), 34cl (Lou Linwei), 35 (Buzz Pictures), 38bl (Brian Atkinson), 38br (travelstock44), 40t (Roger Bamber), 40b (Jeremy Hoare), 43b (Profimedia International s.r.o.), 46t (Roger Bamber), 47 (Martin Mayer), 48l (Pictor International/ImageState), 48c (Nick Emm), 48cr (Rex Argent), 48r (D. Hurst), 50b (Lou Linwei), 51bl (Tim Graham), 51tr (Neil Setchfield), 52t (Roger Bamber), 56r (Steven May), 56l (S.T. Yiap Imagery), 56c (foodfolio), 56cl (Motoring Picture Library), 57 (Neil McAllister), 58c (Colin Underhill), 58t (Roger Bamber), 59br (Dwayne Brown/Brownstock), 59bcl (Stepan Bahensky/Profimedia International s.r.o.), 60 (Roger Bamber), 64b (Robert Harding Picture Library Ltd), 71l & 71r (FocusRussia), 75tr (Jeremy Nicholl), 75b (Bryan & Cherry Alexander Photography), 75tl (Jeremy Nicholl), 79 (Ros Drinkwater), 80 (Ricardo Beliel / BrazilPhotos), 81t (Profimedia International s.r.o.), 82b (Terry Whittaker), 88bcl (Andreas von Einsiedel), 97 (Dennis Cox), 98bc (Adam Butler), 99 (Ulrich Doering); Cartoonbank p 12l (Jack Ziegler); Cartoonstock pp 12r (Mike Shapiro), 18l (Jerry King); Corbis pp 13t (Massimo Listri), 16cr (Tom Stewart), 19 (Layne Kennedy), 30b (Stefan Schuetz/Zefa), 34c (Caroline Penn), 34cr (Catherine Karnow), 36 (Matthias Schrader/dpa), 38tcr (Tony Waltham/Robert Harding World Imagery), 38tcl (Janet Jarman), 39 (Jerry Arcieri), 51tl (Jose Fuste Raga), 51br (Ahmad Yusni/epa), 51tc (Stephane Cardinale/People Avenue), 52b (Alan Schein Photography), 59tcl (Jean Pierre Amet), 59tl (Al Fuchs/NewSport), 59bl (Layne Kennedy), 66 (China Photos/Reuters), 67 (Louis Moses/Zefa), 73 (Louis Moses/Zefa), 74cr (Liu Liqun), 74cl (Andrei Liankevich/epa), 76b (Larry Williams/Zefa), 86b (Jerome Sessini), 88tcl (Hugh Sitton/Zefa), 104r (Alexander Hubrich/Zefa); Getty Images pp 4c (Michael Blann), 8tc (Stephen Simpson/Photographer's Choice), 9t (J W Burkey), 21tl (B2M Productions/Photodisc), 21tr (Zubin Shroff), 21br (Christian Hoehn), 24 (Sunny/Taxi), 25tr (Ghislain & Marie David de Lossy/The Image Bank), 32 (Michael McQueen/Photographer's Choice), 41 (Miguel Riopa/AFP), 42 (Sean Gallup), 44bl (National Geographic RF /Joel Sartore), 44br (Richard Kolker), 45 (Jasper James), 49 (David Woolley), 50c (Nathan Bilow), 53 (Dave Hogan), 64t (Robert Clare/Photographer's Choice), 65 (Jerry Driendl/The Image Bank), 68b (Panoramic Images), 69 (Jerry Driendl), 70 & 76t (Robert Clare/Photographer's Choice), 81b (Panoramic Images), 82t (Robert Clare/Photographer's Choice), 83 (Steve Allen/The Image Bank), 85b (Reza Estakhrian), 88br (Siri Stafford), 88tr & 90 (Robert Clare/Photographer's Choice), 92 (Paula Bronstein/Reportage), 94t & 96 (Duncan Smith/Photodisc), 98b (Zubin Shroff/The Image Bank), 98t (Duncan Smith/Photodisc), 104c (Altrendo Images); Ted Goff p 18r; Jupiterimages p 7 (Frederic Cirou/PhotoAlto); Photolibrary.com pp 20r (Simon Wilkinson), 88c (Robert Harding Picture Library Ltd); Punchstock pp 4tr (Alistair Berg/Digital Vision), 5 (Andersen Ross/Blend Images), 6 (Image Source Limited), 8tl (Photodisc), 9b (Joe Sohm/Visions of America, LLC), 10tr (Alistair Berg/Digital Vision), 10cl (Bilderlounge), 11 (Blend Images Llc), 13b (It Stock), 14 (Photodisc), 16tr (Alistair Berg/Digital Vision), 16cl (Radius Images), 17 (Stockbyte), 20tl (Photodisc), 21bl (Comstock Images), 22tr (Alistair Berg/Digital Vision), 25tl (Veer/Somos), 25br (Image Source Pink), 26b (Brand X Pictures), 26t (Photodisc), 28 (Alistair Berg/Digital Vision), 29 (Stockbyte/George Doyle), 30t (Alistair Berg/Digital Vision), 37 (Image Source), 38tl (Photodisc), 43c (Image Source), 44cr (Stockbyte), 44tl (Photodisc), 48cl (Comstock Images), 50tl (Photodisc), 55 (Pixland), 56cr (simple stock shots), 56tl (Photodisc), 58b (Stockbyte), 59tr (Robert Michael), 59cr (Jeremy Woodhouse/Blend Images), 63 (BananaStock), 68t, 74tl & 80t (Photodisc), 85t (Image Source White), 86t (Photodisc), 94b (Tay Junior/Digital Vision), 104l (Digital Vision); Rex Features p 46b (Dan Callister); Still Pictures p 44cl (Shehzad Noorani)

Credits

The publishers would like to thank the following sources for permission to reproduce their copyright protected texts:

Page 05: From **"Top Seven Leadership Mistakes"** by Kristine Geimure. Copyright © Woopidoo 2007. **Page 11:** From **"Getting staff thumping to the same beat"** by Andy Moore, The Scotsman. Copyright © Andy Moore 2006. **Page 24:** From **"Citizen Complaints Increase despite Growth of Charter Mark Scheme"**. Copyright © Touchpaper Software plc. http://www.touchpaper.com 2006. **Page 27:** From **"People whose ideas influence organisational work"** by Charles Handy. Copyright © Onepine 2005. **Page 35:** From **"Partnerships feel the Indian heat"**, by Peter Marsh. Copyright © Financial Times 2006. **Page 39:** From **"In India, 'next great' industrial story"**, by Anand Giridharadas, Copyright © The International Herald Tribune 2006. **Page 40:** From **"Inditex and fast fashion"** Copyright © The Economist Newspaper Limited, London (June 18 2006). **Page 45:** From **"Dressing across cultures"**, by Bernadette Sukley. Copyright © Expatica Communications B.V. 2006. **Page 46:** From **"The incalculable value of building brands"**. Copyright © Chief Executive 2006. **Page 50:** From **"Problem with your country's image? Mr Anholt can help"** by Oliver Burkeman. Copyright © Guardian News & Media Ltd 2006. **Page 50:** From **"Malaysia –inviting"**, by L.S. Sya. Copyright © brandchannel 2004. **Page 53:** From **"New Bond film is a 'giant advert'"**. Source: BBC News http://bbc.co./business. 18 November 2002. **Page 64:** From **"Private Sector: Thriving but faced with uncertainties"**, by Geoff Dyer. Copyright © Financial Times 2006. **Page 69:** From **"Concepts in Chinese Culture"**, source from alibaba.com http://resources.alibaba.com/article/2492/Concepts_in_Chinese_c ulture.htm. Copyright © alibaba 2007. **Page 70:** Graph taken from **"US knocks UK off pole position for foreign direct investment"**. Copyright © The Independent, 2007. **Page 74:** From **"Doing business in Russia. A look into the nation and its business culture"**, taken from http://www.suite101.com. Copyright © Bhumika Ghimire 2006. **Page 86:** From **"A glimmer of light at last"**. Copyright © The Economist Newspaper Limited, London (June 24 2006).

Best Practice Upper Intermediate Coursebook
Bill Mascull / Jeremy Comfort

Editorial Director: *Joe Dougherty*
VP, Director of Content Development: *Anita Raducanu*
Director of Product Marketing: *Amy Mabley*
Executive Editor: *Bryan Fletcher*
Development Editor: *Sarah O'Driscoll*
Production Editor: *Maeve Healy*
Manufacturing Buyer: *Maeve Healy*
Compositor: *Oxford Designers & Illustrators*

Cover Image: *Getty Images*

Copyright © 2008 Thomson Heinle. Thomson, and the Star logo, are trademarks used herein under license.

All rights reserved. No part of this work covered by the copyright hereon may be reproduced or used in any form or by any means—graphic, electronic, or mechanical, including photocopying, recording, taping, Web distribution or information storage and retrieval systems—without the written permission of the publisher.

Printed in Italy.
1 2 3 4 5 6 7 8 9 10 — 11 10 09 08 07

For more information contact Thomson Learning, High Holborn House, 50/51 Bedford Row, London WC1R 4LR United Kingdom or Thomson Heinle, 25 Thomson Place, Boston, Massachusetts 02210 USA. You can visit our website at elt.heinle.com

Project Manager: *Howard Middle/HM ELT Services*
Contributing Writers: *Gill Francis, Adrian Pilbeam, Kerry Maxwell, Rebecca Utteridge*
Photo Researcher: *Suzanne Williams / PictureResearch.co.uk*
Illustrator: *Mark Duffin*
Text Designer: *Oxford Designers & Illustrators*
Cover Designer: *Thomas Manss & Compnay*
Printer: *Canale*

Credits appear on page 175 which constitutes a continuation of the copyright page.

For permission to use material from this text or product, submit a request online at www.thomsonrights.com

Any additional questions about permissions can be submitted by email to thomsonrights@thomson.com

ISBN: 978-1-4240-0065-4

The publishers and authors are grateful to the following teachers for their advice during the development of the book:

Silvija Andernovics (Latvia), Martin Goosey (Korea), Anna Kucala (Poland), Angela Lloyd (Germany), Luisa J. Panichi (Italy), Wayne Rimmer (Russia), Andy Roberts (Switzerland), Simone Sarmento (Brazil), Hajime Uematsu (Japan), Julio Valladares (Peru), Julia Waldner (Germany), Steve Wasserman (UK)